To Play, To Live

JOHN CALLINAN

WITH JOE Ó MUIRCHEARTAIGH

www.**HERO**BOOKS.digital

HEROBOOKS

PUBLISHED BY HERO BOOKS
1 WOODVILLE GREEN
LUCAN
CO. DUBLIN
IRELAND

Hero Books is an imprint of Umbrella Publishing
First Published 2021
Copyright © John Callinan and Joe Ó Muircheartaigh 2021
All rights reserved

A CIP record for this book is available from the British Library

ISBN 9781910827192

Cover design and formatting: jessica@viitaladesign.com
Ebook formatting: www.ebooklaunch.com
Photographs: Callinan family collection, Inpho, John Power and Gerard Sullivan.

Dedication

To Mary, my dearest sister, who for eight years endured
cancer but never lost the joy of life,
and passed from us in May 2020

To Sophia, our first grandchild, who arrived
unexpectedly early in February 2018 and has illuminated
our lives with her determination
to experience the joy of life

Contents

Acknowledgements

TO JOE Ó MUIRCHEARTAIGH, who listened to my ramblings in the winter of 2019 & '20 and has managed to give them coherence. And to Liam Hayes of Hero Books, who thought there was a story and suggested a 'quieter' Clare hurling book – I hope it is not too quiet!

To the places of my childhood...

Devine's, the Lane, Quay Road...

And the Quay with its boats and nets.

Burke's crag and its pond freezing over on occasions.

The wildness and hazelnuts of Ballybeg.

The shops... Barry's, Considine's and the Corner House.

Newhall Lake, the Fair Green, the Forge, Michael's, Madden's and St Joseph's, the corner itself.

The street.

The school.

The village.

Thanks to the people of my place.

My father, Eamon and my mother, Mary.

My siblings, Anne, Mary, Brid, Martina and Eamon.

Aunt Winnie, Ger Ward, Liam Barry from over the bridge, and Joe Barrett.

To the 'Corner Boys', the priests, Dónal Carey, John Hanley and later in St Flannan's, Fr Seamus Gardiner and Fr Willie Walshe.

And to the hurling magpies, all and every one of you.

I thank you all for being, supporting, talking, encouraging, challenging, educating, maintaining, caring, fighting... with and against.

To hurling supporters everywhere, particularly those from Clarecastle and Clare – and I hope nobody will be offended if I mention one in particular, Syl Addley.

Syl Addley from Killaloe, who has managed a great and successful family and business life around Clare hurling.

To my uncle, Peter Hayes, who left Clarecastle in 1940 to join the army and remains alive and well in Dublin, living in Raheny.

To my great and old friend Paschal Russell. The only good advice he ever gave me was at half-time in my first Clare Cup match, having returned with high ideas from college. 'Go where the ball is going… not where you think it should be going,' he told me.

To my college friends and to my flatmates, Tommy Quinn, Alan Higgins, Fergus Gannon and particularly the late Sean Liddy who 'minded me' in Galway, Ballycastle, Cork and in numerous establishments in Dublin. You left us all too soon in 2012, Sean.

To Frank Lillis, my wedding Groomsman who recently left us, again, too early. And to Brid, Frank's wife, who interviewed Siobhán.

To Siobhán's flatmate and old friend, Dr Michelle Moloney. And to Jack Rea particularly, for not refusing me on my first appearance in Kennedy's.

To my teammates on Clarecastle, St Flannan's, UCD, Parteen, Munster and Clare teams with whom I played. I thank you all and hope I made a contribution.

To my legal colleagues in Clare, my colleagues in Limerick and, most particularly, my recent partner and now District Judge Marie Keane for their toleration of my hurling passion.

To Siobhán's parents, Tim and Maura, and her siblings and their loved ones who I hope won't be too upset if I particularly mention the late great Paddy Doyle from Ferns.

To Aoife and Eamon, whom I love so much and to, more recently, Louise and Sophia whom I have also come to love.

To Siobhán, who has put up with my hurling and other mood swings, who reared Aoife and Eamon and, on many occasions, said nothing when there was nothing to be said. Thank you for introducing me to West Cork and Ballydehob.

Thank you for your support, friendship and love for the last four and a half decades.

John Callinan
March, 2021

◀ ◁ ◆ ▷ ▶

I NEVER SAW the Clare hurling team of the 1970s in the flesh and in live action on the field; I never even saw them live on television, but I didn't need to be up close, personal and know them to feel a real connection to the never-ending journey they were on.

The highlights reel on Teilifís Éireann and the radio commentaries of Michael O'Hehir, who seemed to want them to win as much as they did themselves, were all I needed to be sucked into a story about a team and county that so badly wanted to crash through hurling's glass ceiling.

I'm sure I wasn't alone.

This is because there was something about that Clare team. They were speckled with stardust. Though the holy grails of Munsters and All-Irelands eluded them, they were a big team, with big characters, who helped bring a splash of colour to GAA country just after the country moved out of black and white.

Characters like manager Fr Harry Bohan, his young and ambitious coach Justin McCarthy, his trainer Colm Flynn, who provided a link to the 1967 Munster final, and his players who became folk heroes to an adoring Clare public.

This public drank with the team in Tulla after Dr Daly Park became the graveyard for the ambitions of many visitors; they were with them after the heady days of those National League wins and cried with them after heart-breaking Munster final defeats.

Those defeats didn't make them any lesser of men and hurlers. They were swashbucklers. From Seamus Durack in goal through to Pat O'Connor at corner-forward they captured imaginations. The tearaway Ger Loughnane, the exotic looking Jackie O'Gorman, Sean Stack's pure stick craft, *Sideline Cut* Mick Moroney, *The Case*, *The Hacker* and many more.

And 'Johnny' Callinan – even though he goes by John or Cal, never 'Johnny'.

The professional man. The solicitor. The thinking man's hurler. The GPA activist. The Magpie. Nearly half a century on from when 'Johnny' played his first Munster senior final for Clare, it was a privilege to be asked by him and his publisher, Liam Hayes, of Hero Books to pen the story of his hurling life.

Being a Dub, of Kerry stock, I'm a football man – at least that's what I'm told – but to be a football man you have to be a GAA man first and that's why collaborating with John on this book has been a great honour.

He's Clarecastle; I'm an adopted Éire Óg Inis man; the clubs aren't supposed to like each other, just the way any rivalry should be. 'Ye're from the Fishing Village,' we'd say and then – with enough drink in – 'ye're a garrison village that played soccer before ever holding a hurley'.

I don't know what they'd say about us.

But the respect is there beneath the banter.

And that's another reason why writing this book was a great opportunity. It was an education and illuminating – talking through the highs and lows with John; hearing his deeply personal stories relating to hurling and to life; consulting archival material near and wide, be it online or in hardcopy in the Clare County Library or the Newspaper Library in Dublin, as well as tapping into the knowledge of great GAA men like Seamus O'Reilly of the *Clare County Express*, records man extraordinaire Leo McGough in Carlow, Mike O'Brien of O'Callaghan's Mills, Senan Lillis in Wexford and Fr Tom Hogan in Birr.

All the while, it was almost like taking a step back in time. Reading previews and postscripts of games and John's recollections brought me as close as I've ever come to seeing the Clare team of the 1970s in action.

I was invested in that time again – just like we all were back then, whether it was those breaking the gate down in Thurles to get into the 1978 Munster final, or me listening to Michael O'Hehir as they chased their dreams.

The most cherished dreams never came through, but it was some journey.

Writing this book was some journey too.

Being locked down in the West Kerry Gaeltacht area of Baile na nGall, that has been a temporary home for many a Clare hurler that chose primary teaching as a way of life, comes highly recommended.

'Imíonn an tuirse ach fanann an tairbhe.'

Joe Ó Muircheartaigh
March, 2021

PROLOGUE

Prologue

When we were being shouldered up through the village, I spotted Johnny and Eamon Callinan alongside O'Meara's shop… opposite his mother's pub where Johnny grew up himself. You could see how emotional Callinan was. I got emotional too. It was brilliant to rekindle all of those memories.

— Anthony Daly, 1995

MAY 14, 1964

IT WAS ONLY my second time in Dublin, but whereas the first was fun and adventure, this was a journey into the darkness and the unknown.

My father, Eamon had just died – he had been ill for a while, in and out of hospital in Limerick and finally Dublin, but it was still very sudden and a huge shock. He was just 42 and a strong man, and I wasn't with him when he passed away.

It meant the 150-mile road trip to Dublin and back with his remains was the beginning of a long goodbye and an uncertain future for my newly widowed mother, Mary left with six young children ranging in ages from 13 down to two and a business to look after.

Dad had brought me to Dublin for the first time less than two years previously, to the new frontier for a hurling fanatic; when I became the envy of all my hurling peers on the street and around the village by attending the All-Ireland final between Tipperary and Wexford.

The first Sunday in September.

Where my daydreams actually brought me.

NOW, I WAS going to the same parish – up the Liffey quays… then O'Connell Street… around by Parnell Square, but instead of following a straight line down Denmark Street to Mountjoy Square and on to Croke Park, we were veering to the left for the Mater Hospital.

It was just a few pucks away from Jones' Road, but the difference between the two places and the two visits, two years apart, couldn't have been more stark, particularly because I was so young and didn't really know what was happening.

I was a seven year-old going to Croke Park that first time, wide-eyed and in awe that my father would bring me to the biggest day of the year. His signal to me that I was coming of age; my age of reason coinciding with the age where I could step up to the same level as him and attend All-Ireland finals.

Like the player winning a first All-Ireland, I was convinced it would be like this every year. Myself, my father, the All-Ireland. Again… and again.

A wonderful ritual of habit.

The build-up, the journey… the everything about the best day of the year.

Now, suddenly it was all gone. There'd be no more All-Irelands with Eamon Callinan, the larger than life Ennisman, who had crossed the great divide between town and village and was embraced by Clarecastle as one of their own.

Hurling man.

Hackney man.

Barman.

Board of Works man.

Man about village. To me he was huge. A man of 6'1", with big shoulders and a big chest and a hero. My father was named after Eamon de Valera, but he was why I called my own son Eamon.

At the time of his death, was I heartbroken? Was I bereft?

I don't know, because I don't think I understood it. I had a sense that this just wasn't right, but as to having a sense that my father was actually dead, I wasn't sure what that really meant. How could I understand?

There was nobody there to counsel me, not that I thought I needed counselling.

Hurling did that, and in its own way filled a vacuum. Being out and about with friends, growing up with them, hurling with them. Everyday. Going home to eat and sleep and then away hurling again. It's what we all did.

And it was hurling on many different levels that I was thinking about on the way up to Dublin that day. It was an escape, thinking about that All-Ireland final journey with my father that was a cherished memory… being in the Cusack Stand with him.

It's not like I was saying to him on All-Ireland day that I wanted to emulate the likes of Billy Rackard, Nick O'Donnell, Donie Nealon, Theo English or John Doyle; but I was telling him I wanted to be a hurler.

Him telling me, why not.

Those hurling thoughts would have consumed me all the way back home. Through the towns and villages until we came to our own village, with the funeral cortege stopping ceremoniously below the bridge… Droichead an Chláir, the traditional port of entry by road to Clarecastle from the south that's just a few yards from our house and from the old hurling field across the road.

I wonder will they play the game.

Surely not… how could they play a game of hurling… today?

IT WAS THE local street league final where the only criteria for participation was that you could hold a hurley, wanted to play and were able to stay out of harm's way. It was the ad-hoc All-Ireland that went from the training grounds of the Main Street where I lived, and the Quay Road behind me, to the hurling field for the grand finale.

To all of us, but especially for me, this was bigger than a day out in Dublin for an All-Ireland final. Much bigger. This was about local bragging rights in the village and much more as my team crossed camáns with the lads from St Joseph's Terrace for the title.

They couldn't play without me.

Don't even think about it… didn't happen.

I WAS CONVINCED, but still consumed by it.

I had to know for sure as the funeral started moving again, going past our house and pub where there was another pause and then up the street to the church.

Fifty-six years later and it's one of my most vivid hurling memories. My father was being brought to the church, years and decades before his time, but I was still hurling in that moment, pucking the ball over and back in my mind as to exactly what was happening in my absence.

I WAS WALKING up the church yard behind his coffin, but looking around as I went. I wanted to catch the eye of my best friend, Ger Ward. He'd know.

He was one of the crew, another hurler. Eventually I saw him with his back to the church, and he with another pal and hurler, Haulie Russell.

Over I went, jumping out of the line to get the news. The confirmation I was looking for and expected.

'Did ye play?

'Ye didn't… I know ye didn't.

'Ye called it off for me… fair play.

'When is it on?

'I'll be there!'

Then the pause, and the few seconds of dead air.

'We… we did play and we won.'

My heart sank, but more than that I was absolutely livid with Ger, Haulie and the whole lot of them, even the lads from St Joseph's Terrace. In that moment – and it's frozen all this time – I was heartbroken for a second time that day.

I wanted so badly to play that game, for myself, but also for my father. The fact that the lads didn't wait for me and put the game back for a few days so I could be part of it made me angry and disappointed. I shed a few tears later that they'd gone ahead without me. It was emotional, because even at that stage hurling meant that to me.

It's not like they needed Clare County Board or Central Council approval to do the right thing – instead they did the wrong thing. The winning or the losing of the game didn't matter, but just to be part of the occasion, the rough and tumble of it and the few pucks I might get was everything to me.

At nine I had no idea whether I was a good hurler or not, but I just wanted to play and as I jumped back into the line to walk into the church behind my father's coffin that's what I was thinking about.

It's one of my earliest hurling memories and I wasn't even playing. It's still there because getting the chance to play the game and be part of it was what it was all about – that's how I felt that night and it's a philosophy I've carried with me ever since. It's the thrill of the game, the primal and tribal elements to the simple act of pucking a ball. Everything that goes with it. I just wanted to be part of that at all times.

Hurling it.

Pucking it.

Living it.

I didn't that day, but the day should have waited for me.

◄◄◆►►

It was in the village of Clarecastle that one of the biggest and most emotional of the welcomes took place. There was complete bedlam. A pipe band met the Clare party at the edge of town, the MacCarthy Cup glinting in the orange glow of the bonfire. The six local lads were shouldered high and carried triumphantly. As fireworks exploded and the traditional band played 'Olé… Olé' on the accordion, the entire village went crazy.

– Noel Smyth, *Irish Independent*

SOMEHOW, THAT BRIDGE in Clarecastle remains as a recurring point of reference that best explains how important and constant the theme of hurling has been throughout my life.

The symbolism of my father's funeral stopping there silently for a few moments before crossing the River Fergus is a memory that's hugely powerful to this day, for myself and my family, but on a deeply personal level for me because it's interconnected with the game.

That's because of the ritual attached to the crossing of any river.

For those of us from the street beyond, the bridge was the division between urban and rural; we were townie sophisticates in our own minds on our side, those on the far side were from the wilds of the country.

But, more importantly, the bridge was also the place where people gathered. For my father's funeral procession, but also for hurling processions.

When Clare won the All-Ireland title in 1995 the team bus stopped at the bridge, where the Clarecastle contingent were literally airlifted from hands to hands over the bridge to the biggest night in the village's history.

I was there with my son, Eamon, having brought him and his sister, Aoife to the All-Ireland the day before. He was seven, the same age as I had been when going to the final 33 years previously with my father. Now I was the same age as my father was for that 1962 final – a 40 year-old with a dodgy knee, clambering up onto a gate-post and then the pillar to have a front row seat for the party.

It was a slice of heaven; I felt closer to the place anyway.

The road below that I had first held a hurley on, trained for the street league on, became a hurler on. All for the playing of the next game, be it on the street, Devine's field across the road, or all the way to Semple Stadium and Croke Park… but also for this.

The thrill of being alive and present to see Clare win an All-Ireland and see it coming home to the village. For this stage and this spectacle.

As everything stood still, my thoughts were going into overdrive – just as they had done in the same place the night my father was being brought to the church. It's because I was consumed by the game.

It was everything, with those two incidents on the bridge over three decades apart crystallising everything for me.

The Magpies. Getting off the bus and floating along.

The captain, Dalo.

Sparrow, Tuts, Nev, Morrissey… Sheedo. Six of them; six of us.

Six Magpies… men I had won senior club championships with. *What do you think of that Newmarket? How many do ye have?*

None!

All in jest, of course, because we were all in this thing together and the inter-club rivalries that had held Clare hurling back for far too long were long gone. Still though, the Blues had beaten the Magpies so many times in county finals during my time growing up, and I'd be lying if I said there wasn't a cosy satisfaction in having this over our near neighbours and bitter rivals of old, even if it was never used.

It wasn't, because we were too busy drinking pints. Loads of pints. In our pub, Callinan's, in Power's, in Navin's, in Frawley's and in the Coach House where

Vincent Browne was doing his RTÉ Radio 1 show from that night.

NO WONDER IT was the longest and greatest night in the longest hurling year Clare had since 1914.

If it had ended in Thurles when Clare won their first Munster title since 1932 it still would have been the greatest year, because Thurles had been the graveyard of Clare's ambitions for so many years. My ambitions, too.

Losing the Munster finals in 1972, '74, '77 and '78 – the same old story in the 1981 final after finally beating Cork to get there, before the Rebels finally put me out of my Munster final misery for a final time when we travelled in hope once more for the 1986 decider in Killarney.

But now and gloriously so, all that pain was over.

Finally, we had a journey home from Thurles when we'd be singing instead of crying or cursing into our pints, and with the prospect of Croke Park to come after that.

This is what it could have been like for me as a player. But, when it happened for the class of 1995 there were no wistful regrets, just elation.

I'm not sure everyone appreciated how brilliant it was. There was a little bit of resentment. Some of the 70s crew felt that the team they were on was usurped by all that happened in 1995. I couldn't understand this. I still can't.

Some may have felt that the successes in that long and hot summer that stretched until September took away from their achievements, and that manager Ger Loughnane had paid no homage to the team of the 70s. Whether he did or didn't never bothered me.

I didn't care and used to tell some others… 'Do we need to be told how good we were… we know we were good, we knew our place in Clare hurling'.

I was at a wedding a few years after the 1995 success at which some members of the Clare team were present and part of a speech from Fr Harry Bohan was along the lines… 'You'd swear there was no hurling in Clare before 1995 came along'.

The success of 1995 was what I hurled for, what we all hurled for, what Fr Harry managed and gave so many years of his life for.

We wanted it to be us. And, while we were very good, we weren't good enough when it mattered most.

We had achieved so much, yet we had failed. But between all the highs and lows we still had a great time in trying to kick that door down.

WE WERE DOOR-OPENERS.

That's how I see us.

When we were playing, we came to a plateau and we needed to move up a bit more to win Munster and All-Ireland titles. We didn't, but at least there was a Clare team in living memory that had contended. That was important when the team of 1995 came along, because what we did and achieved kept the flame burning.

Climbing up to get the best vantage point the night the Liam MacCarthy Cup came to Clarecastle for the first time brought that fact home to me. Eamon and myself placed ourselves over on the parish priest's pier and we could see the cavalcade coming down. We were screaming at Dalo as they came towards us.

I was sure that Dalo went past and didn't see us. In that second, I was disappointed. *Maybe I should have waved more and shouted more to get his attention.*

I wanted that attention. It was hugely emotional, even more so when Dalo told me afterwards that he saw the two of us and that it meant a lot to him. I can safely say it meant more to me. The Munster and All-Ireland successes that year were the biggest compliments that Anthony Daly's generation of Clare hurlers could pay all of us past players of the different generations that had gone to the well so many times only to come away bereft.

We weren't forgotten, if anything we were more loved and beloved.

MY GENERATION GOT that love, because there was something about that Clare team of the 70s. A quality and derring-do that stirred something within the psyche of the county at the time, whether one was a hurling fan or not, and penetrated those way beyond the county boundary too.

We were rock 'n' roll, and we lived it up as we hurled, even if we were always fated to be to hurling what The Rolling Stones were to The Beatles. Second best (and Duke was Jagger). Second best in Ireland, but second best to a great Cork team that won three in-a-row, something that hadn't been done since the last time they did it in the 50s.

Still, what we had we gave, because it's all we ever wanted.

All I ever wanted, since being in Croke Park with my father for the first and only time, playing those street leagues and wherever the game took me after that.

I was chasing it right up to my last day with the Clare team in Killarney in 1987, and beyond for a few more years with the club. It was some ride.

PART ONE

Busy Growing, Busy Hurling

« CHAPTER 1 »

I know there were many ardent Limerick hurling followers kicking their heels restlessly on the beaches at Ballybunion and Kilkee when the all too brief message flashed across the air... 'And now here is the result of the Munster hurling final... Limerick 2-16, Clare 2-6.

— Camán, *Limerick Leader*, 1955

GROWING UP AND immersed in hurling from an early age you'd be forgiven for thinking that the game in Clare started and ended in 1955 – that it was the beginning of the end and the end of the beginning.

It was also the year that I was born.

The year explained away by hurlers on the ditch as the annus mirabilis that morphed into horribilis thanks to 60 minutes that defined a generation and as the years passed, somehow dragged down everyone who wore the jersey.

The curse... Biddy Early.

The Poor Clares.

The bullshit.

All that folklore that supporters and headline writers used as a convenience to justify the county's failings and second-class citizenry within the game in Munster and beyond.

It was a lazy default setting, because all the elements of Greek tragedy were there. Clare were the coming team. In Croke Park before a crowd of nearly 30,000, they beat a great Wexford team to win the Oireachtas Tournament, with big Dan McInerney holding the bigger Nicky Rackard scoreless... and Jimmy Smyth being our Christy Ring.

Then Clare beat Cork and Tipperary in the 1955 Munster championship – the first time the big two had been beaten by Clare in the same year, a feat magnified by the fact that it has only happened once since. All that was left was a Limerick team of no-hopers for a Clare team that was going to win Munster and the All-Ireland.

As a newborn, I wasn't brought the 20 miles down the road to the Gaelic Grounds by my father to be present when things turned to dust, but I may as well have been there for the decades that talk of 1955 was allowed dominate hurling conversations in the county.

'Mackey's Greyhounds'. Dermot Kelly. Dónal O'Grady. Clare were too old; Clare's hurling was too slow for the hot day of summer, the same type of mud that was thrown at us in 1977 and '78.

1955 meant nothing to me.

Dónal O'Grady was the man who drove me to the Munster final in 1978; Jimmy Smyth and Dan McInerney were men who were in the dressing-room after that final when the place teemed with people. That was it.

We were just too busy for history. Busy growing up, busy hurling.

I WAS THE fourth of six children.

Anne, Mary and Bríd came before me.

Martina and Eamon after me, and we were reared over the pub that we called 'The Shop', on what we called 'The Street' in Clarecastle.

Tom Hayes was the name originally over the door of the pub – he was my mother's father, who had come from Newmarket-on-Fergus around 1912 and taken a lease on the property in the part of the village that's still referred to as 'The Street'.

My father then married into the pub, but he also came from the same background, the Halfway House that was the midway point between Ennis and Clarecastle, before the spread of suburbia ate into the green fields and eventually joined the two places together, physically, if not spiritually.

He was named after de Valera, because his mother had been a huge supporter of Dev since he came to the county in 1917 and was elected MP for East Clare. She was so devout that when he'd pass the door of the Halfway on his way to Ennis on August 15 every year to attend the County Show, she'd sit outside waiting for him.

And, she'd see him off in the evening when he was going home. It was hero worship. He could do no wrong.

Tom Hayes' house was very different to the Halfway House, though. It wasn't a de Valera house. My mother gave de Valera credit for one thing – keeping Ireland out of the war, but that was it. It was a very simple choice, you were either pro-Dev or not. It was very binary.

She was not a fan. Everyone in the house followed on from that. My father, if he had lived, might have brought a different influence.

CLARECASTLE WAS A port village, but the last boat that I remember was around 1967 – the boats to service the coal yards of Sutton's, Power's and McInerney's in Ennis were long gone and the viability of bringing relatively small boats all the way to Clarecastle was just not there anymore.

There was one famous attempt at exporting from Clarecastle, from the only factory in the village, the clay pipe factory beyond Lissane. It made drainage pipes from the mud, but the problem with shipping them was that they were brittle and they broke.

It was a seafaring and fishing village and it had a culture that at different stages of the year there'd be money around the place. The money mightn't have been consistent, but it was there.

The fishing aspect of the village was huge when I was growing up. You'd be hurling away, but as young fellas we would know the times of the tides and know when the fishermen were coming in. We'd throw the hurleys to one side and go down to see the fishing boats.

FOR OUR FAMILY it was a comfortable upbringing.

I don't recall ever wanting for anything, but at the same time I don't recall having anything extravagant. Still, there was a lot of poverty around the place, but

I don't remember anyone hungry. Then again, would I have seen or noticed such a thing?

My mother worked away in the pub and my father worked there at night, as well as being in the Bord of Works and driving a hackney – a Ford Consul that I went to a lot of matches in during those early years. An aunt of my mother's, Winifred Bowles, a former teacher, lived with us as well.

The village was very much a *village,* and the village thing was brilliant. If you were an outdoor person, it was great.

We were townies, we were corner boys and because we were all living close together, we were always together. The boys hung around with the boys… the girls with the girls. We were even in separate schools.

Ger Ward from the Quay Road was my best friend.

I would have eaten as many dinners in Ward's as I did in my own house. Haulie Russell, who was also from the Quay Road, and Michael Hegarty from Madden's Terrace were other friends.

Hego was a few years older than me and was the leader of the gang, with a crowd around him all the time. He went on to play underage and senior for Clare, and win a senior championship with Clarecastle in 1970.

Growing up, he brought us quieter fellas to places we wouldn't have gone. It was craic around the street, particularly at the corner with Hego. Always.

The other places we found ourselves were down by the Quay, or in the hurling field across the road from my house. They were the choices. We hurled and also kicked a bit of football, mainly soccer unless someone – particularly Dónal Carey who lived over the bridge – saw us in those years before the Ban was lifted.

For most of my friends the first thing was hurling. It wasn't planned and structured – it's more like that hurling in some shape or form was such a central part of our lives that we didn't notice it.

THE QUAY ROAD was where I first held a hurley in anger.

I was the only one from my age group, from The Street, so I was what you'd call an 'isolated player', a well-known concept in Clare GAA, and allowed play with the Quay Road in the informal street leagues that we'd have.

St Joseph's Terrace had a team; Madden's Terrace and St Michael's were some of the other teams. There was no team from the outlying areas. There was a tacit acceptance among everyone that I'd play for Quay Road.

We'd play each other regularly – not every week, but nearly every week. It was intense stuff, at least we thought it was intense. We wouldn't be togged, there were no boots, just our shoes and short pants, sometimes long pants.

If we turned up with 20 players and the opposition only had 15, it was tough luck on them. Whatever number you had, you played with, so there was no mercy shown. Having it as 15-a-side, 12-a-side – there was nothing as controlled as that in what we were doing. It was ad hoc.

In those gatherings, sliotars were as rare as hen's teeth, unless we'd managed to rob one here or there. Those matches were generally played with a wind ball… like a handball or a sponge ball. Not that I saw the ball much in the early years.

At seven, eight and nine years of age you'd only be hoping to get an odd puck of the ball here and there, and not get killed. It was tough, but how tough was it at the end of the day? You'd get cut in the knees or the shins. We didn't break many hurleys, even though calling them hurleys would be flattering them somewhat.

Most of the hurling was on the ground.

It was pretty rudimentary stuff. You got a hurley wherever you could. When we were at school, all the hurleys were left up against the wall or the drainpipe outside, and you just picked one up when you needed it.

The big thing at the time, in total contrast to today, was the complete lack of supervision of children at that age. We were always gone. Nobody ever came looking for us. We were always up to something, but we always got home.

I REMEMBER THE Sheridans up in Madden's Terrace won a television one year, so for the All-Ireland everyone went up there, but we ended up only listening to the matches from outside because the house was too full.

Navin's pub was also a place to go to try and see the games. Pat Navin was the first person in the village to get a television. All the kids could come in at 5pm to 6pm every day to watch *Rin Tin Tin*, but we'd all be gone by news-time.

Hanging around the forge of blacksmith, Timmy McMahon, across from the church was another favourite haunt. We were drawn there. Timmy Smith, we called him. The horses, the bellows… but most importantly of all, if we had a damaged hurley he'd be able to fix it for us.

Hurleys were so hard to come by and when you had one it was kept together by Timmy. He was a character.

Through my father's friendship with another Timmy and a real character as well, I got to go to the 1962 All-Ireland final. Tim Murphy, who was married to an aunt of Anthony Daly's, had gone to America as a young man and was an agent for the selling of Joe McGrath's Irish Sweepstakes tickets. He was a good bit older than my father, had a few bob in his pocket all the time and knew how to enjoy himself.

He got the tickets for that All-Ireland, two tickets, but I was brought along to Dublin for the experience. It was a great expedition. We drove to Limerick and then trained it from there. I missed two days in school for an All-Ireland – but John Hanly, as a hurling man and principal in the national school, didn't mind and would have given his full blessing for me being away.

An All-Ireland was more important than school, a great education in itself was his view.

We stayed in a Bed and Breakfast in the Gardiner Street area of town – a big old Georgian house, but we weren't in it much over the four days. It wasn't just about the match, but everything around it and they made sure to have a good time. They had a few drinks every night, going out on the town… so I had to go with them.

There was holy water thrown on us by my mother's aunt, Winifred, or Winnie as she was known, before we left Clarecastle, and there was holy water thrown on us when we eventually made it back.

It was great to be at the game – the Clare county final between Sixmilebridge and Ruan was played the same day, but instead I was at the real thing and among the 75,000 crowd in Croke Park.

Did I have a craving to be out there myself?

For sure I wanted to be as good as those Tipp and Wexford players – players that nearly 60 years later are looked on as some of the greatest ever – but I'd be lying if I said I wanted to emulate them.

That time, even as a seven year-old, I knew and instinctively felt that it wasn't something Clare hurlers aspired to, because they just didn't get to Croke Park very often. If I was a young fella from Kilkenny, I might have had a yearning for it, but not as a young Clare lad.

The biggest memory, apart from being shunted in over the stile was the minor game – Tommy Walsh was playing for Kilkenny; he was centre-forward and had this shock of blond hair that made him look like a blond Beatle. He's still remembered because five years later, at just 23, his county career was ended after he lost an eye when being injured in the closing minutes of the 1967 All-Ireland final against Tipperary.

On All-Ireland final day in 1962 he became my county hero, even when he was a minor. He made a huge impression on me. It was the hair, because there's a thing about blond hair – just like Cork's John Horgan stood out, and Jean Pierre Rives, the famous French wing forward on the rugby fields in the 1970s and 80s, always stood out.

It was all about the hair, and that it was long and flowed. But just like Horgan and Rives, Walsh was a bloody good player.

For me, he *made* the day, way more than the big names in the senior game could ever do – winning captain Jimmy Doyle, Tony Wall or Billy Rackard, who played half the game with a broken hand. The senior game was held up as one of the greatest ever as Tipperary won by 3-10 to 2-11.

Writing in *The Irish Press*, Mick Dunne called it... *A magnificent and deliriously spellbinding game...* and that... *a selection of the richest superlatives in the most comprehensive dictionary fall short of adequately describing the game.*

All of that went over my head. The only person I could see was Tommy Walsh – he scored 2-2 and to me everything he touched turned to gold.

Two days later it was still *all* about Tommy Walsh for me, as my father and Tim Murphy finally had enough of Dublin and we headed for home – on the train was Mickey Burns, one of the Tipp wing backs, and another player from the subs was also on the train. They hadn't made it back for the Monday night celebration in Thurles and they were a bit the worse for wear from the celebrations over the previous two nights.

I remember getting their autographs.

THE NEXT TIME I came down from Dublin was with my father's remains.

We got a taxi up to Dublin with Jimmy Kelly from the Market in Ennis. He had a big black Ford. Then we came down behind Joe Daly's hearse.

My older sisters were much more conscious of what was going on than I was – it was as if, at just nine, I was at the cut-off age and they were acting in my best interests and not telling me about what was going on.

My father got ill when he was 40.

It was a heart issue, a thickening of the blood in and around his heart that could now be easily dealt with by modern medicine. I didn't realise how sick he was and that's why I don't think I was brought to see him in the weeks before he died.

After going to Dublin I wanted to go in and see my father, but I wasn't allowed. Would I have understood if I had gone in? I don't think so. I saw the coffin afterwards, but I hadn't seen my father in the coffin.

On the day of his burial, a sunny Friday afternoon after High Mass in Clarecastle Church, his remains were brought to Clareabbey. He was a Clare Road man and his parents and siblings were all interred in Clareabbey.

I travelled with the cortege up the old lane, past Leyden's to the edge of Clareabbey, but was kept away from the graveyard; I was left across the railway tracks, playing or occupying myself.

I missed out on something I would have cherished being part of – the ritual of people waiting around after burial and filling in the grave. It's a hugely symbolic thing at funerals, especially in the country.

That I missed it was something I thought about a lot over the years.

Back in 2016, I remember being at the funeral of Munster rugby legend, Anthony Foley, because of knowing his father, Brendan quite well. When he was buried in Killaloe, members of the Munster team were helping fill in the grave. Paul O'Connell, Ronan O'Gara and others stepped up, but standing over on his own well away from it all was Dougie Howlett.

I didn't know him, but went over to him and said, 'Why don't you take a shovel?'

His answer was… 'We do that too at home'.

He went over and played a part in it. I was thinking of my father; it would have been a great connection to have with him, to have been part of that final process.

I was just too young, but being shielded from the whole thing meant that his death went over my head a bit. It had a bigger effect on my older sisters.

But his passing did mean that I grew up a lot faster. I assumed an importance in the family that wouldn't have been altogether healthy for me. I had no real teenage years as, after my father's death, I went from being this young fella to having this responsibility for my mother, while I went on to playing adult hurling before I had any real teenage life.

My mother internalised her grief; she hid her grief from us and got on with it, because she had to, but it was very hard. And it got harder in subsequent years, because one day out of the blue she got a letter from the local ground rent landlord.

IT WAS ABOUT two years after my father died when Fred Herriot, an accountant from Limerick, wrote to my mother and the O'Meara family across the road, serving them with notices to quit. In effect they were being evicted from the properties they'd owned for over 50 years.

He had inherited local ground rents on the properties that were owned by two members of the O'Brien clan from Dromoland Castle, who lived between our pub and the bridge. This was a bombshell and it came when I was getting to be of an age when I understood what was going on.

So, we had a situation where my mother was in danger of losing everything – she'd lost her husband, but got on with trying to run the pub and bring up the six of us, but now we could be turfed out onto the street.

She had to fight it and did, thanks to getting a good solicitor that our neighbour, Dónal Carey introduced to her at the wedding of another neighbour, Peter Hanly.

Kevin Smith was a college friend of Dónal's in Dublin – a dyed in the wool Fianna Fáil man, but this wasn't about politics. The solicitor could have been Dev's own son, Vivion for all she cared; she just wanted someone who would take on the case and, more importantly, win it. Kevin was from Cavan and built up a great practice in Dublin, doing really well for himself.

I can vividly remember it. I wasn't at the Circuit Court sitting in Ennis because of school, but I remember that an earlier legal opinion of Isaac Butt SC was used. It was a huge deal.

The eviction proceedings were thrown out and my mother and Mrs O'Meara came out stronger as protected tenants. It meant that instead of being out on the street, we had a roof over our heads and that my mother still had her business, and life as we knew it could go on.

There was a great party in the pub that night.

It was huge victory against the head and proof that sometimes the underdog could actually win. It was fighting City Hall – the widow tenant with very little against landlordism – and winning. This success was a major influence in my choice of career as a solicitor. Kevin Smyth, although now deceased, remains one of my Legal Heroes.

Even at that stage it could have been a metaphor for my hurling career – in those street leagues all the way through to club and county level.

Taking on City Hall in hurling was taking on tradition. Kilkenny and Cork were that outside of our county, just like our next door neighbours, Newmarket-on-Fergus were in Clare.

It was all about trying to beat them.

« CHAPTER 2 »

Clarecastle was a hurling village when I was growing up. Before that it was football that was played here, just because it was cheaper to play football. The big area was the Fairgreen and we hurled there every day, with the school across the way... a two-room school, one for the girls on top... the boys on the bottom. At break time we were allowed across the road to hurl because there was no traffic. We had a great youth.

– John Hanly, Clarecastle

DÓNAL CAREY WAS and still is a hero to me.

The part he played in helping my mother beat the bailiffs from our door was a simple act of kindness that I've never forgotten, and never will. It was one of many such acts, because the links between the Callinan and Carey families have been constants; they've been there all my life.

Dónal, or Dan as a lot of local people call him, was there for us when we needed him.

Always. He became a huge influence in my life after my father died. In many ways, I don't know what we would have done without him.

THERE HADN'T BEEN any obvious connection between the two families.

I was a member of the Legion of Mary, as were Dónal's parents, who were very prominent in the organisation, but that wasn't a link between us in any real sense because nearly every mother in Clarecastle would have encouraged their children to attend the Legion of Mary. Michael Hegarty was also a member and as Bishop Willie Walsh said to him jokingly many years later at a Clarecastle medal presentation, it was probably the first secret or subversive society of which he was a member.

The real connection with the Careys was forged on the street, and through the basic action of neighbours helping each other out, because it's what people and communities did.

Years later, when Dónal entered politics, first getting elected to Clare County Council in 1974 and eventually Dáil Éireann in 1982 for a 20-year stint as a TD, I campaigned for him – out of duty, but also because I really wanted to do it. He deserved it, just as I canvass to this day for his son, Joe who has followed Dónal into the Dáil.

Dónal was 17 years older than me.

When I was six, he was 23 and my father would have been in his late thirties, so there was nearly the same gap between Dónal and my father, and myself and Dónal. But there was a great bond there between the two of us despite that age difference. An unbreakable bond.

When Dónal got married to a Carlow woman, Evelyn Forde in 1973, I was his Best Man and that said a lot about the closeness between our two families. His brother, Michael, who was a priest, married them, but at 18 I was the one he chose as his Best Man… a Best Man to my father figure.

And he was just that to me – a real father figure in every way, and that included the hurling field.

THE FIRST REALLY big game I went to with my father was the 1961 Munster final between Tipperary and Cork, when I was literally thrown in the car and brought to Limerick. There was a huge crowd there, with over 60,000 making it the largest ever attendance at a Munster final.

It was also dangerous.

Off the field and on it. The crowd were in on the edge of the field from all sides, having packed into the ground hours before the game.

Tipp hammered Cork, but it was all about the bust up near the end between Christy Ring and John Doyle, when in the melee that broke out Tom Moloughney got struck. Ring got the blame, with Mick Dunne's report stating… *There can only be condemnation of his behaviour*…thereby kicking off a controversy that led all the way to journalists being barred by the Cork County Board from attending games in the old Mardyke grounds – and court action against *The Irish Press* and RTÉ.

Dunne said he wouldn't be bothered if he never saw another Munster final – he was obviously never at county senior championship games in Clare in the 60s.

I was just six watching that Munster final, but within a few years was immune to rows, because the game was so rough and there were so many of them. Much rougher than my first Munster final.

You forgot about rows, though.

You moved on. It was all about getting to go to the matches, because it was always a great expedition, wherever they were being played. We'd go early in the morning.

The lads heading to the matches with my father – people like John Ryan and Matt Cunningham, who had a shop hear the Halfway, and John Joe Shannon – would be in the car with a good few pint bottles and sandwiches for the journey, and I'd be stuck in the middle of them.

It was the same, but without the cargo of drink, when Dónal Carey took on the exact same role as my father when ferrying me to matches. In the early years he had a box Renault, a red one that replaced my father's Ford Consul. For those of us in Clarecastle who were interested in hurling, he was brilliant.

A taxi-man and our hurling man.

He did everything for us. He had a huge interest in the game, but apart from that, as secretary of the Clarecastle club he was effectively in charge of the underage on his own.

There were three or four of us he'd bring to all the games, club games that the seniors were playing, county games as well. He was as big an influence as my father had been in earlier years, in a nurturing way that I wasn't really aware of, because I was so interested and consumed by it, and in a way took it for granted.

Clare could be playing at the opening of a field in Cork or Tipperary and we'd load in, and off we'd go. Michael Hegarty was a regular, so too was Ger Ward. I always assumed there was a space for me in the car.

When I started playing juvenile for the club, Dónal might end up bringing eight fellas up to Ruan in the car – and he'd have to make three trips, because he was the only one doing it. He did it on his own, with no parents going to matches at that time to help.

And even if some of the parents wanted to go, there weren't that many of them who had cars. Later on, Chris Keane, an uncle of Anthony Daly's, was like Dónal in that he didn't play but had a huge interest and was another big influence.

And if Dónal wasn't going to games, we'd make sure to get a lift from someone else. We'd hang around the corner and someone always picked us up. We weren't like the young lads of today bringing our hurleys with us and going out on the field at half-time to puck around. The only way we'd be out on the field with a hurley was if we picked up bits of broken hurleys thrown around the place. The pickings were meagre.

Myself and Ger were the real fanatics – we had to see every game, especially the senior games and when it came to the big games I'd be hanging around the dressing-room, and in it if I got the chance. We were rubbing off the team, so as kids we automatically felt that we were part of it.

In school, John Hanly was a different influence, a more direct influence, but the man who gave me the real start and promoted the grá was Dónal. But John Hanly was still huge. At school he was commonly known to his pupils as Johnno – though to most of us he was always Mr Hanly.

He was involved in the training of the Clare team in the 60s when I was in primary school. I had him in fourth, fifth and sixth classes – to get me ready for secondary school, but also to make me ready for hurling in St Flannan's where he'd gone himself and had been an illustrious player in the 40s.

He'd have conversations and discussions with us that were semi-philosophical.

He was a Christian man and a socialist, and still is, but most importantly of all he was a hurler. We'd heard about what he did with Flannan's, and we knew he could still hurl because he played with us during school time. Dermot Fitzgerald was the biggest in the school in my time and he used to mark Johnno in those games.

But what he did most of all was make hurling available for us every day we were at school – he was so encouraging about the game. Hurling was always there. It wasn't a case of us being better off outside hurling than inside learning our lessons, but he did stretch the limits.

He made hurling a huge part of our education; the game was special in his school curriculum, catering to our interests, as well his own.

It was as simple as that and he was very open about it.

WE NEVER WON anything in primary schools competitions, even though we had the benefit of everything Johnno knew as a coach; skills that led him to play a lead role in organising the famous coaching courses in Gormanston College with Fr Tommy Maher, Donie Nealon, Ned Power and Des 'Snitchy' Ferguson.

He was a thinking man about hurling, but it wasn't enough to bring us any success. I remember Stonehall NS beat us one year – it wasn't the first time a team from Newmarket beat Clarecastle, but the excuse we came up with at the time was that they were all over-age. I'm sure they weren't, but it didn't stop us using it.

We didn't care, though – the important thing was that we were hurling. First it was in the school yard and then we got a small field, on the right hand side of the boys school. It was more a piece of green grass than a field, but it was enough. It's not that we were doing drills or anything sophisticated, it's just that we played… and we played.

The first year I made the team was in second class, when I was eight, around 1963. Looking back on it now, there's a pride that I made the cut then, because I was on a team and hurling before my father died.

It was important to me.

I was in goal, then corner-back the following year and the last few years I was a full-back, because John Hanly always believed in building his teams from the back!

He was nakedly macho about what he did. The hurling was just for the boys – there was no camogie whatsoever at that time. Our lives were so separate. I hardly knew a girl who was the same age as myself growing up.

I went to national school at four and fell in love with the first woman in my life. Miss Costello – Mrs Brooks afterwards. She was an angel.

Alas, there were no angels in St Flannan's when I went there.

◄ ◄ ◆ ► ►

St Flannan's College was put on this earth for three purposes... one, to win the Harty Cup in hurling; two, to win the gold medal in Greek; and three, to dispatch priests to the diocese. It was a tough regime. The most benign comment you'll get was that it was character forming.

– Michael D Higgins

IT WAS HARDSHIP.

That was the belief around daily life in St Flannan's College and certainly there was truth to it, but I looked on it differently. I looked at it from my point of view, the selfish one, of how great it was to go there.

Like any school, it was of its time. But, more importantly for me, the college came at a time of huge change in the landscape of education in Ireland. That process was started by Dr Paddy Hillery when he was Minister for Education in the early 60s, but for me secondary school coincided with the most progressive act in the history of education – Free Education brought in by Donogh O'Malley in September 1966. A year to the month later, I started in St Flannan's as part of the first intake of students under the scheme.

It was huge. The best way of giving context to it is that there would have been 12 or 14 boys in sixth class in our national school every year and if you had one or two of those going on to secondary school in St Flannan's College, it would be considered a *big* thing. There was only a handful ahead of us from the village who had gone there... Paschal Russell, and Patrick and Joe Power had gone there before me; so too had Gerald Barry, the now world-famous composer, but he never hurled.

Those from Clarecastle who had won Hartys or All-Irelands were even fewer. John Hanly and his brother, Willie were on the 1945 team; John was there again for the triumphs in 1946 and '47, while Anthony Daly's father, Pat Joe was on the 1952 team. Frankie McNamara was on the 1962 team beaten by an Ennis CBS side that included Gussie Considine, Jimmy Quinn and Bill Murphy from the village. That was it.

Still, I looked on St Flannan's as a bigger version of Clarecastle. We were a solid group as first years from the village. In that first year of Free Education eight or nine of us cycled up to St Flannan's, while the others from our sixth class went to the Tech.

My routine was strange.

I cycled to school, then after school trained and then went to study. At 7pm I'd be down to the Halfway House pub to my aunt for supper and back up to the school at 7.45pm for study, and then home at 9.30pm. I did that five days a week.

As an institution I thought that every day was very tough going, but it wasn't, because being a day boy you were semi-detached from what it was really like for the boarders, who spent every minute in the school.

They used to moan and complain about the conditions, but I didn't know what it was like. All I knew what that I didn't agree with boarding schools then, and I still don't. Psychologically being a boarder must be hard for any student.

I remember on Shrove Tuesday my mother would make lots of pancakes for me to bring into school and share out among the lads – when I got there, you'd swear some of them never got fed. I don't think they were starving, but that it's just that they were getting something different to eat.

They'd ravage what was in front of them. It was a survival of the strongest and the fittest to get a few pancakes.

Just like it was to get on the hurling teams, because it was hugely competitive from the word go. The fact that we hurled every day tells its own story. It was an extension of life as we knew it under John Hanly in the national school.

HURLING WAS A ritual and rite of passage.

The phrase in Flannan's all the time – a cant or a mantra among teachers and students – was... 'Did you go up the field?' And, in reality, you didn't really have to mention field... 'Did you go up?' was enough.

Everyone knew what it meant and certainly there was less thought of you in the school if you didn't go up and weren't interested. There was quite a macho attitude to it.

It was expected of you, but that wasn't uncommon in boys' schools. If you were in St Jarlath's in Tuam it would have been to the football field, or in Clongowes and Blackrock College to the rugby field. To each their own.

For us, it was the hurling field with a bit of football thrown in... if Fr Seamus Mullin and Fr Ollie O'Doherty had their way.

I went up the first week.

We went up to try out for the team. There were trial matches and next was the big announcement that there would be a first year league.

There wasn't a first year team playing in outside competition, but we were kept going with this league There were six teams – nearly everyone was hurling and while you mightn't have teams of 15 it was definitely 13-a-side. Four of them were captained by Clarecastle lads… myself, Ger Ward, PJ Corry and Tony Murphy.

At one stage it was proposed by Fr John Shalloo that there would be compulsory games; that everyone would have to 'go up the field'. Fr Shalloo was steeped in it – he was an uncle of Sean Hehir, while his own uncle John Shalloo was on the Clare team that won the All-Ireland in 1914.

I was completely in favour of what he was proposing, that everyone had to tog out and be part of it. Whether you hated hurling or you had no aptitude for it didn't matter, you'd have to hurl. Very enlightened!

You'd have to go up.

It was bordering on being in an 'Elite Guard' in that you had to be devoted, but I was all for it.

Fr Shalloo, who was president of the college in the late 60s, may have had young priests and teachers like Seamus Gardiner and Willie Walsh to take up the hurling mantle at that time, but they weren't disciples of his in terms of approach when taking us hurlers under their wing.

GER LOUGHNANE AND Colm Honan were a year ahead of me; Sean Hehir was a year ahead of them, while Sean Stack was in my year when he came from Limerick CBS for his final year to try and make all the difference for us in our efforts to finally land a Harty.

I got on the under-15 team in my second year and we won the Munster title when beating Sullivan's Quay in May 1969. We had a nephew of Tomás MacGiolla, Robert Gill from Youghalarra, in goal for us. Loughnane was centre-back on that team, with Honan at midfield and the captain. He seemed massive with his head of curly corn-like hair, probably because the rest of us were so small.

Among those of us up front were Whitegate's Jacko Tracey, Ennis' Brendan Gilligan, Tim Crowe from Sixmilebridge and myself.

Tracey and Crowe scored two goals each in the final, while I got the other in a big 5-8 to 3-4 win that should have set us up to go on and win Dean Ryan and Harty titles in the following years.

I remember afterwards the *Clare Champion* headline said... *Flannan's Future Looks Bright* – the school authorities would have believed that, too and we were paraded out from class to get a picture taken outside the front door.

It was very staged, but great to get that far and win something.

It was my first ever medal. Alas, that was it. It was my *only* medal in my time in the school. We lost every other final we played in.

It wasn't for the want of effort though, or privileges, because if you were a Harty Cup hurler in Flannan's you were treated as being a breed apart – a better class of person, who'd make a better class of man. More of the 'Elite Guard' thing, an outlook on life that chimed with the hurling.

I was in that privileged group, because of making it on to the teams from the word go. I'd have been small for that under-15 team in 1969, but I was getting on the club minor team at 15, while at 16 I was able to make the cut at Harty level, as well as going for trials with the county minors.

Stepping up to Harty hurling was like going from junior hurling to Croke Park on All-Ireland day – not the jump in standard between grades, but the way you were looked upon by the school and your peers who didn't make that grade.

When you were on the Harty panel there was a ritual, where everyone from the various classrooms on the squad walked across the yard together to the refectory for what was called beef tea. This was a soup, that in our minds was the gruel they'd been giving students since 1914. It was only the Harty Cup team that got this special ration.

It was massive stuff. It was a privilege to get it. White bread to go with it, and the boarders on the team looked on the bread as white gold because it was the only time they got it. Us day boys didn't mind the brown bread, because we weren't used to it, but if you were a boarder it's what you were getting all the time.

The simple act of giving white bread to the Harty Cup panel was the school's way of saying... 'You're members of the school's elite guard, and you're better than everyone else'.

It was from a different world.

Again, more of that special status of being a hurler. We were like the young kids in the old Readybrek advert after eating it – we were insulated, we were super confident because we were being treated better than the rest of the school. And, we felt we clearly were better.

It was not healthy; it may have seemed brilliant to us while it was happening, but in terms of promoting equality it was not a good thing; it was anything but equality and parity of esteem – it was elitist and exclusionary.

We would walk back from the refectory and… think about any classic image anyone has of the public school system in England! It was the haves, and the have-nots.

Being on the Harty team meant we were considered a different class of person and there was no apologies for that. It was blatant.

WHEN I WAS captain of the Harty team, I had to go into the refectory on the day of the match to whip up the fellas who were coming to the match to support us.

I was one of the first day boys to captain the side.

The refectory was an intimidating place to go, full of screaming adolescents and there was a somewhat uncomfortable smell in the place. I found that these lads didn't need whipping up, instead they needed calming down as they were getting out for the day.

It was strange. It was another rite of passage as a Harty player.

This special treatment was there every day for the Harty season. I suppose from the management and the school's point of view it was to place us apart and to show us we were different. It was psychology on their part – separating us from the crowd, putting pressure on us to perform.

The only thing was, when we were out – when the Harty season ended – we were immediately back amongst the masses. We were treated like everyone else. As good as anyone else, or as bad as anyone else. It depended on your outlook and how you judged the daily grind and regime of the school.

This was the regime, whether you won or lost. Unfortunately, in my time we lost, as the Harty Cup famine that had stretched back to 1958 started to grow.

We should have ended it.

We should have done a lot better with the players we had.

« CHAPTER 3 »

St Flannans' glittering constellation of well-known inter-county stars entitles them to the favourite's tag. This is particularly true of the Saints midfield combination of John Callinan, who captains the side and Sean Stack, two Clare minors of the most promising calibre.

– The Clare Champion, 1972

THE BIG PLAYER when I went into St Flannan's was Joe McKenna.

I was very small as an underage player, so Big Joe was Gulliver to Lilliputian me. A giant not just in hurling terms, but most of all in hurling.

The only time I saw St Flannan's greatest ever, Jimmy Smyth at the school was when he came back and played a Past Vs Present match. He'd have been on the teams of the 40s that won all those Hartys and All-Irelands and for the priests, who knew all about his history, he was a hurling God.

The history didn't mean much to us. He was in his forties… I was 15.

My generation looked on him as an old man. That wasn't out of any disrespect, just that we were into our own thing. We were into ourselves.

Smyth played full-back in that game. Others to play were the likes of Donie Nealon and Len Gaynor. McKenna went in on Smyth; they had a good tussle, but in our eyes our man McKenna was well able for him.

Coming from Shinrone in Offaly, McKenna was in the school because at that time most of the boarders came from the diocese of Killaloe catchment area that took in most of Clare, a chunk of North Tipperary and parts of Laois, Offaly and Limerick.

Talk to Willie Walsh and Seamus Gardiner about the five Harty Cup and All-Ireland titles they won between 1976 and '87 and they'll tell you that the team Joe McKenna captained in 1970 was one of the ones that got away.

Little did I realise then the impact he would have on my hurling life, and also on my personal and professional life – Joe has been a friend, and client of mine, for over 40 years.

Jim Power was full-back on that team. Peter Scanlan from Waterford, who was a proper hurler, was centre-back. Colm Honan was midfield with Liam Heffernan from Nenagh, while captain McKenna was wing-forward, and Jacko Treacy, who succeeded him as captain the following year, was in the full-forward line. Ger Loughnane couldn't make the team, while Sean Hehir only came on as a sub when they were beaten narrowly by Farranferris in the semi-final.

The same quality and more with it was there when I made the team the following year. Loughnane was centre-back, myself and Honan were midfield, and Tim Crowe and Jacko Treacy were up front. Waterford minor, Peter Scanlan was still there. The goalkeeper was Limerick minor Ger Ryan, while Liam Heffernan and Dan Brislane were Tipp minors. We had about 10 county minors drawn from four different counties.

We were very strong and there was an expectation amongst ourselves that we could and would win the Harty Cup that year. We hammered St Colman's in the first round in Emly, when Jacko hit 3-3, to set up a grudge semi-final match against Ennis CBS.

I'd been at the famous 1962 final between the two sides in Cusack Park. There were over 7,000 present that day, but I could barely see the match. I thought it was like an Old Firm Celtic Vs Rangers thing and that this is what it would be like every year – it would be nine years later before the schools next met.

Beforehand there was a row over the venue.

The CBS wanted it in Cusack Park, obviously because that's where they'd beaten us in that famous final nine years before, but we wanted Tulla.

Both sides dug in their heels – just as they would in the match.

A month before the fixture, the chairman of the Munster Colleges Council, Brother Murray visited the Park – even at that stage he declared the pitch unplayable, but the CBS's Brother Hyland argued that it would be ready. 'The pitch in Ennis is the worst in Clare,' countered Seamus Gardiner. 'It is a joke locally.'

Tulla it was. We got our way; the big boys from Flannan's got their way. That's the way it was perceived. The game had already started. A grudge match for sure, with a month of a lead-in to give plenty of time for everyone to stoke up any aggro between the two sides.

OVER 7,000 TURNED up at the end of February.

It was my first introduction to Tulla on a big day. The cars parked for what seemed like miles in the direction of Ennis and Scariff.

The hill full. The noise, the famous concrete sideline seats that would freeze the joints of the most hardened Antarctic explorer.

The crowd in on the field.

We went one further than the team of 1970 thanks to two goals from Colm Honan. However, the victory came at a price. Players were rarely sent off back then, but things boiled over midway through the second-half and Dónal O'Dwyer from Tipperary – we called him Psycho – got marched by referee John Moloney.

Tony O'Donnell from Crusheen had a good pull at him and then Dónal just reacted, had a swipe of his own and caught him on the elbow. The school authorities nearly expelled him for getting put off – the over-reaction was incredible.

It was a hurling game. He got provoked and he just reacted; Tony only got booked, yet Dónal nearly had to find another school to sit the Leaving Cert.

Missing out on the Harty final in his last of four years playing was already too much punishment, because at that time you got a month's suspension for being sent off. It meant he was out of bounds for the final three weeks later when we were going to win the Harty Cup.

That's what we believed.

We were convinced of it. Thirteen years since the school's last title and in the new 13-a-side game that had been introduced the year before we had the speed to burn them. That's what we thought.

And we had the experience – they had no one from the previous year's team that beat us by three points in the semi-final, while we had seven of that team, with Loughnane and myself thrown into the mix.

At 16 I was the only fourth year to make the side that year, but I didn't feel out of place.

It was set up for us to win, but we flopped. They hammered us by 4-12 to 2-4. I managed a point for my efforts, but that was my first big disappointment in hurling. Many more would follow.

With what we had, the quality of players we had, we should have won, but we just didn't deliver.

It was worse the following year. I was made captain and wasn't looking forward to it, but we got a couple of fellas back… Liam Heffernan from Nenagh, Tim Crowe from Sixmilebridge, but the big one was the other 'Bridgeman, Sean Stack.

He had been in Limerick CBS, but we got him. You could say the school poached him – they wouldn't have been blatant about that, even going so far as to deny it if anyone made the allegation, but the important thing was he was wearing St Flannan's blue and not Sexton Street maroon that year. Sean's career, working in the hospitality industry, was cut short and he was persuaded to have another crack at getting to college when he joined us in November 1971.

MYSELF AND SEAN were midfield and we got back to the final, again beating St Colman's and Ennis CBS on the way, but once more it all fell apart in the final.

Seamus Gardiner and Willie Walsh were old school Flannan's men – they hadn't been involved in club teams and were following on with what had happened for them when they were in the school. That meant it was mainly ground hurling and fairly traditional stuff.

That also meant that instead of helping us, the 13-a-side game actually threw us altogether and meant we were blitzed. In that game you had to be able to pick the ball and run with it. It should have suited us, because there were plenty of us who were fast enough.

I was a sprinter and helped make up the 4x100 and 4x400 relay teams in the school with Colm Honan, Tim Crowe and Michael Tierney, so we had the speed, but that was a game we were not coached to play.

Farranferris were managed by Fr Michael O'Brien and he definitely had it over his colleague priests. They had two Cork minors in that first final, whereas we were in double figures when you added up all the Clare, Tipperary and Limerick lads. It was something similar the following year, but instead of closing the gap it got worse and we were blitzed.

It was awful.

A nightmare summed by perfectly Sean King in *The Clare Champion* when he wrote... *All that glitters is not gold – the cryptic tones of the line from the Merchant of Venice just about summed up the fiasco that was Sunday's Harty Cup final.*

It was a Shakespearean tragedy that played itself out on the hurling field that afternoon in Charleville – we were cursed by fate and possessed of tragic flaws. There was a huge crowd there; we were led out onto the field by the Charleville Brass and Reed Band. There was a parade and as captains, myself and Tom Fogarty were introduced to the Bishop of Cork and Ross, Cornelius Lucey, who then threw in the ball to start the game.

I can't remember if we had to kiss his ring or not – I've no recollection of it anyway. Maybe those days were gone.

Maybe meeting the bishop was the curse, though. Bishop Lucey was a St Finbarr's Farranferris man and while a future bishop in Willie Walsh might have been over us, where was our bishop? Where was our St Flannan's old boy, Bishop of Killaloe, Dr Michael Harty?

He wasn't out on the field with Bishop Lucey.

Clutching at straws, for sure, but it was a case of whatever could go wrong went horribly wrong. They hit us for five goals in the first-half and we were 11 points down. Battered, bruised and beaten with half an hour to spare.

I managed to get a goal in the second-half, but it was another dark day.

Again, we felt we had a chance of winning and overturning the previous year's result, but instead of learning and going to school on that we went backwards and were on the wrong side of a 16-point drubbing, 6-11 to 2-7.

As I was in my Leaving Cert year it was my last Harty Cup game – captain of the team and more than hopeful of joining a select band of Claremen who had led winning sides. Players like Jim Minogue from Bodyke, JJ Bugler from Scariff and Michael Shalloo from O'Callaghan's Mills.

I couldn't have been further away from it, but still, when I left St Flannan's for good later that year, I had become a hurler, even if I had known little success.

I TOOK SCHOOL seriously, so apart from giving me an education and a platform to go onto university it had given me hurling as well. Just like Clarecastle had, whether it was on the street, on the field or the school.

And, I grew up at a good time to be interested in the game, because Clarecastle were a coming team in that period. In 1962 we won an under-16 title, and two years later that team followed on and claimed the minor crown. That '64 team had the likes Paschal Russell, Dermot Fitzgerald, the late Tom Corry, Johnny Scanlan, Oliver Plunkett, George Horan, Bernie Ryan and Jimmy Quinn.

Plunkett was a neighbour, just two doors up from me on The Street. He played for the county minors and under-21s that year and went on to play county senior hurling. When Clare reached the National League semi-final in 1971, he was one of five Clarecastle players on the team – the others were captain Tom Slattery, Paschal Russell, Jack Moloney and Dermot Fitzgerald.

Oliver was the closest to me and seven years older than me, so he was one to look up to and aspire to when it came to making teams. Fitzgerald and Corry were with him on the county minor team in 1964, while the following year Plunkett and Fitzgerald were joined by Bernie Ryan and Johnny Scanlan.

They beat St John's in that 1964 minor final in Newmarket.

Ger Ward and myself got a lift down to the match, but we had to walk back. It was a long walk for a nine year-old, but we didn't care. Eventually John McInerney was passing up from Newmarket and he came across four or five of us struggling up the road. We were within a mile of home when he picked us up.

It was a huge win, something to remember, because we had beaten the Town. That always made it better, because any time we played the Town it was like a county final. It was a great night of celebration.

Our place would have been one of the pubs of call.

It was a hurling pub. There were always hurlers there. Haulie Daly was the most visible of the old hurlers growing up. I'd have known he was a hurler, but I just thought of him as an old man. He was 40 but to me he was *ancient*.

He was Anthony Daly's uncle and a hero in Clarecastle, because he was so steeped in it. He *was* Clarecastle. His father, Michael was a founder member of the hurling club in 1912 – his uncle John was a trailblazer in football, being on the Clarecastle Robert Emmet's team that won the senior championship in 1908.

Willie McAllister, Tolly Guinnane and John 'Poet' Russell were others. They had the same hurling upbringing as myself, playing on the parish league teams – for some reason in their time they called the teams the Rockies, the Barrs and Rovers. You'd like to think it wasn't in homage to Cork, but it was, most definitely.

Of the older Clarecastle players, people like Jimmy 'Dutcher' Moloney and Paddy 'Conjurer' Moloney, who'd played on the teams that won championships in the 40s, are the ones I remember most in the pub.

Paddy was a great friend of my father's and apart from having a few pints he loved playing darts. I used to mark the board when they were playing. As a kid, getting that job was like carrying their hurleys for them going out on the field to play a county final. It was big, but for me it was huge. You had to be quick to mark the board – it helped my mental arithmetic.

It was a Newmarket pub also. My grandfather, and then my mother when she took over with my father, would have had a lot of Newmarket customers dropping in as they made their way home from Ennis.

The Newmarket hurling team were always there after county finals and much to our dismay growing up, they played in a lot of them and won them all. To them it was always Tom Hayes' – one of their own and a Newmarket man, my grandfather.

He used to slag my uncle that Clarecastle had to amalgamate with Ennis to beat Newmarket in a county final – the one they won way back in 1928 – and that they could never beat them on their own.

He was right.

NEWMARKET ALWAYS BEAT us in finals and we hated them. They always seemed to win the games that mattered. They won the county title the year I was born and then started that great run in the 60s, most of them at Clarecastle's expense in finals.

They beat us in the 1964 final and filled the Canon Hamilton afterwards in our place. As a Clarecastle man – as a young Clarecastle hurler – it was seriously embarrassing for me. I got stick over it.

The corner boys thing was there at that time and I was a part of the set as much as anyone.

Some unused or gone off fruit was thrown at the Newmarket cars as they passed by us on the street before they then stopped at our house.

And some of it would be directed at me. I don't remember getting a kicking, but definitely I was told about the fact that Newmarket lads were in our village and in our pub. I remember having to stay up the street out of the way until all the Newmarket lads had finally gone.

It was a tough time.

It was tougher on the field, but I loved it. I was hooked. Some of the games between Clarecastle and Newmarket at that time had little to do with hurling – there was a lot of fighting, with some hurling breaking out in between some of the bigger rows.

The biggest was in 1967 in a group game in the championship when Newmarket hammered us by 6-11 to 5-3. The game was lucky to get that far, because according to *The Clare Champion… Such was the savagery of the combatants that had it not been for the intervention of the Gardai under John Lavin the game might never have been finished.*

It really was that bad, with the reporter Sean King giving the Clare county championship one of the most memorable introductions when remarking… *had an American recruiting officer been present he would have been impressed by the ostentation of the unflinching commandoes from Newmarket and Clarecastle, and would have inevitably enlisted a portion of them for combat guerrilla warfare along the Da Nang battle front. Picture an expanse of irresponsible hurley swinging and ruthless man-to-man tackling and then marvel that somebody was not fatally injured in this dirty ill-mannered encounter.*

That was the way things were.

The year I stepped up to senior level for the first time saw the two teams go at it once more in an infamous Clare Cup semi-final that Clarecastle actually won.

Blood-curdling scenes at Cusack Park, announced the headline, And beneath it… *No adjectives could describe the squalid scenes fought out in a vicious mood of hatred and contempt.* All because… *All hell broke loose, as the bloody warfare of Vietnam and Belfast was enacted – all in the name of sport.*

But if that was bad, it was still nothing compared to a game against Crusheen back in 1964 that I went to with Ger Ward. We were both only nine and ended up in the row, almost right in the middle of it, before being plucked to safety.

It was a replay, so there would have been a bit of tension before a ball was pucked. We won the game with a late, late point and then it all kicked off as the players came off the field. There was a verbal altercation between Joe Considine and a few Crusheen people, and it just set them off.

It escalated into a war that eventually led to a number of people being treated for their injuries in Ennis General Hospital.

MYSELF AND GER, like everyone else, had drifted down towards the dressing-rooms that were against the wall at the town end of the field. They were sheds with a lean-to roof.

After it started someone quickly thought about our safety, picked the two of us up and threw us on top of the roof.

We had a bird's eye view of everything that happened.

We were very safe, but very close to it all – it was marvellously exciting and I don't remember being scared, but it was savage stuff. The door was being battered with hurleys, and whatever bit of glass that was in the windows was smashed.

The Clarecastle players were in the dressing-room, but some of the players were caught outside. A priest was hit; and Mickey Fitzpatrick, who was a man with epilepsy, was also struck.

The attack on the dressing-room was only stopped when the door suddenly flew open. Anthony Daly's father, Pat Joe, Pakie Guinnane and Paddy Russell came out the door and hit whoever was in front of them.

A bit of an area around the dressing-room was cleared and more came out then. It was Clarecastle saying… 'We're out now… if you want to fight us, come on!'

We were looking at a mini-war.

I believe that the lads broke their hurleys in the dressing-room, because that would make them easier to use when they went out. They were probably safe in the dressing-room had they stayed inside, but they were being attacked.

We were watching all this. They drove the Crusheen lads back!

There was someone wearing a cloth cap with the peak open and he got hit and the blood came out through the cap, almost instantly. That actually stopped it. It was a case of… *Oh f***… this can't be allowed to go on.*

A couple of priests intervened and it finally stopped.

Witnessing this should have turned me off hurling because it had nothing to do with the game, but it didn't do anything of the sort.

Still, it was horrific.

Was there much of an outcry? There was probably talk about it in the pub afterwards, while *The Clare Champion* didn't hold back in publicising what had happened, but it was never going to be used against me to try and dissuade me from hurling.

At no stage was my mother saying, 'Where were you… were you safe? It's awful what those fellas were doing… and you're not playing that game'.

It was already too much part of my life; I really wanted it.

In truth, I couldn't get enough of it.

« CHAPTER 4 »

Watch out for Clare's hurlers. Although there may be little conclusive evidence of an upsurge in the county's team, startling developments are expected in the Banner County. The setting up of an action committee to act as searchers for talent for the county team, help in the transport of players for training sessions and trial games, which will be staged at intervals of six weeks, and generally to generate interest and pride in players, has already had significant results.

– John D Hickey, Irish Independent

JULY 11, 1971

I WAS MAKING teams in the club and at school. And I was making them out of my age and from that Dónal Carey gave me my first ever shot at making the Clare minors.

It was 1971.

He'd just call… 'There's a trial in Tulla, you're going… are you ready?'

That was it, and off I went. It helped that he was a selector with Clare teams in those years – he was with the minors and then with the under-21s afterwards. Donal always promoted and encouraged Clarecastle players to go forward for county underage teams. Was that nepotism? I hope not, and don't think so!

For me, it was all about trying to get a jersey, and be a county minor that year.

It was a blue jersey with yellow trim – that's what Clare wore for a good few years up until 1971, with the saffron not coming back until the following year. The game was in the Gaelic Grounds, and we were playing Tipperary.

I DON'T RECALL us doing much training, with the team brought together in the weeks before the game after a couple of trials.

My first start in a Clare jersey was at left half-forward.

My first point as a county hurler came when I landed a sideline in the first-half.

Over on the other wing there was an all-St Flannan's clash with Dan Brislane from Toomevara marking Colm Honan. They were both boarders and they were great mates. It was a bit weird, but you just got on with it. Honan certainly did that day.

He was wearing glasses – his eye was in though, because he scored 2-1 and we hammered them by 12 points, 3-13 to 1-7, to put Clare into a first Munster minor final in 19 years. It was a big deal for everyone involved.

More than that, Clare beating Tipp at any level was huge and we made sure to sew it into them. That was a strong team. Sean Stack and Sean Hehir were midfield and dominated, Enda O'Connor was the full-back, Martin McKeogh was at centre-back and a real star in the making, Ger Loughnane was on the wing, while in the half-forward line you had myself and Honan.

That's seven players who became the core of the senior team under Fr Harry Bohan a few years later, while our final opponents Cork had just one player who progressed afterwards onto senior in any meaningful way – a fair player, one Jimmy Barry Murphy! He was full-forward and although he got a goal, he was well held by Enda O'Connor in the final.

That was virtually it though. Martin McKeogh was brilliant at centre-back once more, but the rest was a whitewash. This was like the Harty Cup final nightmares, but worse. If Fr Michael O'Brien in Farranferris had it over us in the Harty, Fr Bertie Troy did the very same to Clare at minor level, with help from Fr O'Brien.

We were all over the place and just weren't able for them. Éire Óg's Michael Skelly was in goal and he was replaced at half-time by Newmarket's Christy Ryan, but it didn't get any better. They scored six goals and beat us by 17 points.

IT WAS ONE of only two games my mother ever went to, club or county.

I didn't even know she was going and she was back before I knew she was there. It was as much for the trip to Killarney as going to the game. Clare people loved going to Killarney for games because it wasn't Limerick and it wasn't Thurles. Women didn't go to matches then; you'd nearly be embarrassed if your mother was on the sideline watching you play.

It was the day of the famous dry ball and Babs Keating in the senior final. I'd say she was long gone from Fitzgerald Stadium when that happened, but I had a great view of it because after our game we were in the corner behind the goal, the only place we could get.

Clarecastle's Michael Slattery was the referee and Babs played a central role in all my memories of the second-half that day. He hit 3-4 – he scored the goal which began Tipperary's revival and then was a central figure in one of the most famous incidents in hurling. I had a perfect view of it when Tipp won a 21-yard free.

Babs had a cut over an eye and ran over to Donie Nealon, Tipperary's coach that day, who was standing behind the Limerick goal. Babs borrowed a towel to wipe his eye.

The sodden match sliotar had vanished into the crowd.

Nealon plucked a dry sliotar from his pocket and handed it to Babs. A second or two later the match sliotar was fired back from the terrace. Donie caught it and shoved it in his pocket.

All too spontaneous for a conspiracy, but on a day of biblical rain and flooding, a dry sliotar fired from 21 yards was a very different proposition for the goalkeeper than a ball that was heavy and soft with rain.

Babs rammed it to the net and Tipperary went on to win by a point when John Flanagan grabbed a late score in a Munster final classic.

I saw it all unfold – little could I have imagined that a year later, I'd be playing in a Munster senior final myself.

A child in a man's world of senior hurling, but somehow it happened.

◄◄◆►►

I started off with a Morris Oxford and it had bench seats so a load could fit into it. When I changed it for a Renault, which was a much lower car, it used to be nearly on its axel going to matches because there were so many in it. John was nearly always with me – he was only a small fella so he'd squeeze in. He was very enthusiastic about his hurling. The only thing was the lads in Clarecastle didn't understand a ciotóg hurler – all the time they'd be trying to change it to the orthodox, but John stuck to his thing and when he went into St Flannan's his skill improved enormously. You could see he was going to make it.

— Dónal Carey, Clarecastle

THE NOTION THAT the darkest hour is before the dawn is something that the teams I was on in the early 70s put to the test. That's because there were plenty of dark hours that were followed by too many false dawns.

There were those Harty finals in 1971 and '72, when the aggregate total of the beatings that Farranferris dished out to St Flannan's sat at 30 points.

There was that Munster minor final defeat in 1971.

But, maybe the worst of all, there was the Dean Ryan final defeat in 1972.

We were playing St Colman's in Emly and finally our luck seemed to have turned in big finals after those back-to-back defeats in the Harty. We led them at half-time by 2-4 to 0-2.

We had a wind, but we were much the better team in that first 30 minutes. Ambrose Power from Quin and John Ryan from Newmarket got the goals, while I chipped in with four points. But disaster struck in the second-half when they hit three goals in five minutes in the closing stages to beat us 4-3 to 2-7.

We just collapsed, just like we had in every other final.

Again, I was captain, but instead of never wanting to hurl again, I sprinted off the field, grabbed my clothes and hopped into Seamus Gardiner's car and headed the 25 miles in the road to the Gaelic Grounds for another match.

The Dean Ryan final was over at around 4.30pm – Clare were playing a Munster under-21 semi-final against Cork at 7.30pm, so I'd no time to dwell on what had just happened. Of course, I was gutted, but I was picked corner-forward for the 21s. How mad was that?

Again, Dónal Carey was involved in that – he was a selector on the under-21 team that year. We stopped in Hanratty's in Limerick for something to eat on the way.

We weren't given a chance of beating Cork. They'd won the previous four All-Ireland finals, with Mick Malone winning all four medals, and Seanie O'Leary trying to emulate him. They also had Jimmy Barry Murphy, Martin O'Doherty and Brian Murphy. Cork had arrived in their limousines and it was very intimidating, while we were arriving in dribs and drabs, in different cars and from different directions.

It made them look much more of a team than us. They probably believed that as well.

And so did we.

That's how it looked for most of the game as Cork were coasting. They led by 2-6 to 0-6 at half-time and with less than 10 minutes left the gap was out to 10 – 3-8 to 0-7. Jim Rothwell, who never made it as a senior afterwards, scored three goals that night. We were being hammered yet again.

But then something happened.

Finally. It was crazy stuff. What happened and what was said about it was colourful in every way. Sean King in *The Clare Champion* described it as… *A rally that would go a long way to putting General Custer's last stand to shame.*

There was more. He said it was… *like a great forest fire roaring its way through a prairie of grassland.*

We scored 3-2 without reply to win the game.

Michael O'Connor, Timmy Ryan and Paddy Hickey got the goals, while Timmy Ryan and Enda O'Connor got the points, with Enda's winner coming in the last seconds. He had started at full-back, while Jim Power was put in the corner on Seanie O'Leary. Cork then put Seanie in full-forward and it kind of released Enda to go up the field.

That changed everything.

It could prove the turning point as far as our fortunes on the inter-county field are concerned, mused King. He was right, because things were starting to happen for Clare that year, both on and off the field.

FOR THAT GAME, the Clare County Board brought two players home from England – Con Woods and Colm Honan, who were in college in Strawberry

Hill doing physical education. Bringing players home didn't happen very often in those days, if at all, because the board wouldn't want to spend the money.

Instead, it was about spending as little money as possible. It was always about where money could be saved and not spent.

But it happened, because earlier that year an Action Committee had been set up to promote Clare hurling. It was an organisation that was independent of the county board, but at the same time was able to influence the board. There were some heavy hitters on it.

Fr Harry Bohan was the chairman. Others involved were Clarecastle's Michael Slattery and Cratloe's Basil Boyce, who were joint-secretaries. Former Clare players like Des Carroll, Pat Henchy, Matt Nugent, Sean Guinane, John Daly and Naoise Jordan were members, as was former board chairman, Jack Daly and that year's senior captain, Gus Lohan.

When the committee was launched earlier in the year one of the members gave an interview to John D Hickey in the *Irish Independent*, but it was on condition that his name wouldn't be used.

I didn't know who Fr Harry Bohan was at the time, but in hindsight it had to be him. The language he used and the way he lowered the blade... into the opposition... into Clare supporters... into everyone.

He threw down the gauntlet to all-comers and didn't care about standing on toes.

We are sick and tired of being the underdogs in Munster hurling. We've been kicked around for so long that we've decided not only to bark, but to bite. Believe me you will see a new Clare in this year's championship. We've got the hurlers and the hurling, and with the spirit that is fast developing in the county we won't care a damn about any county come the summer.

For far too long we've been what I call motor car critics. We went to matches in which our county were playing and the game over, we got into our cars and all the way back home we criticised the team, the selectors, the County Board. But what did we do – sweet damn all. You see, we were too busy divorcing ourselves from the defeat, passing the buck.

Well, the days of passing the buck are over in Clare... If Clare fail to make the grade, we will all fail and we will admit it, not look to find scapegoats and thus absolve ourselves.

I feel we have already taken the most difficult step to end the Tipperary-Cork monopoly which our approach – it was the attitude of second-class hurlers – has done much to create. Damn it all, we have as good hurlers in Clare as they have in Tipperary and Cork and, furthermore, we are going to prove it in quicker time than many people think possible. We will show them. There is not an acre of Clare we won't search for hurlers.

This is what I was coming into.

It was electrifying. I just went with it. I'd only turned 17 three weeks before that under-21 semi-final against Cork and two months later the seniors ambushed Limerick in Cusack Park to reach a first Munster final in five years.

THAT DAY I was playing with the minors – Limerick hammered us by 12 points, but it was all about the seniors' win over a Limerick team that fancied their chances of going all the way that year.

Seamus Durack was brilliant in goal; Noel Casey, Milo Keane and Jimmy McNamara got the goals, and Timmy Ryan hit 0-7 in a morale-boosting 3-11 to 2-10 win.

It was huge shock.

It was even a bigger shock to be in amongst them. I was there because that time the under-21s trained with the seniors and our Munster final against Tipperary was on just two weeks later.

That final was played in Cusack Park on a Sunday evening – it was put back so as not to clash with the Munster football final that was on in Killarney earlier in the day. I was corner-forward, a position I always hated, with Seamus Durack in the other corner.

It was a controversial game. We had dominated in the first-half but somehow found ourselves 2-5 to 2-3 down. Going in at the break, one of their officials came over to the wing-back, Anthony Quinlan from Silvermines, who was marking Timmy Ryan. I was five yards behind them and heard it all. The official hit him in the small of his back.

'That fella is soft… give it to him!' he said.

Quinlan had already given it a good few times before that.

I went into the dressing-room and Timmy's hand was badly hurt. He went over to Dr Tom McGrath. The hand was probably broken but the team needed him out there for the second-half.

I challenged the Tipp official on what had happened down in the West County Hotel afterwards.

He denied it. That was the game.

There was more controversy in the second-half when Clare selector, Jim Woods, who was one of the linesmen, ceremoniously walked over to referee, Frank Murphy and handed him back his flag – he was refusing to continue because Murphy had overturned one of his decisions.

Still, we could have won.

We really battled in the second-half. I was moved to centre-forward and got three points. This was inside the last 10 minutes and we led with less than three minutes to go.

But it happened again – it was like the Dean Ryan final. There was a very bad goal conceded after a mix-up between the goalie and the full-back line. That killed us.

With that, my Clare year should have been over, but within a few days I was called up to the senior squad on the back of my performance in the under-21 final.

I was playing against the seniors in training already so I jumped at the chance. It sounds arrogant to say I wasn't that surprised to be called up, but I wasn't. You have that irrational confidence when you're so young.

It was all happening for me, and there seemed to be no big deal about it.

But it was a *big deal*.

FIVE YEARS BEFORE that, when Clare were last in a Munster final, I hadn't even started secondary school. Instead, I was a child at the Gaeltacht in the Aran Islands listening to the match on the radio.

It was supposed to be total immersion in the language, so we weren't supposed to be listening to any English, not even Michael O'Hehir's commentary.

That didn't stop us though and the rule was broken. Someone had a transistor and we went to some secluded spot and listened in. Jimmy 'Puddin' Cullinan and Larry Kiely were sent off, that's what I remember from the game. And of course another defeat.

Now I was in the same dressing-room as Puddin, training for a Munster final.

We played a challenge against Kilkenny in Piltown a couple of days after the under-21 final and I was given a few minutes, even though I never expected to be playing in the final. Being part of it was enough.

There was a bit of a buzz about the thing, for once. We ate in the West County after every training session. There was esteem around Clare hurling for those few weeks.

To me, it didn't really matter that the final was yet another disaster – we were beaten by 22 points, 6-18 to 2-8. It was bizarre, in many different ways.

Early in the second-half Denis Coughlan was sent off for hitting Pat O'Leary. The Cork supporters went apoplectic – for the remainder of the game a large section of their supporters in the 25,000 crowd slow hand-clapped the Limerick referee, Sean O'Grady, while after the game he was escorted off the field as bottles were flung in his direction from all angles.

In the middle of everything that was going on, with about 10 minutes to go, Haulie Daly came over to me and told me I was going on. I replaced Jimmy McNamara.

He thought it was my last year minor and wanted me to have the same record as Jimmy Smith, who played minor, junior and senior in the same year. He made sure I played minor, under 21 and senior within a couple of months.

If he had known I was a minor the following year he wouldn't have put me on at all.

Was this pure parochialism; a Clarecastle man, Haulie Daly looking after his Clarecastle clubmate, John Callinan? Still, I always claim that we were 30 points down when I went on and we were only beaten by 22 points, so I was worth eight points to the team! I also started in the senior championship the following summer, under Matt Nugent, when I was still a minor.

Afterwards, John D Hickey in the *Irish Independent* wrote… *Minor John Callinan showed no trace of stage fright when called into the Munster senior final when Clare were reeling.* I was delighted with myself.

I remember being under the stand after the game and shaking hands with all these Cork players – Ray Cummins, Justin McCarthy, Charlie McCarthy, Seanie O'Leary, the lot of them. I was in heaven, even though we were obliterated.

I'd played in a Munster senior final.

My excuse now is that at 17, I was still only a child.

One fella had his hand out – he wasn't one of their superstars. I didn't know him, but instead of shaking my hand he just put his hand on my head, patted me and said, 'Hard luck, young fella'.

It showed what they really thought of us; that it was men versus boys.

A couple of years later I got to play against him in a National League game in Tulla and I gave him a good roasting.

However, I had played in a Munster final.

The fourth Munster final I played in during 1972 – the Harty and Dean Ryan Cup finals, and the under-21 and senior finals.

I lost all four.

PART TWO

Daydream Believing

« CHAPTER 5 »

As regards commitment, motivation, fanatical fervour and attention to progressive training methods, the Sigerson and Fitzgibbon Cups can easily match any other GAA competition and far outweigh most of them. Third Level GAA is an institution and those who have been involved as players, officials and supporters have the happiest of memories of their association with great competitions.

– Eugene McGee, UCD

'THERE YOU GO… this is your room. Is that okay?'

'Ehh, okay so… alright!'

It was a double bed in a small room on Upper Kilmacud Road in Dublin. My new home; my digs for the year as I was starting out in University College Dublin the following morning.

For sure, the room was fine; so too was the Kilmacud area in the suburb of Stillorgan, while the college campus in Belfield was only down the road. A short cycle on the bike or a hop on the 46A and I was there.

But the bed.

The bed.

The double bed. It was for two people and I'd be sharing that bed with another fella for the college year. The Airbnb rental agents, who pack the punters into their properties these days, would be proud.

There you go… this is your room. Is that okay?

It was okay, because that was the deal in the digs as the landlady packed them in and doubled her money. It was half-bed and breakfast, with a dinner thrown in every evening.

IT WAS A massive culture shock.

I mean, sharing a bed with another student, when you think of it? I don't remember the lad who was sleeping next to me, only that he was doing arts in UCD.

Still, it was the life.

In the city. The freedom of college life.

Meeting women.

Having women in your class. And hurling, with college life and social life shaped around hurling and the GAA, just like it had been in St Flannan's and in Clarecastle.

It was a hectic time. Busy. Very busy.

Hurling busy.

In 1972, between school, club and county I played for eight teams – throw in kicking a bit of ball and it was double figures. Now it was time to track down the hurlers on the vast UCD campus.

Before that, it was the mission to get there – the little matter of sitting a Leaving Cert in the middle of all the hurling and deciding what I wanted to do with my life. There was a big educational belief in our house, an interest in education and that feeling and encouragement that it was very important. My mother saw to that and cultivated it.

It helped that there were plenty of influences nearby – the Hanlys across the road were teachers, and my grand-aunt, Winnie had been a teacher in Newmarket-on-Fergus. She pre-schooled us all, so I was well ahead of most others when I went into primary school.

In St Flannan's, I was in the A stream and I genuinely tried to be the good boy there at all times. I had promised my mother that I'd behave and work. The night I got my Leaving Cert results I came home well drunk from a night out in Ennis, but that was it.

There was an expectation always that college was an option for me after leaving school. My three sisters hadn't gone, because of family circumstances after the death of my father, but for me it was always a case of… 'What are you going to do?'

There was a first cousin of my mother, an Oblate Father in Dublin, and when he'd visit I'd be threatened with being sent to Belcamp College as a boarder, where there was no hurling. It was an idle threat, because my mother couldn't afford to send me to Flannan's, never mind Belcamp.

IN MY EARLY years in secondary school I thought of nothing else other than being a priest. There was a heavy religious influence there in the background – in the school and outside it. Looking across the road from our house, the parish priest was on the left, the Hanlys were in the middle and the curate's house was on the right.

There was Canon Michael Hogan when I was growing up and then Fr Paddy Loughnane, a first cousin of Dr Bill Loughnane and related to Ger Loughnane as well. Fr Ned White was chairman of the club for a long number years – he was a Tipp man.

There was Fr Patrick O'Meara, Fr Thomas Comerford and Fr Sean Moriarty, so that influence was there all around me.

With boarders in St Flannan's, if the Dean of the college thought you might be 'priest material', the seed would be planted and everything would be pointed for you in that direction.

You'd be a prefect, you'd read at Mass every Sunday. You'd be in the choir and would wear the college blazer at official school functions and would get the honour of sitting at the top of the refectory table.

As I was a day student, I didn't really have that same level of attention, but the career guidance teacher at the time, Fr Rueben Butler would point us in the direction of the clerical way of life, if he knew that the interest was there. The Diocesan Vocations Officer would do the same.

Up until I was 15, I went with that – I was very comfortable with the idea of being a priest, but other considerations finally came to the surface for me. In the end, I felt the pressure-cooker atmosphere of producing people for the priesthood in St Flannan's was wrong and it was something that I reacted to and finally railed against.

There were five or six from my Leaving Cert year that went to Maynooth, but it would have been a lot more before that and the numbers were starting to get very thin on the ground.

Fr John Callinan?

IT COULD HAVE been me, but in the end that wasn't for me and I opted for law. The only reason I can think why I opted to study law was the eviction case that my mother had to fight a few years earlier.

It wasn't that I had vocation for the law – after all, we broke the law in the pub all the time because we did 'after hours', just like most pubs. There was no respect for the law there in that narrow sense.

But that court case had a massive impact on me, because it showed in this instance that the law worked for the small person; in fighting that case it was like taking on City Hall and winning. There was nothing else influencing me towards the law other than that.

I was not very good at figures, so accountancy was not for me. I wasn't good enough at maths to be an engineer. I wasn't creative enough to be an architect, while I didn't want to be a teacher, nor go into the Civil Service or the bank.

I wanted to go to college though and again Dónal Carey influenced me heavily. He had gone to college. He was in Dublin and he was in Cork for a while as well. He always advocated college as a way of life and it seemed attractive.

It was fine by me, so I applied for law and got it, and managed to qualify for a county council grant.

FOR 10 DAYS AFTER I started my course, I met nobody I knew.

I knew there were St Flannan's fellas in UCD but the place was so big that I met nobody. Even then, there were thousands there between the Science Block and the Arts Block.

The big thing for me was the Freshers Exhibition, but there was a delay in that it wasn't on right after we all started. When it eventually came around, I went down to the hurling club table and this fella came up to me.

'John, we have been expecting you!'

It was Jack Ryan, the son of former GAA president, Seamus Ó Riain, from Moneygall. And he was an All-Ireland winner, being a sub on the Tipperary team that won the Liam MacCarthy Cup the previous year.

He was also a former St Flannan's man and he married Séan Ó Siocháin's daughter. Jack became a very good friend of mine for years. His brother, Seamus, who captained the team when we won the Fitzgibbon in 1975, was there as well, and I was made to feel welcome by them all. Another brother, Eugene was two years ahead of me in Flannan's.

It was a huge relief, psychologically and emotionally.

Without hurling at that time, it would have been very lonely and very hard being up in Dublin. In my law class, there was no other hurler, no one who admitted to playing hurling anyway. There were a lot of 'Dublin 4' types in the class.

You definitely didn't walk around with a hurley in your hand, like lads do now. The Mayo footballer, JP Kean had a couple of goes at doing veterinary science in UCD, but ended up doing law and he was in my class. At least there was another GAA man with me.

I give a lot of credit to all those lads in the hurling club I fell in with at that time. They put the arm around me in the big city.

They were a great cement for me in Dublin. I remember after getting to know the lads – I was in the old UCD bar that was just a pre-fab – there was this assumption that because I hurled and because I was from Clare that I was a de Valera man.

That was the first time I declared forcibly that I wasn't and was anything but a Fianna Fáil man. I hadn't yet started campaigning for Dónal Carey and Fine Gael at election time, but I was political; a lot of us were, because you couldn't but be aware of what was going on.

When I was in St Flannan's I was very conscious of the riots that took place in Paris in 1967 – also the Civil Rights marches in America, and then in the North when the whole Troubles kicked off in 1969.

I was very interested in that whole movement of change and protest that was taking place at that time. Bobby Kennedy… Muhammad Ali… Vietnam. I was taking all that in. And Bloody Sunday in the North… I was very much aware of all these things that were happening.

I was reading James Baldwin and Martin Luther King. I had rows with my mother in the pub because she was quite selective in what Travellers she would serve and what Travellers she wouldn't serve. My view was that everyone should be served – end of story.

Everyone was equal, and what was the difference between being selective on who could come into the pub and the segregation on the buses in America during the campaign for Civil Rights?

My attitude was that everyone who came through the door had to be served. Her attitude was quite simple, very direct and to the point.

'You're not ever going to be a publican… so get out of my sight!'

All these things were happening, so it wasn't just all hurling – and it wasn't so much hurling was coming at me, as I was at hurling. What else do you do? As Brian Cody said when questioned about the commitment lads make to the game… 'What else would they be doing but training'.

I was of that mindset and wanted more of it in UCD.

THE GAA WAS very strong in the college at the time, both hurling and football. However, the two codes were quite separate. I did play a few Dublin county league games with the footballers when they were stuck, all the same. JP Kean brought me along to games when the likes of John O'Keeffe, Kevin Kilmurray and Ogie Moran weren't available. I remember going down to a tournament in Claremorris, driving down with Galway player Mick Judge.

The footballers were really strong and the fact that Kevin Heffernan insisted on the senior championship being finished early in the year to leave the rest of the year free for the Dublin county team's All-Ireland run always gave UCD a great chance of competing with their best 15 on duty.

I went to some of those famous football games between St Vincent's and UCD in the club championship – they were some battles, because Vincent's weren't just the epitome of Dublin, they *were* Dublin, while UCD were this collection of culchies.

There was a real hatred there. Open hatred.

I LOVED THAT whole college scene though, and being in college… and the hurling.

I got my own bed in second year and was staying in a flat in Lennox Street, and was in Rathmines and Rathgar in other years. The freedom was great.

Alan Higgins from Lucan and Tommy Quinn from Clarecastle were living on Richmond St, while up the road from us were Sean Hehir, PJ Fitzpatrick and Dinny Burns from Cork. There was a great GAA community in the area.

We were always meeting people from other counties, with the GAA as the common bond. The UCD hurling team, for instance, had very big Kilkenny and Tipperary influences. We also had a really good player from Kildare, Pat White who had gone to school in St Kieran's.

We used to train at night in the Iveagh Gardens at the back of Earlsfort Terrace and Newman House in St Stephen's Green. There was a green area that wasn't very big but there were lights and it was an incredible place to train. I even remember training in the snow there one night – the first time I experienced the magic of training in the snow!

I made the Fitzgibbon team in my first year, but we were beaten by Maynooth in the semi-final in Athenry. They had Sean Stack, Sean Silke and Iggy Clarke, as well as Willie and Paudie Fitzmaurice – they were a decent team but it was still a bit of a shock that they beat us. I got a goal that day, but Paudie Fitzmaurice beat us on his own by hitting 11 points.

The Fitzgibbon was very competitive at that time. Cork were reasonably strong, and Galway were good too, as they had players like Niall McInerney and Joe McDonagh, but UCD and Maynooth became the two big teams.

That was Maynooth's first title and we had great battles with them.

There was also a great social life associated with Fitzgibbon and that was as important as the hurling itself. The following year, Queen's University were the hosts but in those years Belfast was literally a no-go area with the Troubles, so they moved it up to Ballycastle. We played Maynooth in a final up there, but Paudie Fitzmaurice beat us again… this time by hitting 0-7.

Tomás Ó Fiadh, later a cardinal, wasn't a popular man with the UCD crowd that time – he was fairly triumphant when Maynooth beat us in that final. One of the Maynooth mentors, Jim Gleeson, a friend of mine who was in the priesthood at the time, said, 'Tom must have been hard for ye to take?' He was.

We just had to take it.

We drank to soften the blow, and the Fitzgibbon banquets were great. There was loads of drink. We stayed in a protestant hotel in Ballycastle that was dry, but we still managed to bring a couple of crates of beer back with us.

Some bright spark had decided that the UCD and Maynooth teams should share a bus to and from Ballycastle and Belfast.

I was just 18 and I had way too much to drink – I was drinking with the late Sean Liddy, and Paddy Barry, who was going for the priesthood. They were marking each other in the game and were huge men who could hold their drink.

They were drinking pints of lager and when someone went to the toilet, they'd get a glass of vodka and put it into the man's pint. I wasn't able for this and was very unwell coming home and had to ask the bus to stop in Belfast to let me out.

I had to walk up through the Maynooth fellas to get out of the bus and get sick.

It made me feel sicker again.

◄ ◄ ◆ ► ►

There was a great hurling community in UCD at the time. We were always on the look-out for new players coming in and anyone that wanted to hurl was taken in. We knew even before Johnny Callinan arrived that he was going to be a top player for us. He always delivered the goods for UCD.

– Jack Ryan, UCD

EUGENE McGEE SPRINTED out onto the field.

He was a serious man, always businesslike and direct. No nonsense.

He had the magic bottle and immediately went to work on my head as the blood poured. I didn't care about my head and any superficial wound that I had.

'Eugene, it's my leg… it's my f***ing ankle… it's gone!'

It was a Fitzgibbon Cup semi-final against UCC on a frozen O'Toole Park in March 1975 and Mr UCD football, Eugene McGee was the hurlers' first aid man and the physio rolled into one.

I was in agony.

We were on our way back to the Fitzgibbon Cup final and another shot at beating Maynooth and preventing them from winning three in-a-row. The game was on the following day in Croke Park, but I wouldn't be playing. It was a big blow.

Afterwards, it was suggested that I was targeted off the ball – which was untrue. I was catching the ball but I got hit with the flat of the hurley and came down awkwardly on the frozen ground and went over on my knee and ankle.

But Cork's Dinny Burns, playing for UCD, was definitely singled out deliberately that day. I was watching from the sideline; Dinny was going to make a catch and there was this wild pull. It was savage stuff.

That same evening, Dinny and I came from hospital into Kennedy's near Kelly's Corner where the team were meeting to get organised for the final. I was on crutches and Dinny had his arm in a cast and a sling. It wasn't a good start, but we still won the following day, because Matt Ruth gave a masterful display on Sean Stack.

That weekend was the first time in my life that I saw Matt shake himself as a hurler. There was so much hurling in him. In that semi-final in which I got injured, we beat UCC by 3-12 to 0-4 and he hit 2-6 of that total. Then in the final he hit two goals in the first-half and we never looked back, winning by 4-8 to 2-7.

Matt gave an exhibition that day in Croke Park. I don't think he would have done that if the rest of us were playing. He was the coolest, drollest, loveliest fella you could meet. He'd be pulling the hurley along behind him like Chunky O'Brien, as if the bloody thing was an inconvenience and too heavy for him. Frank Cummins used to throw it over his shoulder as if it was an extension of himself and like a sword, but Matt was barely able to hold it.

He was right half-forward and Sean Stack was left half-back.

You'd often hear professional soccer players talk about what fellas can do in training. Matt didn't. He'd shake himself for five minutes in a match and *produce* it.

He wasn't the most athletic, but when the fire would ignite, he was brilliant. One of the goals he got came after he collected the sliotar 60 or 70 yards out and shrugged off Stack and Silke – these weren't mugs he was up against – and then blasted it to the net.

HE WAS CAPTAIN the following year and the captain usually trained the team – but Matt instead asked me to do the training for him. It wasn't scientific training. It was mainly boot, bollock and bite.

It was Mike Mac stuff.

That time you'd be doing a couple of laps – I'd be on the outside driving them on, but Matt would be on the inside going the shortest way he possibly could around the field. He'd go inside the flag always. It really annoyed me, especially because he was the captain.

For the yard, or maybe the two or three that he was stealing, what was the point?

'JESUS MATT!' I'd roar at him, exasperated and frustrated.

'You're the feckin' captain'.

But in the match, he was different and I can thank Matt for my Fitzgibbon medal.

It was a great period in my life – my education, but also my hurling education, because of the engagement with the Kilkenny fellas, the Tipp fellas; everyone I met through hurling and the Fitzgibbon weekends.

Playing with them and against them, you knew you were as good as them.

Winning with them.

Trying to beat them.

Raising the banner in the big city.

« CHAPTER 6 »

One of the few bright sparks for me was provided by the refreshing form of Clarecastle's John Callinan – he must have been the youngest player to play in a Munster final. Callinan did enough to show that he is definitely a name for the future. The Clarecastle man must be an automatic in manager Matt Nugent's plans.

– Sean King, The Clare Champion

MAY 26, 1973

'WELL?'

'WELL YES… what do you want?'

'How did we get on?'

'We lost!'

I was in a phone box near Ireland's first ever shopping centre on the southside of Dublin, in Stillorgan, calling my brother Eamon, who was back home in the family pub in Clarecastle. He was seven years younger than me, but although only 11 he still held the upper hand in what was the briefest of conversations between us.

The call home was to find out the result of the first round of the Munster minor championship between Clare and Limerick in the Gaelic Grounds. We were hammered by 18 points and I wasn't there. It was an ignominious end to my career as a Clare minor hurler.

I had been selected to start at midfield with Leo Mannion of Ennis Dalcassians as my partner, while the pre-match analysis hailed the fact that... *It is not every county minor team that can boast the services of an experienced senior player*, adding that my... *experience of the big time should be an invaluable asset to Clare.*

Not much good having that asset in Dublin instead of Limerick.

Eamon wasn't impressed. I wasn't impressed, by the result, or my own actions. Apart from giving me the 5-16 to 3-4 result, there was nothing else to say.

There was no chat, no small talk – no mention of my mother, my sisters, the lads around the village. Just the sums of the game. That was it. He was very mad with me and showed it. He slammed down the phone.

He probably wouldn't have even answered if he'd known it was me. Eamon was and still is the quietest man you could meet.

This was a disgrace to Clare hurling, stated the Champion. *An annihilation that will not be easily erased from the minds of the petty handful who stood on the sparsely populated terraces of the Limerick Gaelic Grounds, to witness another ridiculous shambles, as far as Clare hurling is concerned.*

It was worse for me, something never to be erased from my mind.

It was my third year as a Clare minor, having been there in 1971 and '72. I was still a minor in '73 – a flagship player and by far the most experienced member of the team, but I was nowhere to be seen.

That no-show is a black mark from my last year as a minor, a mark I put against myself, with the only thing to compare with it being my final year as an under-21 in 1976 that was another unmitigated disaster.

I'D MISSED OUT on playing in the under-21 grade in 1975 because of the injury I received in that year's Fitzgibbon Cup semi-final; we beat Tipperary in the first round but were then hammered by 16 points by Cork in the semi-final.

The following year we had decent team – I had the most senior experience, followed by Pat O'Connor, while we also had players like Pat Morey, Brendan Gilligan, Tommy Keane, Deccie Coote, Con McGuinness and Liam Corr.

For the semi-final against Tipperary in Ennis I arranged a lift down from Dublin with Michael Slattery. At the time I was still based up there and was studying for my solicitors' Law Society exams.

We left for the game in plenty of time, but the Friday evening traffic was terrible and I missed the start of the game and only came on as a sub 10 minutes into the second-half. At least we won, and I played well when I came onto a team in which Pat O'Connor was the standout performer with 1-3 on the night.

The final was played on a Wednesday night... July 14.

That time, I was staying in a flat with the late Sean Liddy from Newmarket, Tom Quinn from Clarecastle and Dubliner Alan Higgins. They were heading off for the match around lunchtime, but I had been notified by hurling board secretary, Mike McTigue that Sean O'Leary from Inagh, who was working in Croke Park, would bring me to the game.

Partly because of the debacle of being late for the Tipperary match, I decided to toe the official line and go with what McTigue told me. This turned into a worse nightmare.

We arranged to meet in the Ormond Hotel on the quays, but Séan never showed; instead he left a message to get a taxi to Naas where he was collecting Vinny Daly, who was in the army cadets at the time.

It was a Wednesday evening and because of the heavy rain the traffic was chronic. Myself and my future wife, Siobhán didn't get to Lawlor's Hotel in Naas until about 5.50pm. We didn't leave there until 6pm, because Vinny had gone off up the street to get himself some chips.

It got much worse.

There were six of us in the car on the journey down – myself and Siobhán, Vinny, Sean and two women he had with him. I was fuming, sitting sullenly in the car as we seemed to crawl through Newbridge... then Kildare and Monasterevin... Portlaoise... Roscrea and Nenagh, before finally reaching the Gaelic Grounds at 8.15pm.

Sean was quite sanguine about it – he felt they wouldn't start the match without me, but the Munster Council had no intention of waiting for John Callinan and Vinny Daly and it began on the appointed time of 8pm.

When I arrived, Con Woods was there to meet me, and gave me a hurley – I saw the last few minutes of the first-half.

I came on in the second half; the team played really well on the night but we were beaten by two points. I have had plenty of disappointments but that was one of the worst given the circumstances.

After that, I didn't want to talk to anybody or have anything to do with anybody. I know the following day I met up with Anthony Scanlon from Clarecastle, who was on the panel, and then linked up with Brendan Gilligan in Ennis before doing a tour of the pubs in the town.

I didn't have the money to do a tour of any pubs to drown my sorrows when Eamon put the phone down that night of the minor game, but I know it was absolutely and totally to my discredit that I failed to show.

I CAN HAVE my regrets of not winning a Munster or All-Ireland with Clare at senior level in my long stint with the team, but that is something I had little control over. I played in Munster finals and plenty of them, and we just didn't get over the line.

You can have all the regrets you want about those disappointments, near-misses and what-might-have-beens, but my one big regret from all the years playing was not playing minor in 1973. Unlike the under-21 in '76, when I was depending on people for a drive and it was a bit out of my own control, I had control over that.

I could and should have played. I should have been in Limerick.

College exams were earlier than Leaving Cert exams and given the opposition we had that night my thinking was simple and reasoned in my own head... *F*** it... we'll beat Limerick without me.*

We had prepared well for the minor that year, taking part in a Munster league in the spring when I alternated between playing for the seniors and minors, as well as fitting in the Fitzgibbon Cup and playing Railway Cup for the Combined Universities.

In that minor league we played Limerick a couple of times – the first time in the Gaelic Grounds they only had 12 players, but when we gave them some of ours to make up 15, they beat us. That was just a blip, however, because we beat them in Cusack Park the day before I was playing against Kilkenny in the National League.

What a pity this county can't produce players of the calibre of hurling and football star, John Callinan, who last Saturday was the mainstay of the team, bemoaned the *Champion* after the Munster league defeat in the Gaelic Grounds.

What a much bigger pity for me, that I didn't show up the next time the sides met in the Gaelic Grounds. It was awful. I was trying to do the right thing by my mother in studying for my first year exams, but look, there were repeats if I didn't get my exams.

There were no repeats when it came to playing minor for my county – it was my last year; I'd never be a county minor again. It was so, so wrong.

Beating Limerick easily enough in that Munster league game led me to half-rationalise that I could avoid the championship match in the safe knowledge that we would win and I'd be back for the semi-final against Tipperary.

The exam wasn't until the Monday, so it wasn't as if it was the following day. The danger of a broken finger or hand?

Rubbish, because there's always a danger of a broken bone.

After nearly 50 years, it still hangs there over me. I should have done right by the team that I would have captained was I there. We had a decent enough team. It's a black mark against my name, put there by myself.

Maybe I had become a bit detached from the scene being up in Dublin and that's why I took the chance. I wouldn't have been the first or the last fella to get distracted by college life.

But that couldn't condone it, or give me a free pass. Lads afterwards that I met would have held it against me – and they were right, because I held it against myself. I should have gone down, I should have played.

These were lads who were on the team and the line was… 'Callinan, you would have come down if it was the senior team', or… 'You're a Clare senior now… you're too big for the minors'.

It was easy to make that accusation against me, that I had got above myself, because my hurling life had been a whirlwind for the previous year.

Playing senior for club and county, college life… *life*.

AFTER MY CAMEO appearance in the Munster senior final against Cork, attentions had quickly turned to the county championship to see if we could knock Newmarket-on-Fergus off their perch.

We thought we were good enough, but never got that far because of another confrontation with Crusheen – it wasn't anything like the all-out war between the sides I witnessed as nine year-old in 1964, but it was hugely controversial.

Around that time jaundice and hepatitis had gotten into our house – two of my sisters got it and were hospitalised. I also got it and Dónal Carey brought me to see the Clare team doctor, Dr Tom McGrath in Kildysart. Straight away he told me it was obvious I was sick, because I was as yellow as the wall.

It was very debilitating, but I still pressed ahead and started the quarter-final against Crusheen. That time the team would gather at the old turnstiles in Cusack Park before going in, and I was asked how I was feeling? At 17 you always feel you're on top of the world, because you have that confidence of youth. Truth is, I felt terrible, but I wasn't going to say that to anyone.

I started centre-forward that day, with Ger Ward right half-forward and Michael Slattery on the other wing. We were leading by 1-2 to 0-4 after Christy 'Wax' Guinnane knifed his way through the Crusheen defence for a great goal in the 14th minute. We were hurling well, but it all kicked off in the 20th minute.

One of our lads put in a long ball that Tommy O'Donnell caught in the Crusheen goal – he was playing from the town end up and he cleared it out to the left half-back position. Ger Ward came onto the ball, caught it on the hop and when he was going past the half-back, Frank Vaughan he got a good flake of the hurley, but not on the head or anything like that.

Ger was like a waif and he went down and had every reason to go down, but next thing it all kicked off inside in the goal area.

I saw Mick Moroney running in and he roared at Tommy to go down – this is a mixture of what I saw and heard – and the referee, Mick Spain ran in and asked his umpires what had happened.

Apparently, Eugene Moylan had made a visit into the goalie – as all corner-forwards were supposed to do at that time, because the man between the sticks was considered fair game. Spain put off Vaughan for the tackle on Ger Ward and then eventually put off Moylan for getting himself acquainted with Tommy O'Donnell.

Prior to putting Eugene off, the ref put off Wax, who was 5'7", 15 stone and black haired. Then he put off Dermot Fitzgerald, who was well over six feet tall and blond, before finally getting the right culprit and marching Eugene, who was also six feet tall and blond. Putting off all three, as it appeared for a minor offence, caused consternation.

It was crazy. Michael Slattery lost it completely and you couldn't blame him. Earlier in the game he had been felled off the ball by a bad foul and nothing had been done about it by the referee. Then there was this fiasco.

Bad enough having one put off… but three? The people who were sent off in the wrong, Dermot and Wax, may have been re-instated as the referee finally turned to Eugene Moylan and got it right, but it was a comedy of errors, only that no one was laughing.

Spain was credited as being a top referee – he was only two weeks away from refereeing the All-Ireland final between Kilkenny and Cork, but he lost the plot and didn't know what he was doing on that occasion.

As well as playing, Michael Slattery was our trainer and he started roaring, 'Call it off… call it off, get off the field!' I wasn't sure if that was the right thing to do. I said this to Frankie McNamara, who was playing midfield and was Slattery's brother-in-law.

We were the last two off the field.

We were deemed to have walked off the field and forfeited the match, but Crusheen wouldn't take the match. It was never played and it meant that St Senan's – an amalgamation of Cratloe and Clonlara – got a bye from the semi-final to play Newmarket in the final.

I used to joke with Tommy O'Donnell and Mick Moroney afterwards, saying it was all Moroney's fault and that Tommy wasn't touched and just went down. 'Aren't you still alive, how could you have survived if you were really hit?' was my line. It was true.

It was another sad episode in my hurling education – a fracas that once more laid bare the hostilities that existed between some clubs at that time, when the potential for things to blow up was always there.

The Clare Champion report on that game summed it up when concluding… *No marks at all are due to the section of supporters who saw fit to throw stones at Michael Slattery as he lay injured on the ground and to that certain section on the embankment whose derisive shouts did anything but encourage the players to hurl. That kind of stuff the GAA can do without.*

People blamed us for walking off the field, but my mentor Dónal Carey, who was chairman of the club that year set the record straight when turning on our detractors at our dress dance at the end of the season. 'People seem to think that Clarecastle has not served the county well,' he said, 'but I would like it to be made known that when other players turned their backs on the county team, the Clarecastle club helped out and Clarecastle has never let the GAA in Clare down'.

As things turned out though, it was just as well we walked off the field that day – I could have done without that game, because of my illness, and it was fortuitous from a health point of view that the match was abandoned.

IF I HAD played the full game I might have paid the consequences with my own health. The day afterwards, Dónal Carey brought me back out to Dr McGrath and I was grounded for a few months and didn't puck any ball.

Because of the illness I missed the first four rounds of the National League. Matt Nugent had come in as manager, and he was also given sole responsibility for team selection. Clare had made a great start in the league.

Victories over Offaly and Cork, as well as draws with Limerick and Tipperary had lifted things again after the Munster final hammering. I was back for the fifth round game against Galway in Pearse Stadium, coming on as a sub in a big win that put us top of Division 1 with Kilkenny going into the Christmas break. Just like my championship debut I came on for Jimmy McNamara.

My first full start in the league came the following February against Wexford in Cusack Park when I got a point, my first ever score in a senior jersey – we lost though, with another defeat in the final game against Kilkenny meaning we missed out on the knockout stages.

My no-show for the minors could have knocked me out of contention for a place on the senior panel for the championship, but all was forgiven when Matt Nugent gathered everyone together to prepare for our semi-final against Limerick in late June.

When he took over the previous autumn, the St Joseph's legend had been given sole responsibility for the team – manager, coach and selector. There was no one with him, but the Clare Hurling Action Committee that he was a member of made a move about a month before the game to try and get him some help.

They turned to Michael Hennessy, who had trained the Clare team that won the National League in 1946, and tried to get him to come on board as a trainer/coach, but he was too busy with his taxi business in Shannon Airport to commit.

It was left to Matt alone.

He was an absolute gent, but we had no real time to evaluate him as Clare manager other than knowing he was this famed hurler who brought that authority of being a legend with him. It's not that he was very authoritative in the dressing-room, as he wasn't roaring and shouting and banging tables. But he did have a real presence and authority about him.

I remember he was the first fella I heard use the phrase – we must have had a good win in a league match – that after… 'A clap on the back… a kick in the arse is never too far away'. It shows you how raw and naive I was at the time.

I never thought that there'd be such cynicism in the game of hurling. I wasn't long learning how wrong I was.

He picked fellow magpie, Paschal Russell and myself at midfield for the Limerick game. We were up against Richie Bennis and Eamonn Grimes, two very seasoned players at that stage of their careers. I had only turned 18 in April.

Paschal may have been 25, but hadn't played that much championship hurling with the county – his only two games before that were against Cork in 1969 and Tipperary in '71.

I REMEMBER MATT coming over to us before the match, just before we went out onto the field in Thurles.

'You pick up Grimes,' he said to me.

'You'd have the speed for him… to go with him!'

He said nothing to Paschal.

There was that low-level of 'tactics' in hurling at the time; no deep planning or strategy, but more of a… 'It will be alright on the night' type attitude to the whole thing. Maybe other teams were the same, and there was this ad-hoc approach to things everywhere, but we certainly had it.

For that 1973 Munster semi-final, this plan was a disaster. That was the start of Richie Bennis' great year for Limerick that would carry them all the way to winning a first All-Ireland in 33 years. And he carried them more than anyone else. Captain Eamonn Grimes may have got the Texaco Hurler of the Year award, but it was Richie's year – he was unbelievable. He was a big unit and a big hurler.

Limerick were a seasoned team. Clare caught them in Cusack Park the previous year, while there was the wet ball incident against Tipperary in Killarney the year before that again, so they were on the go for a few years and it was a case of now or never for them.

They were raging favourites, but we pushed them all the way and in the end we were only beaten by two points – 3-11 to 3-9. Paschal and myself were switched during the game. And I just couldn't manage Bennis. They were putting loads of puck-outs right down on top of him. Jackie O'Gorman was behind me and roaring, 'Take it from the feckin' elbow Callinan'.

Jackie's girlfriend at time, whom he later married, was Joan Bennis – Richie's sister. Richie was roaring back, 'Come out and do it yourself Gorman!'

That's exactly what should have happened. The two lads, who were jawing back and forth at each other, should have been let at each other.

Would Bennis have caught all those balls with Jackie breathing down his neck?

As someone who'd been around the squad since the 1967 Munster final, Jackie was senior enough on the team to make the call himself on the field, simply by saying, 'Drop back wing-back… let me in there'.

There would have been nothing said about it, but as a teenager making my first full start in the team, I wasn't going to suggest it or make the move. Something should have been done though, because Richie was almost unplayable that day.

I got a poxy goal for my efforts, a long ball floated in that went all the way to the net, but Timmy Ryan had one disallowed and that could have made all the difference. We were well in the match. Whoever was on Grimes, myself first and then Paschal, did alright, but it was Richie. He beat us.

We were livid afterwards, especially when the year panned out the way it did. Limerick winning a first Munster title since 1955 and then taking their chance in the All-Ireland against Kilkenny.

It's not that it could have been us, but we had the feeling we weren't a million miles away, even though in terms of preparation we hadn't done an awful lot.

And we were without Mick Moroney, who would have been midfield if he was available. He wasn't because he was serving a six-month suspension over something that happened in the previous year's Junior A final between Crusheen and Ballyea, when he wasn't even playing but got involved from the sideline.

Apart from ruling him out of the championship game, it cost him a trip to America as an All Star replacement. I wonder if the same happened to one of Limerick's best players, would he have been suspended for six months by his own county board and would the county team have been left badly damaged.

PART THREE

Harry's Game

« CHAPTER 7 »

Clare has had great hurlers and teams in every decade since the foundation of the GAA, to match the best. Is it any wonder hurling is still a live topic within the county? We seem to have been unlucky. However, we have had our heroes, and great hours. Is it too much to expect that we will make the breakthrough? I do not think so. Let us rally behind what is a very promising young team now and help bring back that coveted MacCarthy Cup to the county.

– Harry Bohan, September 1973

WE'RE ALL CREATURES of habit.

Sometimes it can be a good thing, other times it holds you down, weighs you down and never allows you to achieve. Break the cycle. Break free.

Be the best you can possibly be.

This was one of the perceptions built up around Clare hurling for years. That it was being held back by forces from within – the Clare County Board looking after their own interests, the players' actions themselves.

Then you had different factions within the team.

The Newmarket-on-Fergus crew, and the Clarecastle crew… on it went with those from other clubs. A collection of different groups, never a team.

When they came together to play for Clare, it was in name only – of the same team, but not a team in the true and proper sense of the word. Togging out in different parts of the dressing-room; not pulling together on the field.

It may have been exaggerated to explain away why Clare never won anything, but it was there. There was *something* and it wasn't right.

AROUND THE TIME I joined the Clare senior set-up Tom McNamara from Crusheen famously told a county board meeting that he had... 'Yet to meet an honest Clare selector'... adding that they were just... 'parochial-minded and more concerned with filling cars than picking the best team'.

When we played that championship game against Limerick in 1973 there was a picture taken beforehand – there I am on the very right of the front row, with Clarecastle's Patrick 'Jack' Moloney and Paschal Russell to my immediate right, and with Sixmilebridge's Niall McInerney and Noel Casey together in the back row.

Nothing sinister maybe, but maybe it was an indication of how rife the club stuff within the team was – it was always there just below the surface and I saw that from the very first day I was in a senior dressing-room in the championship, in the Munster final against Cork in Thurles.

I was sitting with my own people. I did that because they were the only lads I knew to talk to, but also because it was what everyone did.

There were a few from Clarecastle in the dressing-room – Jack Moloney, Michael Hegarty, who was sub goalie to Seamus Durack, and Tom Slattery, who was team captain in 1971 because we won the championship the previous year.

Gus Lohan was the captain in 1972 after Newmarket won their title back and there was a huge Newmarket contingent – two other defenders in Billy and DJ Meehan, Pat O'Leary at midfield, with Jimmy and Paddy McNamara as well as Jimmy Cullinan in the forwards.

It was the only time I witnessed a row in a Clare dressing-room, and the first I was ever in as a senior. I was sitting down after the game and delighted with myself that I had played. Martin McKeogh also came on; I'd no idea how he was feeling but I soon found out about the third sub that day, the late Niall McInerney, and his thoughts.

HE WAS THE first to come on, replacing the injured Lohan midway through the first-half, and he played well.

Louis Halpin was going around the dressing-room afterwards. He is a gentleman and was never an offensive man. He was doing as any selector would do... 'Hard luck ....we'll come again...'

Louis was going along the wall and then he came to Niall McInerney and he said the same again...'Well played Niall... hard luck'.

Next thing Niall grabbed him and stuck him up against the wall.

'You fecker... if I played with Newmarket I'd be playing on the team'.

Niall was actually from the Newmarket parish – it was the 'Gaza Strip' near Ballycasey between Newmarket and Sixmilebridge. And there was a lot more venom between Newmarket and Sixmilebridge than there was between Clarecastle and Newmarket. It went back to the digging of the graves in Kilkishen, before Newmarket and Sixmilebridge played each other in the infamous Clare Champion Cup final in 1962.

I was over at the other side of the dressing-room and next thing Hego was roaring... 'Go on... give it to him!' That was the Clarecastle Vs Newmarket stuff coming out of Hego, who would have been well up for such a fight.

That was the only time I witnessed club rivalries and perceived slights between one club and the next breaking out in the dressing-room. And at 17, I thought this was par for the course and it would be there all the time, always ready to break out.

But it wasn't. That was the only time.

It never happened again, even if Niall McInerney's days with Clare were numbered. He played towards the end of the following season's National League and started right half-back against Limerick in the championship in 1973, but after he was replaced by Ger Loughnane in the first-half he never played for Clare again.

Niall left the following year. He was a huge loss.

There was the belief at the time that the toxicity that existed between clubs was very damaging and holding Clare back. Basically, you had to be from a certain club.

Niall declared for Galway and the rest is history.

He was an All Star in 1975, the same year he won a National League and played in an All-Ireland final, while he finally won his All-Ireland in 1980 when he collected his second All Star. Maybe it would never have happened if Niall felt he hadn't got such a raw deal from Clare in 1972 and '73.

At least such a repeat was banished from Clare dressing-rooms after that.

HARRY BOHAN IS the man credited with breaking up that cosy cartel of clubs being independent republics within the team, but it had started to change in 1973 during Matt Nugent's season in charge.

Then when Harry came in, there was no going back – he was really conscious of not allowing cliques or clubs rule the roost, and he blew old ways out of the water.

Under the old order, everything seemed fractured.

Apart from sitting in different parts of the dressing-room, it was as if you were identified by your club only, never the county you were actually playing for and supposed to represent.

A case of, if a Newmarket man was talking he was talking as a Newmarket man first and last; same if a Clarecastle man was talking, an Éire Óg man and so on. They were never talking as Claremen and bridging that divide, which is supposed to be what it is all about.

Harry's gift from his earliest days was that he was always talking as a Clareman. And although he'd be talking about 'Fakle this and Fakle that' he was *speaking* as a Clareman. There was a big difference. It was the power of the collective and bringing everyone with him in the one direction and all together.

He was only 34 years of age when he took over the team; you could say he was nearly of the same generation as most of the players. County boards were never that, they were so far removed from that.

Only a few months before, the board had looked for Michael Hennessy to train the Clare team. Hennessy had done an awful lot for Clare hurling, playing for the county in the 30s, coaching the county to its last national success in the 40s, refereeing a couple of All-Ireland finals, but he was well into his sixties at that stage.

A new approach and something different was needed. That's what Fr Harry provided and represented. He stood for the modern era. He was different, something Clare hurling had never seen or heard before.

Aside from the Feakle lads, none of us would have known much about Harry, apart from him being on the Hurling Action Committee that was established the previous year. He wasn't a Matt Nugent or a Haulie Daly, who had played with Clare. They had huge cachet because apart from years of service on and off the field, they'd actually achieved something by being on that 1946 National League winning side.

Harry had none of that. He hadn't played for Clare, and he had no hurling reputation preceding him like his predecessors. He'd been to St Flannan's like a lot of us, he'd played a bit with Feakle, lining out with them in the 1958 county final, but at that time we didn't even know that.

All most of us knew was that he had these half-mad eyes, longish hair, was a big man and he smoked cigarettes.

And yes, he was a priest. We knew nothing beyond that.

It wasn't long after we had got together that we got to know all about him though – what drove him and what he wanted for Clare hurling. There was a meeting organised in Anglim's of Tulla, probably after one of the first training sessions we had under Harry that September.

WE WERE VERY open to someone like Harry.

Ger Loughnane can say what he wants now, but we were open to him. The O'Connors, Honan, myself, Durack, Loughnane, Stack and Hehir – that group with Durack being the oldest – we were very ambitious, without ever thinking we were ambitious.

Most of us were going to college and we'd held our own in Fitzgibbon and Third Level competitions. Yeah, we didn't have too many medals to show for what we'd done, but we had a sense that we were good.

We were welcoming to a fella like Fr Harry coming in, a fella who was different from the old regime and the old ways of Clare hurling. That toxic atmosphere of different cohorts in the dressing-room – we witnessed him finally blow it all away.

That was the first thing at that meeting. I'll never forget it.

'WE'RE ALL CLAREMEN HERE!' he thundered.

Then he started on about winning Munster and All-Ireland titles, and across the room Colm Honan caught my eye. I'm sure the expression on both of our faces told the same story – we'd never heard anything like this before. We were bemused.

This was the New Testament in the hurling sense.

Scripture from the young priest – like going from the Tridentine Latin Mass to English Mass at the stroke of a pen.

No one ever spoke in those terms before… that we weren't just there to make up the numbers and be fodder for the blue bloods like Cork, Tipperary and Limerick in Munster, and Kilkenny and Wexford beyond that.

Another myth or attitude that was blown away was that the achievement was to get on to the county senior team. Rubbish.

That couldn't be the achievement, the yardstick or the boast; yes, you must get on the team, but it was all about being on a winning team.

I was very taken by it. And, if all the lads who were part of it place their hands on their hearts, they'll say the exact same thing. It was inspiring. Here you had this larger than life character and what he was saying was coming from the heart and it was coming from the toes.

He was an evangelist.

He really meant what he was saying and he spoke at length about his vision for the future of Clare hurling. And right from the very beginning he was able to hold his audience. From the word go, that made Fr Harry very attractive to us.

I DON'T KNOW how religious any of us were, but here before us was this modern priest. He had a pint and he was of the people. We were attracted to him; attracted by what he said and attracted by what he did.

He said he was going to take on the Clare County Board, because it was all for the betterment of the team and where we wanted to go. Immediately we were at one: this was the kind of stuff that we wanted to hear. Even at that stage, all of us had seen the way things were – those age-old cliques that were around the GAA in the county.

There was going to be no more of that.

You had the O'Connors from Tubber, and you had Honan from Clonlara. I used to slag them, saying, 'Jesus lads, I don't even know the colour of your jerseys'.

It was the truth, I didn't know.

We never played those clubs, and the likes of Clarecastle, Newmarket and other big clubs never rated players from those clubs.

Now we knew there was going to be a spread of fellas. If they were good enough, they would play. Suddenly Clare hurling was more 'catholic' from that point of view.

Harry had a lot going for him, because he was so young and energetic. He was proactive. He'd always be asking how we were getting on in college. We were being treated as adults, as human beings.

It was holistic.

While he was mad into the hurling and wanted nothing only Clare to succeed, he looked beyond that. He was an educationalist; he was a visionary in a lot of things he did.

He was not of the county board. He was of us – part of the team and straight away it was very obvious that he was not one of them. He spoke that way that first night.

He'd taken on the board by insisting on food after training and demanding more hurling balls. That might seem small stuff, but Matt Nugent hadn't done that. Matt might have been livid with the county board but he wouldn't have taken them on in that way.

With Harry, there was a meeting of minds. He was with us and he was with us all the way. We were energised before we pucked a ball.

We couldn't wait to get out there.

◄◄◆►►

Vincent Loftus stood very adjacent to the goal, a position he should not have been allowed to occupy by the stewards. One can understand Loftus' excitement causing him to make his illegal entry, but one cannot but point an accusing finger at the stewards or officials who permitted him to take up the position.

— John D Hickey, *Irish Independent*

I DIDN'T GO to the 1973 All-Ireland final when Limerick had their big day, but I can say I was represented in Croke Park on the day by a woman who, five years later, would become my wife.

Siobhán O'Donovan was Kilmallock and Limerick, loud and proud. She still is, and whenever Limerick have a big day the flag is put out – too often these days – in all its glory, whatever protestations or misgivings I might have.

We had yet to meet, but I've heard plenty about it since.

She was in the Cusack Stand that day – with her uncle, Tommy O'Riordan of Kilmallock, Leitrim and Ballyboden St Enda's fame – when Limerick ended a famine of 33 years. And she was back in Croke Park when the famine of 45 years was ended in 2018. I was with her.

Afterwards, she met a couple of her O'Riordan cousins, her sister, Majella and husband, Mike Hayes, in the Gresham Hotel on O'Connell Street. Nearly all of them had been at the 1973 final, so it was a reunion that they revelled in. I was the designated photographer and as they gathered together, a young fella passing by decked out in green said... 'Do you want to get into the photograph?'

All of them in the photo, including my wife, shouted... 'NO!'

I shouted no as well. They didn't want me and I didn't want them.

It was them and us. They're great people, but they *are* Limerick, and I *am* Clare. The lines of demarcation are clear.

Inside I was sore, because I felt Clare should have won that All-Ireland in 2018.

THE EXACT SAME sentiment was there when we played Limerick in our first game under Fr Harry. It was just five weeks after Limerick's All-Ireland win over Kilkenny, the first game of the 1973-74 National League and it was in Cusack Park.

As league openers go, it was a perfect stage. All-Ireland champions strutting their stuff for the first time and doing so against their next door neighbours. Clare doing the same for the first time under a new manager, who was promising to change the world.

A big crowd.

A big day. And an explosive occasion all round.

'That was a right baptism,' commented Limerick's coach, Jackie Power after they'd beaten us by 3-9 to 0-14, while the *Limerick Leader's* Sean Murphy jumped on those words when writing... *Unfortunately, the baptismal ceremony was performed with blood rather than with the usual holy water.*

There was more.

We all agree that the mantle of champions is a heavy burden for the wearers, continued Murphy... *but Limerick had to pay an exorbitant price for success in Ennis. Every one of the 17 players who participated bore the scars of battle as they trooped off the pitch at the end of this unsavoury hour.*

Indeed, spectators could be forgiven for asking if, in fact, they had switched from their traditional jerseys to the green and red of Mayo, so bloodstained was their strip.

It wasn't that bad, but it was tough.

Very tough. Before the game, the red carpet was rolled out for the new All-

JOHN CALLINAN CHAPTER 7

Ireland champions. Out of courtesy we formed a guard of honour for Eamonn Grimes and clapped Limerick out onto the field. County board chairman John Hanly made a presentation to his Limerick counterpart Rory Kiely, while the Clare Hurling Board secretary, Joe Keane said in his programme notes, *We welcome them with the welcome of the Gael.*

As it turned out it wasn't a céad míle fáilte.

The whole idea was to get stuck into them from the first whistle. We did that. It was a perfect opportunity for us. I was playing left half-forward and being marked by Phil Bennis.

Enda O'Connor and Willie Moore were sent off before half-time, but we were leading by 0-9 to 0-4 and playing really well, with Paschal Russell, who ended up with a tally of 0-10 that day, doing most of our scoring.

Then 10 minutes into the second-half, Vincent Loftus was sent off for a pull on Ned Rea. Gus Lohan was playing full-forward and he was brought down from the other end of the field to go full-back. As he was coming down Ned Rea walked up along the sideline on the stand side with a cut on the head, but with the first aid men gathering around it looked much worse than it actually was.

When he saw Rea passing by and saw the blood, Phil Bennis started hitting the ground with the flat of the hurley behind my heels. Phil was no shrinking violet.

He roared... 'HEYYY RICHARD... RICHARD!

'It's time to start taking a few of these f****** out!'

It was bravado after seeing their man bloodied and being helped off the field. The big row that threatened never happened though, but it was very tough.

After he had been sent off by John Moloney, Loftus stood behind the goal and even intervened in the game on one occasion. In a moment of danger, he came back onto the field – it was his instinctive reaction. In the words of the referee afterwards he, 'Stopped the ball with his hurley from entering the Clare net'.

We were a goal up at the time – 0-14 to 1-8 – and the result was a free which Richie Bennis pointed. We looked like holding out with our 13 men, but in the end a couple of late goals from Eamonn Grimes and Mossy Dowling finally gave Limerick the win.

In the dressing-room afterwards Vincent was bending down, taking off his boots and I said, 'Lofty, what happened... what happened?'

It was my innocence of youth. And he looked up at me.

'If he moved again,' he said, 'I'd have hit him again.'

I asked no more.

There was me thinking this is the quiet professional man and banker, who's giving me lifts down from Dublin for training and matches. He was different on the field; he was ruthless, he was a strong man on the team.

There was no remorse for being sent off – it was a case of… 'It had to be done'. Taking a player out of it was a newish phrase to me. It was another part of the learning curve.

A steep learning curve.

But I was eager to learn; we all were.

« CHAPTER 8 »

Going into the 1974 Munster final it was all new to us. I was on my own over the team and had no selectors. Johnny Callinan and Martin McKeogh were injured that day and were sitting down on either side of me on the bench. Limerick beat us well, but we didn't let the defeat get us down.

– Fr Harry Bohan

'YOU DID!'

'I didn't.'

'You feckin' did!'

'I feckin' didn't.'

'Were you wearing 15?'

'I was, but it wasn't me'.

'But it was the number 15 who hit me… who DID me!'

IT'S A CONVERSATION I've had many times with Patsy O'Keeffe, the two of us laughing about it. I meet him regularly and every time it's the same cant.

We re-hash the same old story.

It wouldn't be the same if we let it go; it's the thread played out on a continuous loop over the years and decades. Never any aggro. It's just banter now, but there's no holding back. We're talking about the 1974 Munster under-21 final that Clare contrived to lose to Waterford in Thurles – a defeat every bit as bad as the infamous 1992 loss at the same venue and against the same opposition that brought an end to Ger Loughnane's days as a manager in that grade.

We had seven of the senior team that had beaten Tipperary in the Munster senior semi-final the previous Sunday, and were nailed-on certainties to win, having beaten Tipperary and Cork to reach the final. More than that, we hammered them and in doing so we had made a huge statement.

We had arrived. But, the final was a huge let down.

Patsy was corner-forward for Waterford and at the throw-in, as I was hitting off my left a fella came in and came straight down and broke my thumb.

Martin McKeogh was ruled out of the game with a knee injury and couldn't start, but was helping out with the team and he came into me on the field to see if I could continue.

I just said no, telling him clearly that, 'anybody with two hands has to be better than me'. But I was left on and I played on. You could manage with a broken finger, but not a broken thumb. I may as well have not been out there. You could say that about the team too, because collectively we flopped.

A big Clare crowd had made the journey to Thurles that night, even for an 8pm start, again because of the Munster football final earlier in the day in Killarney. They travelled because this was going to be the night of the big breakthrough – a first Munster championship for the county since the junior title in 1949. Call it a silver jubilee, just to collect the silver cup.

Clare and Waterford shared the same hotel for the pre-match cup of tea and Clare confidence literally impregnated the very atmosphere, remarked the *Waterford News and Star* afterwards... *Clare officials wished you well, with a knowing smile lurking at the corners of their mouth. They had this game won before a ball was struck.*

Maybe it was over-confidence.

Whatever happened, we never got going. John Galvin had a huge game for them at centre-back and they led the whole way through. They were 1-4 to 0-2 up at half-time – I got a goal from a '21' early in the second-half but soon afterwards a second goal from Paul Moore killed us off.

Near the end, in a desperate attempt to turn things around Martin McKeogh came on, despite being on one leg because of his injured knee. That brought to eight the number of senior players who played that night – nine when you include Pat O'Connor, who went on to make his senior debut in the Munster senior final a few weeks later. We were so strong in every line. Ger Ward had a great game, and it was a final that should have been won.

ON A RAINY and overcast night it was getting dark when we were finally put out of our misery. It was awful, and a long journey home.

Up to then it had been a really positive year on every front. After the opening round defeat to Limerick in the league we had our ups and downs, but for every disappointing defeat there was something to pick us up.

Waterford beat us by five points in the second game, but we bounced back to beat Tipperary in the third game in Tulla. Then after Cork hit us for seven goals, we hit Galway for five in Tulla, while we finished off the campaign with a win over Kilkenny in Tulla a couple of weeks after being beaten down in Wexford.

Home wins over Kilkenny were a given as the years wore on and, in all, we beat them on four occasions in Tulla in the 70s, but this is the win I remember most. It was memorable because I scored a goal. I didn't score many, but that was a good one.

Midfielder Con Woods hit a long ball in and as he did I was sprinting in towards the goal. Full-forward Gus Lohan flicked it to me and I blasted to the net. At that time in Tulla, the 'net' was actually a wire mesh and I put so much power into the shot that the sliotar got stuck.

It was nice to put one past Noel Skehan!

We started the under-21 championship with a home game against Tipperary and we hammered them by 10 points. I was marking my best friend from St Flannan's, Liam Heffernan. Even then I used to go up to Nenagh regularly and stay in his house, and it continued for years afterwards. They had a furniture shop on Kenyon Street and we had a ritual of having drinks in the High B and then going up to the tennis club for more.

'Minny' we called him in St Flannan's – it came from Minny Heffernan in the RTÉ drama, *The Riordans*. He was a good hurler and it was strange having him as my direct opponent. I didn't know how to react, so I just shook hands with him and we didn't say a word for the rest of the game.

It was a bit intense and strange, but I got on with it.

I scored 0-4 that night, but it was the goals we got from Enda O'Connor, Pat O'Connor and Jacko Treacy that really made the big difference as we burned them in the end by 3-12 to 1-8. Just like we did in the minor game three years previously, we ploughed into them and showed no mercy.

Apparently towards the end of the game, I was roaring… 'DRIVE IT ON… DRIVE IT ON!'… with a few other choice words thrown in. All this with the game over. Minny challenged me about it afterwards, saying, 'There was no need for that shouting'. I politely disagreed then, and I still do.

The semi-final against Cork was on in the Gaelic Grounds two weeks later and we knew we'd beat them.

There wasn't a huge change in the make-up of both sides since the minor final three years previously – they still had their star man, Jimmy Barry Murphy, but we were missing the injured Martin McKeogh.

But we were very confident and beat them by 12 points – after being beaten by 17 points in that minor final it was a 29-point turnaround. I was midfield with Honan that night. Loughnane and Hehir were in the half-back line. Stack was full-back, while the two O'Connors were up front. It was the best display from any Clare team I played on.

No wonder we were confident going into the final against Waterford.

AFTER BEATING CORK, I remember the trip back to Dublin to college that night with Hehir, Stack and Loughnane. We were as high as kites.

Paddy Hill from Kilmaley, who was on the squad as well, was with us. I remember waking up my two flatmates Tommy Quinn and Alan Higgins in the early hours to give them the result and they weren't a bit impressed.

We were staying in an awful kip of a place on South Richmond Street near Kelly's Corner.

They got up anyway and we had a few bottles of beer at 2am in the morning. We had a big victory to toast. And there was the promise of more victories to come.

Before the Munster under-21 final we had the Munster senior semi-final against Tipperary in Limerick. It was a big day. Clare hadn't beaten Tipp in the championship in 19 years, while later that night the World Cup final was on between Holland and West Germany.

The soccer was definitely more memorable than the hurling. Tipperary were very poor but we just about got over the line against them. Leading by 1-8 to 0-5 going into the last quarter we failed to score for the rest of the game but managed to win by a point when Francis Loughnane missed a couple of late chances to force a draw. Jackie O'Gorman let out a roar in his direction for one of the chances and it worked.

After the victory we all went to the Two Mile Inn just out the road from the Gaelic Grounds to celebrate being in another Munster final, but also to watch the World Cup final.

We were all into it, because we were attracted to that Dutch team and their 'total football'. Everyone was on about Johan Cruyff. For me, Johan Neeskens was the *man* on that great team – the box-to-box midfielder and the runner that I saw myself as when I was on the field. He could do everything except the odd bits of genius that Cryuff had in his bag.

Colm Honan was christened 'Willie' by Enda O'Connor after West Germany's Uli Hoeness – it was because of the similarity of the two surnames and the fact that both had big heads of curly blonde hair.

The senior final was two weeks later against Limerick, but any confidence the under-21s on the team had going into the game took a hammering with the debacle that followed against Waterford.

My whole experience on the night was coloured by what happened to me in the opening minutes, but beyond that it was a devastating defeat and shattering for all concerned. Worse still, I was injured for the Munster senior final, while Sean Stack then broke a finger the Sunday before the game when contesting a ball in training with Timmy Ryan.

When the team for the final was picked A.N. Other was playing on the double – at right corner-back for Stack and right half-forward for me. It didn't stop Fr Harry believing that both of us could still make the cut and be fit in time. The week of the game he brought the two of us into Limerick to see a doctor in a clinic on Pery Square. He wanted a second opinion.

The doctor looked at the x-rays of the two of us.

Straight away he said nothing could be done for me, but he told Sean that he'd strap his finger, give him an injection and that he'd be okay and could start the game. Great that he could play, but it put paid to our grand plans for a night out in Limerick.

BEFORE MAKING THE journey into Limerick, we were both fully expecting to be ruled out of contention. Fr Harry was driving the car, collecting me in Clarecastle and then going on to the 'Bridge for Stack. When Stack got in it wasn't long before I turned to him.

'Have you much money on you?'

'A couple of quid… why?'

'Pints!'

'Where?'

'In Limerick… after the doctor.'

'Great plan.'

It was decided. Our attitude for the whole journey was that we were going on the beer. After getting the doctor thing out of the way, we were going to tell Harry to work away and head home by himself; that we were going to the cinema or something, that we'd make our own way home.

There'd be no cinema. The law student in me was intent on being called to the bar; so too was Stack. As students, it's what you did.

The White House on O'Connell Street, not too far from Pery Square, would have been a starting point. Bobby Byrnes'… Kennedy O'Brien's… Flannery's were other options. Wherever, it was going to be a good night.

Stack being told that he was ready for Sunday's Munster final ruined our carefully laid plans. It was a terrible disappointment, because he was far from right, but also because it ruled out our night.

A few days before the game there was a photograph in *The Cork Examiner* of myself and Stack flanking Fr Harry – we looked like the dregs of student-hood with our long hair, and Fr Harry is there with a face on him like he's just after hearing all belonging to him are after dying.

It was worse on the day of the game.

I WAS SITTING on the bench in my civvies as was Martin McKeogh. And Stack should have been there with us. He played, but he shouldn't have been put out there really.

It was a nightmare.

Jimmy Cullinan came into the team instead of me, but the game was nearly over as soon as it had started. Limerick had three goals inside 12 minutes, and that was that. Frankie Nolan cut through the defence and fired home the first. Two minutes later Stack scored an own-goal with virtually the first big play he was involved in – all because of the broken finger.

Richie Bennis was on Stack and when the first high ball came in towards them from a harmless enough looking lob from Joe McKenna, up went Stack to try and catch it – he hurt the finger again and only managed to deflect the ball into the net. He shouldn't have played, we should have gone out on the beer in Limerick. We were still disappointed about that.

It got worse.

Ned Rea added a third, and then his fourth before half-time. Trailing by 4-8 to 1-5 at half-time, the large Clare contingent in the 36,000-plus crowd could go home. In the end we were beaten by 14 points. Yes it was a big set-back on paper, but looking on from the sideline it wasn't the shattering experience you might expect.

That's because in 1974 I was still just 19 years of age.

I was so young. We were all so young. Sean Stack was 20, Colm Honan and Ger Loughnane were 21… and on it went.

Loughnane became an All Star a couple of months later – Clare's first ever Carrolls All Star – which was a big breakthrough for the county in itself.

Being beaten in two Munster finals within the space of two weeks was hard to take at the time, but not for long because we looked to the next match.

At that age, it was always the next match.

◄◄◆▷►

Ah to hell with it, give them the two points in Tulla
and think of the money we will save.
– Paddy Grace, Kilkenny County Secretary

IN THAT FIRST season under Fr Harry there was a buzz about the team and much of it came from Tulla where Clare started playing the majority of their home National League games from 1973 onwards, because of the deteriorating state of the pitch and facilities at Cusack Park.

There'd been a game in Tulla against Kilkenny in early 1972 that was before my time, but under Harry the East Clare venue became a thing. A huge thing.

Training there and playing there, and winning there. And along the way developing a great relationship and rapport with the Clare public.

We were comfortable there – not in the environment and the state of the facilities, but comfortable in the place itself where we had this feeling about the venue. There was something about it. The big crowds, the cars parked for miles on the Ennis and Scariff sides, the craic and pints afterwards in John Minogue's and beyond. We had great wins there.

That first year, the three league wins we had against Tipperary, Galway and Kilkenny were all in Tulla, and with them something started to grow in the team.

Those wins really lifted us, even if we didn't make the knockout stages that year. The place lifted us. When we started winning there and built up a real head of steam we were always going out before crowds of 9,000 or 10,000. The crowd was nearly in on top of us. The supporters were also on the sideline on the two rows of concrete seats hugging the field, then up on the famous bank.

Going out to play there, we were automatically sticking out our chests. The supporters were turning up and because we were winning and kept winning, it meant the whole Tulla experience gathered a huge momentum.

This aura built up around the place.

It was built by the supporters, but the press also cultivated the narrative that an away team decamping to Tulla in winter was somehow akin to going into battle into downtown Galatasaray – going to face a mob of tribal Clare supporters. I never believed that, but it suited the storylines to build the place up. There was this 'Fortress Tulla' thing and we weren't going to tell them stop talking bullshit.

WE BEAT KILKENNY there more than any other team. We had it over Cork too. I don't think the likes of Seanie O'Leary or Jimmy Barry Murphy ever came to Tulla to play us, preferring to stay away. But the thing that sticks out above everything was the Galway game in February 1979, near the end of our time in Tulla. It was the one.

The craziest game of all.

With three minutes remaining the game was over as Galway led by 2-9 to 0-7, with two Andy Fenton goals sending us hurtling towards a big defeat. It was over, with many supporters from both sides voting with their feet and leaving.

By the time they'd gone and had reached the pubs up in the village we had done what we had done, scoring three goals to win the game. The first came from Pat O'Connor after Micky Murphy set him up. A minute later Brendan Gilligan gathered a long clearance and set me up for the second. Straight from the puck out we got the third. Loughnane made a great catch, thundered up the right wing, crossed the ball to Noel Casey who first-timed it to the net. It was a brilliant goal.

The game finished when I was fouled following a run up the field after picking up the ball in defence. It was an amazing win – a win that had 'old timers' talking about the famous comeback in the 1932 All-Ireland semi-final against Galway, when Tull Considine ran riot in the second-half. We ran riot in a few minutes. We may have lost the previous two Munster finals, but we were on top of the world for those few minutes.

After the game we landed up in John Minogue's and the people who were there before us refused to believe we won. It was pre-local radio and no news had travelled until we arrived. We had a great night.

We had many great nights in Tulla.

Immediately after any game in Tulla we showered quickly, if there was a shower and if it was working. There weren't showers at the start of our run. When we got them, they were very basic. The whole place was rudimentary. The walls were plastered with a bit of black tar-like paint. If you stayed too long in the shower, you'd be moved on fairly quickly because the water would go cold. We weren't going up the town smelling, but we weren't smelling of Eau du Cologne either. We didn't care.

The first decision after coming out the gate was always... 'Right?'... 'Or left?'

It was still manic outside the ground. Would we navigate our way up town by the lower road... or the higher road?

There was food for us back in the Queen's Hotel in Ennis, but no player went back there. The gate checkers may have gone back, just as the county board lads went back, because they wanted their food. Not us though; we wanted a drink.

It was a case of getting a bag of chips that night before we all went home. It's almost pathetic when you think about it now, but that's the way it was and everyone who liked a drink went with that.

Sometimes there might be a bit of food for us in Anglim's but it was never appropriate and didn't pretend to be. The big thing was that we went up and had our pints. Minogue's was the first port of call... then it was to what's now Power's.

Then when it was all over, it was case of making our way home at whatever time it was, as best you could.

WHEN I WAS a student, unless there was someone going back to Dublin the night of the match I always stayed. I never wanted to go back.

Michael Slattery's transport business had lorries going up at 6am in the morning, so I'd fall out of the bed, get into a lorry and fall asleep again, before getting up to Dublin around 9am and heading in for my first lecture.

Tulla had a lot of things going for it from the romantic point of view. The Tommy Daly thing, the windswept hill. It was out in the middle of nowhere. I don't know if teams were four or five points down before they came in the gate, but if they were that wasn't our problem.

The surface wasn't great, but we knew every inch of it.

I remember we played Tipp there the day after my sister Bríd got married and I would have loved if the game was called off. I'd had a couple of drinks at the wedding and there were pools of water on the field, but on the match went. Mick Moroney was taking sideline cuts that day and Tipp lads were getting back out of his way because they were getting drenched.

Forget the rain, the wind and the liquid mud along the touchlines, wrote Padraig Puirséal in *The Irish Press* after one of those Tipperary games... *and difficulties when trying to see though burly wellington booted gentleman in leather coats.*

Everyone but the opposition loved Tulla, despite its limitations. A big thing was the supporters going up to the pub with us after the games. We went in and our backs were clapped and we all loved it. As a result, to this day I meet people of my own age or older who say, 'Jesus, ye were great'. We had *great* days and *great* nights in Tulla. I wouldn't say it was because we were going to the pub with them, but at the same time we were very much of the people. We were accessible, because there was no concept of not being accessible.

We didn't travel in buses; we made our own way to the matches.

It was a generational thing too. Economically things were starting to move. People had a bit more disposal income. People were able to go to matches more and I suppose we were giving them some hope that there could be some sort of success.

And we believed we would be successful, too.

We sensed that in the first year under Fr Harry.

« CHAPTER 9 »

Fr Harry Bohan has preached for so long that Clare are capable of much greater things than they have been achieving. Now, perhaps, they might prove him right.
– Michael Fortune, *The Irish Press*

THAT FIRST DAY, when Fr Harry attracted some puzzled looks amongst the squad by talking about 'days out' in Croke Park and All-Irelands, there were a few in the room that had ticked the first box by having a day out in headquarters when Clare contested a final there.

It was five years previously – 1968, when they were beaten by All-Ireland champions Wexford in the Grounds Tournament final. Jackie O'Gorman, Gus Lohan, Jimmy Cullinan, Jimmy McNamara and Vincent Loftus played that day and were still around.

I'd played there as well and it was a big thing. Just over 10 years after being there with my father and still just 17, I got to shape up against some of the best in Ireland when playing Railway Cup for the first time.

IT WAS 1973 when I was picked for the Combined Universities to play Leinster in the provincial semi-final. That year the Combined Universities' footballers won the Railway Cup – they were very strong with All-Ireland winners like John

O'Keeffe, Kevin Kilmurray, Paudie Lynch and Brendan Lynch playing for them.

Us hurlers were nowhere near as good, but still had county players like Galway's Sean Silke, Dublin's Pat Quigley, who later played with Tipperary, another Tipp player in Seamus Hogan, as well as myself and Niall McInerney from Clare. If we'd had Sean Stack, Iggy Clarke and Joe McDonagh playing that day we might have been closer, but Leinster hammered us. They had a fantastic team with the pick of Kilkenny and Wexford – Pat Delaney, Kieran Purcell, Eddie Keher, Frank Cummins, Pat Henderson, Tony Doran, Mick Jacob and Martin Quigley; they were all there.

Myself and Niall McInerney were up against Cummins and Jacob at midfield.

It was a tough baptism. I remember Jodie Spooner from Roscrea, who was playing wing-forward, hitting Pat Henderson a right belt. Henderson didn't even know who he was. I was telling him to take it easy in case they got cross with us.

It was a great day out for us, but Croke Park was a dark place; and I never thought it to be a great field. We got the gear though, a red jersey with a green trim. It was a 'keeper'. We were allowed to hold onto them, at a time when keeping a jersey was almost a capital offence.

I got back there a good few times with Munster in the Railway Cup, but with Clare there was nothing. No big days as we had hoped. Just a few National League games in the dead of winter with nobody there.

This was summed up by my last visit there in 1984. My wife Siobhán's first cousin was playing in goal for Dublin the same day. Tomás Riordan caught a ball under the crossbar, but as he did Gerry McInerney was loitering. As he threw the ball up before clearing, Gerry just nipped in and flicked it to the net.

After scoring a point I turned to the ref and said, 'He's broken my hand'.

His answer was, 'Didn't you get the point'. That was my memory from my last day playing in Croke Park.

We won well, I was even named Man of the Match, but there were only 1,500 people there, with someone taking the trouble to count the number on Hill 16.

There were 35 there.

THIS WASN'T WHAT Fr Harry was on about when he talked about getting to Croke Park. In that sense, we failed, but we weren't *failures*. We weren't because from the mid-70s we competed consistently with the best and were able to beat the best.

This consistency over a number of years had never been in a Clare team before. It was never sustained. A team might come one year with a big performance, but fade the next year. Our success was that we came every year and we gave it everything.

The first big move after the 1974 Munster final was getting to the 1976 National League final. We got to the semi-final in '75 but Tipperary beat us with John Flanagan's frees, and just like the Munster final I was sitting on the bench injured, the latest big match after the Fitzgibbon Cup and Railway Cup finals that I missed that spring.

The Munster under-21 semi-final against Cork also came too soon for me – maybe I was lucky missing that game as we were hammered by 16 points. I wasn't so lucky in making it back for the Munster senior championship game against Cork as we suffered another big beating, this time by 11 points.

It wasn't a good few months for Clare hurling and it got worse at the start of the 1975-76 National League. It started with our first trip to Croke Park when we could only draw with Dublin. Then we lost to Cork and Wexford, and were left sitting near the bottom of the table with just a point after three games.

We had to beat Galway in the next game in Pearse Stadium, or else we were gone. It helped that Galway were worse off than we were, with the hangover from the All-Ireland final defeat to Kilkenny seeing them lose their first three games.

We won by five points, but it could have been 15. And with that, we had turned a corner.

'That game was our best display in 12 months,' enthused Fr Harry afterwards. 'It has put the entire team in great heart for next Sunday and you have to remember we have never lost a league match in Tulla.'

Tulla took over for us.

We beat Kilkenny and Tipperary there, and went from relegation trouble to the knockout stages. It was the first run of continuous good form we had as a team.

Holding Tipperary to just three points in the final game clinched a quarter-final place against Waterford, but it was the defeat of Kilkenny before Christmas that really set up the team for the rest of that league season.

It was three months to the day that Kilkenny had won the All-Ireland and they came to Tulla with 13 of their All-Ireland winning team – Frank Cummins and Kieran Purcell were the only two they were missing, but they didn't have bad replacements in Ger Henderson and my UCD team-mate Matt Ruth.

It was the biggest two-point hammering we ever gave a team and we did it the hard way. I missed two great goal chances in the first-half that would have killed it.

At least I was there, because Colm Honan arrived late and missed the entire first-half before coming on to get what proved to be the winning goal inside the last 10 minutes. We were also missing Seamus Durack, who broke three fingers in an inter-firm game the day before, with Tom Glynn coming in for him.

Apart from winning the game, we were starting to win the crowd over. It was the Tulla factor, where they always packed in to support us, but they eventually travelled far and wide with us as well.

After we beat Waterford comfortably to reach the semi-final for the second year in-a-row there were only 5,000 in Thurles when we played Wexford, but when it was over you'd think there had been 50,000 in attendance.

We were as good as beaten, trailing by a goal, with many in the crowd having left when Colm Honan shaped up to a free 30 yards from goal in the last seconds. When he mis-hit it, we looked beaten... only to be awarded another free 25 yards from goal.

This time Honan stepped away.

Mick Moroney stepped up. It was the last puck of the game.

The scenes which followed were those we see when some top English soccer player scores, wrote Peadar O'Brien in *The Irish Press. Players hugged each other; they fell to the ground in disbelief; Clare lived to fight another day with the last puck of the match. Moroney, who had to score direct, had risen to the occasion and will be a hero in Clare for many a long day.*

IT SAID SOMETHING that there were over 30,000 at the replay.

We had huge momentum, and the belief was rising. That it was a great game going all the way to extra-time, and more importantly that we won, was huge for the team. Honan was the hero this time by getting us to extra-time with a late point, while Tom Crowe finally finished Wexford off with a goal.

It was bigger than reaching Munster finals in 1972 and '74, because it wasn't just a single, one-off performance that got us there, like beating Limerick and Tipperary in those provincial semi-finals had been. This was a run of form, something that was building ever since we beat Galway in that do-or-die game the previous November.

To an extent, we felt we had arrived.

We had a hurling team and there was no shortage of hyperbole around our second coming to a National League final – 30 years after the first.

The heartbreak seeds of defeat, sown with monotonous regularity over the past three decades of fruitless endeavour, faded and died in the April sun of Thurles, wrote Michael Ellard in *The Cork Examiner… to be replaced by a new flowering bud which reaped a rich harvest for Clare when they mastered Wexford in an epic semi-final replay of the National Hurling League.*

And the fact that we were going in against Kilkenny in the final made it better again. They were the All-Ireland champions, but more than that they were a great team that had won three of the previous four All-Irelands. Still, we were undaunted by the challenge.

We weren't afraid of them, and felt we could beat them.

On top of that, just days after the win over Wexford we got another injection of confidence when avenging that 1974 Munster under-21 final defeat to Waterford. Coached by Joe McGrath from Down we beat them by four points in Bansha, with Pat O'Connor shooting the lights out with 1-9, while I managed 1-3.

THERE WAS HUGE excitement leading into that league final.

I was up in Dublin and missed most of the hype, but with Fr Harry it was about embracing the opportunity in front of us. That was his style of management, his way of lifting things.

He talked about when he first took charge of the team and what he wanted from us – he talked about that first meeting when he built up the team and told us where we could go.

'I showed them a Clare jersey and told them, "I want you to be proud when you wear that".'

It was very basic stuff, but it was powerful.

He was using psychology. Sports psychology.

'One night I asked them what have Tipperary, Cork or Kilkenny got that we have not,' he added, before finishing with… 'Clare want to break into the big time. I told them we would win an All-Ireland. All I wanted was total dedication. Just for the Clare jersey and the honour of playing for the county these men would be prepared to die'.

That's all I wanted to hear.

I loved the training and hard work. In fact I would always have argued that we should have done more. And I didn't think Clare *were* any different to Tipperary, Cork or Kilkenny.

This was our first chance at senior level to prove that fact in a final under Fr Harry.

AFTERWARDS, IT WAS described as a classic hour in… *What must be the greatest ever National League campaign.*

It was Padraig Puirséal who wrote that, hitting out at those who said, 'Hurling is dying'.

Selfishly, from my own point of view I didn't think that. I died out there; I didn't perform at all, contributed nothing and couldn't get a puck of the ball off Ger Henderson.

It was a nightmare personally.

However, we weren't beaten and only for my UCD team-mate Matt Ruth we would have won it and become national champions after three decades.

Just as Fr Harry had said beforehand, we didn't die. We were five points down with six minutes remaining but stuck at it and nearly pulled off a famous victory.

In one of few positive things I contributed on the day, I gave a pass to Tom Crowe, who cut through their defence and palmed to the net for a goal that changed everything. Three minutes later Colm Honan barged his way up the left and set up Noel Casey, who blasted the ball to the net off the upright to give us the lead. We thought we had it until Matt got his only point of the game to bring it to a replay.

They were far from happy after it was all over – we were accused of being dirty and trying to roughen them up. Jackie O'Gorman did hit Mick 'Cloney' Brennan and he had to get stitches after going off. Their full-forward, Pat Delaney was complaining that he got done as well, as was centre-forward Kieran Purcell, who also had to go off with a hand injury.

My answer to them was… 'You played your whole life against mad Wexford fellas, and you're giving out about us!'

Years later, in a syndicate, I had a couple of horses in training with Purcell up in his yard in Windgap – and even after all that time, he was adamant that we were filthy that day.

To hear these giants of men and hurling legends like Purcell and Delaney, with seven All-Ireland medals between them, saying this stuff? They genuinely believed we were rough and dirty and tough.

They felt that we had gone out deliberately to timber them.

Kilkenny feeling that they got timbered? Come off it.

They were well able to timber themselves. It was just that their pride was hurt, that Clare deigned to put it up to them; that a team that wasn't Tipperary or Cork dared to front up to them. That might be subjective, but that's what we believed.

They were put out because we were challenging them, that we had the temerity to do that. We were taking them on, daring to take them on. We weren't just falling into place and feeling comfortable with the narrative that… we were Clare… they were Kilkenny… and we were automatically second best.

That's exactly what Fr Harry was talking about when tackling any inferiority complex when it came to taking on teams like Tipperary, Cork or Kilkenny. That had to end, and it did.

One of the things with Fr Harry was that while we didn't treat people disrespectfully, we weren't doffing our caps to them either. Were we a dirty team?

Definitely not!

Kilkenny were just surprised by our performance, that we faced up to them. They just didn't expect that when it came to the physicality of the game, that we would be able for them.

The replay was a different story.

AS ALL-IRELAND champions, Kilkenny went on the All Stars tour to America after the first game, but they didn't just go for the beer. They trained for the replay in America and trained hard.

Colm Honan was on that tour as an All Star replacement, while we trained at home for the first round of the championship against Waterford on June 6, with the league final replay two weeks later.

We beat Waterford thanks to two Noel Casey goals, another from Tom Crowe and 0-9 from Colm Honan after he returned from America, but we had poked the bear in that drawn league final. Kilkenny were a much different team in the replay and we just fell apart.

Again, there was a huge crowd following us, with over 35,000 at the game and while we were in it in the first-half we were blown away either side of the third quarter. Full-forward Pat Delaney scored three goals between the 42nd and 49th minutes. We were hammered by 15 points.

The same day, the Clare footballers were beaten by Cork in the Munster semi-final, but at least they put up a better showing and were only beaten by seven points. We put on no show at all. After the Munster final defeats in 1972 and '74, this was our third final flop in-a-row.

I managed a solitary point, but again made no impression on the game or on Ger Henderson, who had the measure of me. He was only a young fella then, not one of the seasoned older fellas they had in defence, like his brother Pat, Fan Larkin or Nicky Orr. But he was an 'animal' of a player and I couldn't manage him at all.

They were two nightmare matches for me. Aidan Tuttle, who was a great supporter of the team and a friend of Fr Harry's, was blunt about it afterwards, as only he could be, asking me, 'Why didn't you ask them to take you off Cal?'

I wasn't taken off but I couldn't have had any complaints if I was.

I was terrible. We were terrible.

To make matters worse, just before the end Martin McKeogh hit Eddie Keher, was sent off and later got landed with a six-month suspension. Keher was to Kilkenny what Ring was to Cork – there was an outcry as he walked off the field with the blood pouring from a head wound.

The word afterwards was that Eddie was doing a bit of sledging and that Martin just lost it for a split second and hit him a belt. It wasn't the first or last time it happened on the hurling field, but it wasn't left there.

GAA president Con Murphy stoked things up further. 'We do not want it as part of our games,' he said, when congratulating referee Frank Murphy for sending off McKeogh. Then he presented the trophy to Fan Larkin.

He shouldn't have intervened like that. Apart from losing the game, as far as the court of public opinion was concerned we were in the dock and found guilty.

But there was no trial. We were being labelled dirty again.

IT DIDN'T END there though, because our troubles were only beginning, as we tried to put the defeat behind us and prepare to take on Limerick in the Munster semi-final two weeks later.

We didn't manage that. This time we were well beaten by eight points and the vultures were circling; this time they weren't critics or knockers from outside the county, but from within Clare.

It had been fine when we were winning and when we went on that long unbeaten run to a first league decider since 1946, but when we failed badly in the final replay and then failed again in the championship everything seemed to change.

The boys in the long grass, those county board people that Fr Harry had challenged and stared down and openly criticised, were waiting for this to happen. They were waiting for the experiment to fail. This was their big chance.

They had even appeared out of the long grass before the two goals in 30 seconds by Éamonn Cregan and Johnny Neenan skewered us in the closing stages of the Munster semi-final in Thurles.

Our season was over, but in many ways it was only the beginning.

« CHAPTER 10 »

Had Clare won the National League they would be knighting
Fr Harry Bohan, instead of knifing him.
– Noel Casey, Sixmilebridge

THE KNIVES WERE out after our season ended, but looking back on it now
you could see the blades even before we took the field against Limerick in Thurles
in our attempt to reach a third Munster final in five years.

It was July 4, but far from being born again on what as the bicentennial of
American independence, it soon became clear that this Clare team were looked
on as dead men walking – the Clare team under Fr Harry Bohan that is.

Two days before the match there was a remarkable rebuttal carried in *The
Clare Champion* – an attempt from somewhere to calm the situation and say that
all was well in the Clare camp.

Everything was rosy. It really was.

There was no acrimony after the disappointment of losing the league final
replay. There was no one anti-Harry; the fellas who couldn't get on the team were
obviously the fellas you'd be looking at for any rancour or disgruntlement, but I
never got that at all. It didn't exist.

When you're preparing for a match, as we were, you're in a bubble. Reading what was in the newspapers you'd think there was open revolt in the camp and that we were in meltdown.

Rumours have been rife in the county with regard to incidents involving Clare players and officials, which were supposed to have taken place before and after the game. These rumours are nothing but mere fabrication, but were concocted to damage the image of the Clare senior hurlers after this disappointing display against Kilkenny.

No, there wasn't a punch-up in the Clare dressing-room before the game or at half-time. Neither was there a punch-up after the game, either in the dressing-room or the hotel.

Neither is there any truth in the damaging rumour that team manager, Fr Harry Bohan, was floored by a member of the Clare side, and since this is totally untrue, the rumour that another player was assaulted when coming to Fr Harry's attention can similarly be disregarded.

The Clare hurlers have given much pleasure and pride to Clare GAA followers in their commendable and united run in the National Hurling League. Such scurrilous attacks on the unity of the team and the characters of a number of players are totally unforgivable.

The rumour mongers are no credit to Clare.

If they come from within the county, then my message to them would be to stay at home. Leave Clare hurlers united – even in defeat.

BUT DENYING THAT anything had happened only served to put it out there that there was *something* wrong. Rather than douse the flames, it fanned them.

Then, when we lost the Limerick game, it wasn't long before there was a heave.

There was a plan put together, with the terms of reference being what was the best way to run a county team. Was it with a manager? Or was it by committee?

It was framed against Fr Harry.

We had been hammered in the National League final replay. We had been hammered by Limerick in the Munster semi-final. So it was all about whether the system of having a manager was the right way to go.

It wasn't about Fr Harry, but it was *all* about Fr Harry.

It was a heave against Fr Harry. You could see it a mile away.

How ironic then for me, that it all started in Clarecastle and that the Clarecastle club was involved. The August meeting of the Clare Hurling Board was held in the Abbey Hall in Clarecastle just over a month after the Limerick game. This would tell all, whether the rumours circling about team and management would come to anything; whether people would put up or shut up.

Brendan Vaughan was in his first full year as chairman of the Clare County Board, while Andrew Curtin was chairman of the Clare Hurling Board – both had a big say in the administration of hurling in the county. The proposal about the Clare hurling management didn't come from the top table, but everyone believed it was of the top table.

It sought that there would be no manager of the team for the 1976-77 season. Instead, there would be three selectors and a coach/physical trainer, all of whom would be appointed by the board. The board would be in control.

Implicitly it meant there would be no Fr Harry Bohan, because his position of manager was being abolished. He had been manager for three seasons, but now his services were no longer wanted as manager. That's how we read it.

It was proposed by my clubmate Gussy Considine and seconded by Emmet Henchy of Scariff, and it was carried by just one vote… 11 to 10. In the end, it all hinged on the vote of the delegate from Fr Harry's own club, Feakle. Dan Cunningham, who also happened to be club president, actually voted against Fr Harry. You couldn't make it up.

Straight away there was a war of words.

Brendan Vaughan was accused of using his influence as county board chairman to canvass clubs to vote against Fr Harry. He strenuously denied this, but at the same time was putting forward the credentials of Joe McGrath to be appointed as team coach for the year ahead.

MCGRATH HAD COACHED Limerick to the league title in 1971 and had been brought in to take charge of our under-21s in 1976 – my fifth year with the team, when after wins over Tipperary and Waterford we lost a third final in five years. We were beaten by Cork, but had put in a big performance in the final, only being beaten by 2-11 to 3-6.

Brendan Gilligan was outstanding at full-forward in the final. We trailed at the break by 1-5 to 1-2 – then I made my belated appearance after the debacle of arriving late for the game, and a brilliant goal from Gilligan had us 3-4 to 1-6 ahead at the three-quarter stage.

We should have won from there, but a goal by Pat Horgan inside the last 10 minutes turned it back in Cork's favour and they beat us by two points. Near the end I won possession from the puck out and tried to hit it into Brendan Gilligan, but the ball carried just over the bar. And that was it.

It was a very strong Cork team. They had Dermot MacCurtain, Tom Cashman and Johnny Crowley in defence, with John Fenton, Pat Horgan, John Allen and Tadhg Murphy in their attack. The fact we were so close got people on the board looking for McGrath to step up and join the seniors. There was the belief that he was the man to take Clare hurling forward at senior level.

I didn't know McGrath that well, because I was in Dublin when he was training that under-21 team. But I wasn't impressed with him. When I arrived late for that Munster final, he was telling me before going on that the wet evening would help us and would bring Cork down to our level. This put me off him.

I didn't feel in any way inadequate to any county and I proceeded to tell him so very loudly. He was lucky, I think, that Con Woods was in the dressing-room. There were only three of us there at the time and he helped to calm me down.

Bernie Ryan was Clarecastle's club secretary at the time and he wanted me to highlight the organisational debacle that conspired to make me be late for the final, but in the end I told him to hold off.

Michael Nihill proposed that the position of manager should be retained, but added, 'Neither Fr Bohan or his selectors can sit on the sideline and make changes during a game.

'Harry Bohan has proved himself as regards morale, but Joe McGrath has proved himself as a coach. The Clare hurling team had no coach last year.'

THE HEAVE AGAINST Fr Harry came out into the open that night in Clarecastle. As players, we were never consulted, even though another delegate from my own club, Vincent Murphy, said, 'The conduct after games was disgraceful'.

It was the hurling board taking unilateral action.

Their argument was that players should play and the board should look after management structures, but when allegations were flying around about management and players that weren't true, we should have been consulted.

We would have been very strong on that.

We wanted a say and were determined to have a say.

This was our attitude, even after Fr Harry announced that he was severing all connections with Clare hurling, explaining, 'The current controversy over the method of management is personally abhorrent to me'.

It was abhorrent to us as well. We were all singing from the same hymn sheet on that one. We wanted him and were determined to keep him, but we were floundering as to how we were going to make it happen.

We were very vocal.

Everyone knew that the players were far from happy with the county board and the whole saga united everyone behind Fr Harry and made the bond between players and management stronger. And it had been very strong to begin with.

There wasn't a committee formed and there wasn't anything very structured, but we had a plan and that was to make sure that all of this wasn't going to be done over our heads. I remember attending one meeting. I spoke up and said that what was going on was just bullshit – that we should be training instead of having meetings.

I told the meeting, 'This isn't about whether you want a manager for the Clare team or not'. I was very strong about it.

'This is a vote on whether you want Harry Bohan or not.

'You do or you don't?

'Don't be hiding behind the discussion about what system is the best for Clare going forward. And if you want to know my position… I'm for Harry Bohan.

'And I'm for the managerial system as well'.

Everyone had a view.

THERE WAS A stream of letters into *The Clare Champion* about what was happening. Former players like Dermot Sheedy and Des Carroll had their say. Sheedy highlighted the fact that we were… '30 seconds away from winning the league', while Carroll said… 'We were 'easily the best ever team in the county colours'.

Fr Enda Glynn from Lahinch wrote to say that, 'Fr Harry Bohan is not the fourth person of the Blessed Trinity' but that he was 'gifted in certain directions' and just needed someone to compliment his qualities on the sidelines.

Our hope, as players, was that by agitating in the background the board would reverse the decision, go back to Fr Harry and get him back as manager. It was much easier said than done, but the first chance was the September meeting of the Clare Hurling Board that was held in Broadford.

What happened there only angered the players more.

It was a bureaucratic mess that showed up the politics of the GAA and what we were up against. A motion came from the Feakle club calling for Fr Harry's reinstatement as manager – it was sent to the hurling board by way of a letter, proposed by Toddie Nelson and seconded by Jack Hogan.

Of course, we backed it, because we were as much behind it as the Feakle club. It wasn't so easy though, because a Clarecastle man intervened – not Gussy Considine or Vincent Murphy, this time. It was John Hanly, my old school master, who quoted the Treoir Oifigiúil and said the motion was out of order because each member of the committee hadn't been notified about it.

It was dead in the water.

We were dead in the water, until secretary Michael McTigue said that the detail of the motion which appeared in *The Clare Champion* was notification enough.

However, the motion was soon dead in the water again. It was put to the meeting, but we then had the bizarre situation where the Feakle delegate, Dan Cunningham, who should have been speaking in favour of his own club's motion calling for Fr Harry's return, spoke out again in support of the decision that was made at the Clarecastle meeting to get rid of the management structure.

Again, you couldn't make it up.

There were 42 people at the meeting with a vote, but the two-thirds majority of 28 that was needed to reinstate Fr Harry failed by three votes. That wasn't the end of it though, because the top table refused to count the number of votes against the motion, when just three abstentions would have meant 25 votes was enough for a two-thirds majority.

Then they refused a total recount. It was blocked at every move.

This was despite how vocal the players had been in support of Fr Harry before the vote – within our clubs, in the media and talking to supporters.

But instead of giving it up as a lost cause, this latest setback only entrenched us further. Our attitude hardened; we had to have our way because it was for the good of Clare hurling and our own careers. That was our thinking.

The players themselves are about to take up the matter, reported Tom O'Riordan in the *Irish Independent* a few days later. We leaked that story to the press – that we weren't going to take this lying down.

They are more annoyed than any other sector in the county. They had a phenomenal bond with Fr Bohan. They were just like Heffo's Dubs – prepared to work hard for success.

Now the team heads off to America with little preparation. No doubt a much closer bond will build up between the panel and it will not come as a surprise were they to inform the board about their insistence to have Fr Bohan back at the helm.

It took those two weeks hurling and drinking and meeting in New York to sort it all out.

◄ ◄ ◆ ▷ ►

The hurling board decision, after Clare's heartening rise from the nadir of hurling to the league final, is not only an insult to a sincere and totally committed manager, but it is a bad decision in the view of the players themselves and most of their dedicated supporters. Leadership like that given by Fr Bohan is a rare commodity. Perhaps at this late hour, the hurling board will decide, in the best interests of Clare hurling, that a wrong should be righted and an idiotic decision rescinded.

– The Clare Champion Editorial

PUTTING A NEW roof on Crusheen Church might be a strange pretext for going on the beer in New York, but for the Clare senior hurling team this is exactly what happened for the first two weeks in October 1976, as we left the whole management mess behind us.

The Clare Association in New York was behind the fundraiser which would see us play a series of games in Gaelic Park, and then do a round of social functions, with the proceeds going directly to the roof fund.

It was great to get the chance to go away. It was even better again when the trip was extended from one week to two, after our first round game in the National League against Cork was put back because they were playing in the Wembley Tournament final against Wexford.

It meant an extra week on the beer, and in New York.

Apart from Clare playing in the Wembley Tournament in the 50s, it was the first time a team had ever gone on such a trip. It was a big deal. For the occasion, we were decked out with slacks and beige brown jackets from Moran's of Ennis – we were going to have to pay for the shirts ourselves until a sponsor stepped forward.

We certainly looked the part when we flew out from Shannon Airport.

Twenty-seven made that trip – 24 players, after we dug in our heels when the county board, penny-pinching, initially refused to bring all the members of the National League final squad. Four players were left out, as was Martin McKeogh because he was sent off in the final, but in the end all panel members were allowed to go if they wanted to.

We had a great time. I remember, I broke up the 14 days in New York to visit New Haven in Connecticut and meet with the Geoghegan and Malone families from home. There wasn't any shortage of drink up there either.

We played three matches, won them all and lived it up afterwards and in between. For the two weeks we stayed in the houses of members of the Clare Association – and there was enough money to roof the church in Crusheen with the cash that was collected from the match attendances and a big banquet held in Gaelic Park. I was billetted in Woodlawn, under the roof of the late, great Paddy Markham and his wife, Sally.

It was during this time, as we were literally living in each others' shadows, that we really resolved to get Fr Harry back. He hadn't come on the trip, so we'd effectively managed ourselves on the field. We met as a group of players and had ad hoc meetings all the time, away from hurling board chairman Andrew Curtin, vice-chairman PJ McMahon and county board vice-chairman Tadhgie Murphy, who were also with us on the trip.

Seamus Durack became our leader, while I wouldn't have been too far behind him. The Duke was a great talker and always had strong views, and he was never shy about expressing them.

He wasn't the oldest member of the squad by any stretch – Jackie O'Gorman was the most senior frontline player in the group, with Noel Casey and Mick Moroney also in that bracket.

Jackie and the lads were happy that others took the lead and said we were right to fight for Fr Harry, as well as his selectors Matt Nugent and Jim Woods, who had also stepped down in protest at what had happened. That's why it fell to Durack, with myself, Ger Loughnane and Sean Hehir coming in behind.

THREE DAYS AFTER coming home from New York, the October meeting of the hurling board was held in the West County Hotel in Ennis and Seamus Durack led a delegation of players who went in to address the board delegates.

Durack spoke on behalf of the group, reading out a statement that I also co-signed on behalf of the players' delegation. The statement held nothing back, demanding that Fr Harry be returned as manager, along with Matt Nugent and Jim Woods; to join Noel O'Driscoll, Gerry Browne and Jimmy Corry who had been ratified as selectors at the September meeting.

The statement began:

Mr Chairman and fellow county board representatives.

It is with great regret that we, the players representing county Clare, have to attend a meeting of the county board the try and rectify the most CONTROVERSIAL AND UNJUST DECISION ever taken at a county board meeting with regard to selectors and team management.

We the players are appalled with the decision of club representatives and the hurling board who have completely disregarded last year's system of team manager and selectors en bloc...

The statement concluded:

We think the decision was desperately unfair and unjust and that is the reason we the players are here tonight. Again we repeat. THAT WE ARE DEMANDING FR BOHAN BE REINSTATED AS MANAGER, WITH MATT NUGENT, JIM WOODS, GERRY BROWNE AND NOEL O'DRISCOLL AS SELECTORS, AND ALSO A COACH BE APPOINTED IN AGREEMENT WITH THE MANAGER, SELECTORS, PLAYERS AND HURLING BOARD OFFICIALS.

We also suggest that a review panel be organised to look into the matter of team selection each year and then make their recommendation to the hurling board if changes are necessary.

In conclusion, we wish to impress on every delegate's mind the importance of what WE ARE DEMANDING...

No delegate spoke against the proposal.

As players we had faced down the county board, and chairman Brendan Vaughan proposed that the demand be acceded to. It was a big victory for player power, one that was copper-fastened at another board meeting four days later in which Fr Harry was formally ratified as manager once more.

It was the same day Cearbhall Ó Dalaigh resigned as President of Ireland over the 'thundering disgrace' comments made by the Minister for Defence Paddy Donegan. We felt that the Clare County Board was a thundering disgrace.

At that meeting Fr Harry showed everyone that he was firmly back in charge when he laid out the conditions for his return. One of these was that Joe McGrath would have nothing to do with the coaching of the team.

Again, my old Clarecastle mentor John Hanly wasn't impressed, saying he was, 'against anybody laying conditions before the board'… adding, 'The day we accept such is a sad day'.

That didn't matter. It was a great day; we had won the day off the field and now had to go out from that meeting and back it up on the pitch a week later when we played Tipperary in the opening round of the National League.

We only had a couple of training sessions. The Tuesday before the game was our first night back when we gathered for the start of the new season in Newmarket-on-Fergus. I was happy going in the gate, but within minutes was getting sick.

Colm Honan hadn't gone on the New York trip and he took the session that night, as Colm Flynn wasn't around. He ran us into the ground – it's as if he tried to break us.

There was a light at the lower end of Fr Murphy Park and Honan had us doing wire to wire runs. I was 21, and I was very fit. But the beer in New York had taken its toll, a heavy toll.

I remember running to the wire, grabbing it, trying to get my breath and saying, 'I'll feckin' kill him!'

And for that second or two or three, I meant it.

Honan was there laughing and I could hear him.

It made me madder again.

We badly needed it though, because this was the most important National League opener we had ever played. We were under pressure for the game, big pressure.

The spotlight was on us. We'd gone out on a limb, taken on the county board and taken an axe to them in our efforts to get Fr Harry back. And we had to back that up out on the field. If we didn't, it wouldn't be long before there'd be people rustling in the long grass once more.

THE GAME WAS played on October 31 – winter would be starting a day early if we lost and we knew that going down. We just had to win this game. We dare not lose.

Fr Harry knew that, too; we all knew it. The minute we put our heads above the parapet, the heat was all on our backs.

MacDonagh Park in Nenagh was an unusual venue, but there were 6,000 there, the majority of them from Clare to see what we'd come up with. It wasn't much, however, when we were trailing by 2-5 to 0-3 coming up to half-time.

Phil Fanning and Brendan Kenny got the Tipp goals and we were all over the place, but before half-time we turned it around. Enda O'Connor flicked home a goal after Pat O'Connor's initial shot was saved – and straight from the puck-out I was involved in a move that saw Jimmy McNamara fire home a second goal.

We were back in the game and then took over completely in the second-half, forging a four-point lead at one stage only to make very hard work of it in the end. We didn't win it until the final puck of the game, when Pat O'Connor landed a monster.

Taking a pass from his brother Enda, he nailed an unbelievable strike. He was 70 yards out. It was an over the shoulder point when he was looking down the field towards his own goal. It was a miracle point really, with one leg up off the ground as he struck the ball.

I can still see him hitting it.

When the whistle went, Fr Harry raced out onto the field to Porky, as many of the lads called Pat. Fr Harry needed that win; we all needed it.

It set us off. With that point the pressure we were under was immediately lifted. It was blown away and we were away.

Winter could begin the following day.

« CHAPTER 11 »

There was a great spread of players. We gave them guidelines but we didn't restrict them from playing. I mean you couldn't tell Johnny Callinan or Colm Honan what to do if they got a ball; same with Loughnane, Stack and more. You had personality players; you had characters; you had tough men; you had athletic men; you had fellas with very good skill. You had a great team.

— Justin McCarthy, 2018

NOVEMBER 20, 1976

JUSTIN MCCARTHY WAITED for absolute quietness. You could hear a pin drop in the room as he gathered his thoughts. Then, a few seconds later, he broke any sense of calm by letting off this huge roar, one that really exaggerated his Cork accent.

'YE'RE DIFFERENT LADS…

'YE'RE VERY DIFFERENT!'

'We're different… we're inter-county hurlers… we're different to everybody we know.'

I'll never forget it.

I WAS THERE listening and thinking… *We're not different.*

I'm 21.

Ger Loughnane is 23.

Colm Honan is 23… Sean Hehir is 23.

And on down through the rest of the lads… to Jackie O'Gorman, the oldest at 30.

We have the same hair styles as everyone else… we're in college or we're working like everyone else. We don't really want to be different.

'INTER-COUNTY HURLERS in Cork don't have to be told they're different. They are different and they demonstrate it.

'Everybody knows it about them.'

We had gathered in Anglim's of Tulla to hear Justin's maiden speech.

Just like Fr Harry's state of the hurling nation address there three years previously, it was inspiring and mind-blowing.

No one asked Justin what he meant by his flurry words and the soundbites that he hit us with. It was a case of… *We better absorb this now, learn from it… move on and be different.*

We knew that much.

'You're going out with your friends, fellas you know all your life, lads you grew up with, maybe your brothers, your cousins.

'They're going out on Friday night, you're not.

'You're not, because you're different.

'They want to be like you… you don't want to be like them.'

That meeting, hearing those words! It was the first time I finally admitted to myself… *Yeah, I'm different.* I was probably doing things differently anyway but wasn't doing them differently enough, and I wasn't making that distinction between myself and my peers. I did after hearing Justin that night.

FR HARRY WAS 34 when he spoke to us, in Anglim's in 1973, from his hurling heart. Justin was three years younger again when he spoke to us for the first time. But it wasn't just Justin's talk; it was his actions out on the field that we'd seen for the first time a couple of hours earlier.

Justin had been appointed Clare coach in between our second and third National League games. After the Tipperary game we'd come home to Tulla and hammered Dublin, thanks to a brilliant display from Noel Casey, who hit 2-3 from play – our next game was away to Wexford and Justin was with us for that.

After all the controversy over the management of the team, as players we had conversations with Fr Harry about where we wanted to go as a group – how things could be taken on further, and improved upon. Getting a team coach was part of those conversations.

Fr Harry's 'line in the sand' was that this coach had to be someone coming in on his terms and not foisted upon him, his selectors or his players by the county board. Such had been the case with people at county board level championing Joe McGrath. But it wasn't the case with Justin's appointment.

Justin was sourced by Fr Harry himself. We were absolutely thrilled when we heard he was coming in.

It was a massive move and it was quite a coup to get him. He'd cut his coaching teeth when winning an All-Ireland intermediate title with Antrim in 1970, when he was recovering from a broken leg he suffered in an accident on the eve of the 1969 All-Ireland final. He'd coached Cork to the Munster title in 1975 and he knew Clare hurlers, having played against us in the 1972 Munster final.

It helped also that he was a little bit off-centre. He wasn't your blue blood Cork hurler, one moulded in the cradle at the Rockies, Glen Rovers, the Barrs and so on. He was different and he was his own man, and we knew that he wanted a new challenge to embrace. He wanted to prove himself again. It was what we needed to do as well.

It was a perfect fit.

I'll NEVER FORGET that first time we trained in Tulla.

It was a Saturday.

Justin parked his car inside the gate. Even before setting foot on the field he just looked the part. He was slim and trim with his head of black hair.

He looked fitter than any one of us.

He opened the boot of the car. He had five dozen hurling balls. Usually, we had four or five hurling balls and a couple of good ones for the match. That was it.

Just on this basic level of hurling balls, Justin's arrival was transformative. I remember looking out and it was like Dr Tommy Daly Park was one big field of mushrooms. We never saw five dozen hurling balls in a year… never mind at one training session.

He also had this thing about hurleys.

He had 10 or 12 of his own hurleys and he laid them out on the ground. He was going through the hurleys, deciding which one he would use that would best suit the conditions.

Then when Colm Flynn took us running, Justin told us to leave our hurleys with him. He went through every one of them – he told us most of them were useless.

As a hurler you were a craftsman, so you had to have the proper tools. I wouldn't have been that obsessed with hurleys, but he was. Everyone had one hurley, a favourite hurley and you hated to break it.

From that point on, Justin took care of our hurleys.

It was another part of his attention to detail. He was emphasising the importance of everything being right. His statement to us later that evening about not going out on Friday nights – like having the right hurley – was all part of his mantra of living as a hurler, a county hurler.

He would emphasises that all the time.

'You're a county hurler… and a person apart!'

It sounds arrogant. Cocky perhaps. But it's a statement that wouldn't need to be made in a room full of Kerry or Dublin footballers, or Kilkenny and Tipperary and Cork hurlers, because they had it. They knew it.

But it was certainly a help to me and others in the Clare team to hear those words.

Those words challenged us.

It was also the fact that Justin McCarthy was willing to come and give of himself to us. We were never at training before Justin. He was coming from Passage; he was driving 100 miles to get to Tulla, but no one was ever there before him.

The first drill we did, he had us get our approximate positions on the field and fellas just hit the ball at one another. We had to be really awake and alert to what was going on, or we'd be killed. In 10 minutes, we hit dozens of balls.

And we weren't just hitting them away, we had to hit them with purpose.

Straight away, from the first few minutes of that first training session, Justin had put down a marker – he was immediately identifying the need to speed everything up. It was our striking, it had to be faster.

That would have been the perception about Clare. It's not that we were dwelling on the ball, like a soccer player would, but we were doing things that little bit slower.

The sessions were brilliant and were so refreshing. It's not that we were in the dark ages before that. We'd been around; we'd competed well. A lot of us were in college and exposed to Fitzgibbon hurling, while a lot of us had played for Munster, but straight away there was a wow factor with Justin.

Some people say there were issues between himself and Colm Flynn. His sessions were about 50 minutes to an hour, no more. But we'd be at it, with no let up at all. Colm would come in and do the physical stuff and Justin would be whispering, 'Take it handy with the physical'.

It left a lot of us a bit uneasy, because the younger lads in the group wanted more training. Justin believed that we could do all of our physical training through hurling and that we didn't need specific runs and exercises.

I was on Colm's side on that argument. To me he was brilliant – I'd be saying do more physical stuff, and Loughnane was saying the same. There was real method in what Colm did. He didn't punish us if we had a bad game on a Sunday.

I don't know how scientific it was, but one of the runs was from the gate in Tulla… up the hill. It wasn't long but we had to go hard and it was timed. Running up the hill didn't start in Tullyvarraga with Mike McNamara.

I think the different elements that Justin and Colm brought to the party complemented one another.

FROM THAT FIRST session, Justin would play in the games we had at training. And I was often the one who ended up on him. It was murder.

I'd think I had him, but he had great feet and his hands were brilliant too. We'd play 20 minute-matches. I was physically stronger than him, at least I thought I was, but I couldn't nail him. I couldn't hurl him either.

I'd be calling Honan and saying, 'Come over here… take my place and try marking him'.

I'm not so sure that him taking part in the games came from the best coaching manuals, but he still wanted to play himself. He would go to the alley five or six days a week.

He'd tell us of the absolute pleasure he got at hitting a ball off the wall.

I said to Fr Harry after the first few training sessions, 'Sign him up… get him transferred. We'll play him'. He was still that good. I meant it.

'If you don't sign him up,' I also told Fr Harry… 'I can't be marking him every night, or else I'll lose my place'.

It was a real eye-opener; between the training pitch and the team meeting I fell in love with the man there and then. Straight away our esteem went up. Sometimes the Cork thing would irritate a bit, but you could see what he was doing, building us up, putting us up on a pedestal.

We went with him, because he came with some pedigree.

He had All-Ireland medals. He was a Texaco Hurler of the Year. He was a young and vibrant up and coming coach who had been shafted by Cork.

We had all seen him in action, so we knew he wasn't just a talker. He was able to talk the talk, but he had walked the walk too. He had done it and now wanted to do it with us.

So, it began.

IF THE TIPPERARY game gave us lift-off, his arrival catapulted the whole thing into a different orbit. Again, the Tulla factor became very important, but the first game after Justin coming on board was the real springboard.

We were away to Wexford. On our previous three visits there we'd been well beaten. By 11 points in 1972, by 14 in '74 and 10 in '75. This time it was our turn to pummel them and we beat them by 10.

Then it was Cork back in Tulla where we ground out a win, before finishing off our pre-Christmas run of games with a three-point win away to Limerick. Clare had never won five league games in-a-row before. We had answered a few critics.

We were determined to keep it up. What better incentive for that than Kilkenny in the final game after Christmas. We knew it was going to be a lot different to the league final replay, especially in Tulla.

We didn't need to win, but were never going to lose in front of a packed house – the attendance was given at 7,000, but there were many more there – as we racked up our 13th successive league win in Tulla.

The special atmosphere of Tulla is all it's cracked up to be, noted Dónal Carroll in the *Irish Independent*, further noting, *Clare were firing on all cylinders, and the back-up in each sector underlined the tremendous job Justin McCarthy is doing as coach. Attacks were switched from wing to wing and up the middle to ensure there was no respite for Kilkenny.*

We were a different team.

And after sweeping Offaly aside in the semi-final by 2-15 to 0-7 we earned another crack at Kilkenny in a final in Thurles to show what a difference a year had made.

After seven wins in-a-row, the eighth game took on the importance of an All-Ireland final.

It was huge for us.

It was the biggest game we ever played.

◄◄◆►►

Some of them sat there, as if they could not believe they had won their first title since 1946. The rest cheered. They shouted and they were ready to hug and embrace anyone in the dressing-room. This was their day and they were going to savour every hour of it.

– Peadar O'Brien, *The Irish Press*

I CAN'T REMEMBER who I went to the match with, or how I got back. There was a good reason for the latter though – I was the worse for wear in the excitement of the celebrations that followed immediately after our famous win.

But as far as going to Thurles, it's just as much of a blur. It was very different the previous year. Coco Broderick, a legendary taxi driver from Ennis, was the pilot and I remember the conversation we had when he swung by Clarecastle to pick me up.

'Where's the Ford Consul, Coco.'

'It's in the garage.'

'But it's only a couple of months old.'

'I'm afraid we're going to win and it will be damaged.'

We were going from there to collect Sean Hehir and Jim Power. We were in the equivalent of an Escort and I thought Hehir was going to punch the head off

Coco, as a result of being downgraded in this way. It was alright for me, but Hehir and Power were big men and needed room.

The next time around, the trip to Thurles must have been uneventful.

All I know is that en route I was wrapped up thinking to myself. That's because no matter what people say, a player is only really worried about himself. You hear lads saying… 'I don't mind playing badly as long as the team wins!' But that's bullshit.

You definitely mind. As a player, you're selfish.

You're playing on a team, for the team and you want the team to win. But you're still selfish. I was concerned about my own game, who I was marking and what contribution I was going to make. I was genuinely not worried about others.

Playing is very selfish, and that selfishness begins with your preparation.

WE WEREN'T IN anyway overawed by Kilkenny.

We had beaten them plenty of times and had built up great confidence on that winning run and a much stronger bond had built up in the group.

That winter we trained hard, down in the corner of the Newmarket field under lights. And at the end of the training Colm Flynn's thing was to have a soccer match – they were ferocious, but a lot of fun. There were plenty of skirmishes because fellas weren't able to tackle. Loughnane was a dangerous soccer player… he had no regard for anyone else.

Under the radar I used to play a bit of Premier Division soccer in Limerick with Aisling Annacotty, and inter-firm with Limerick County Council. I loved it.

Soccer after training was a great way of building up the spirit.

I didn't think about whether we were going to beat Kilkenny or not, and I wasn't surprised that we did. I'd have been very disappointed if we had lost again. We had so much to prove from the previous year's final.

Whatever they felt about what we had done to them in the drawn match, we felt we were well bullied the second day. It wasn't visceral. We were inclined to strut and talk the talk, but we didn't do it when it was put up to us in that 1976 replay. We had to do it this time.

And so much went right for us for in the game. Jimmy McNamara's goal after just 75 seconds. Tom Crowe's goal after 12 minutes that put us 2-1 to 0-1 ahead. Tom, from Clonlara, is the only member of the squad who has passed away.

Fr Harry wanted Tom on the team. He was very adamant about picking the man first and the player second. It would be ideal if you could pick the two at the same time.

He liked the way Tom played. I had played Fitzgibbon Cup with him in UCD. He was awkward, but he was hard to mark and was as genuine as they come on the field. He was very persistent, as illustrated by the goal when he got the better of Noel Skehan.

Nobody liked Skehan either – opposition forwards didn't anyway, because he was so good, so to see him getting caught and Pat Henderson running back forlornly as the ball crept over the line was great for us. It was as though everything was acted out in slow-motion.

Arising from that Matt Ruth told me that when they were training for the championship Skehan had a habit of running towards you, pretending to throw it up on his right, but then pirouette and hit it off his left.

One night, Matt ran in on the blind side and tapped he ball into the net and Skehan went crazy – 'Do you not think there are people here looking at that?'

Cool as you like Matt said, 'Yeah, and if I can see it… they can see it'.

Skehan never did that again.

To see Skehan getting done in this way, it was nearly worth more than the goal itself. He was caught by Tom's pure persistence. He was away and just as he was clearing the ball Tom just blocked him, and in blocking him fell and then got a bare touch to it. The ball trickled over the line. It was still very early in the game, but that goal was the winning of it.

The victory exceeded everything that happened in the match, the preparation beforehand and the build-up. It did this simply because it was a final victory, something that this team hadn't had at any level.

And we'd been through a lot. Munster finals at minor, under-21 and senior. Then the controversy with the county board.

Not since Brian Boru hurled the Danes into the sea at Clontarf in 1014 had a victory roar rent the air as it did in Thurles, wrote Mairtín Mac Cormaic in the *Irish Independent,* adding, *Clare's victory over Kilkenny was probably the most important in their history. The 25,000 crowd was about four to one in Clare's favour. If the 32 counties were represented at Thurles, 31 of them were surely willing a Clare victory.*

The reaction was incredible.

IT WAS 31 years since we last won the league, but beyond that it was like 100 years of emotion was released after the final whistle. It was quite overwhelming. It was like 1995, there's no other way to describe what it unleashed in everyone.

At the 1995 Munster final in Thurles – when we were 10 points up – former Offaly player, Paddy Kirwan leaned over and shook hands with me. I said, 'Feck off Paddy', because I was afraid it would go wrong, even with only minutes to go.

It depends on where you are in the tapestry of hurling, but to me 1977 was bigger than '95 in what it unleashed. One minute we were playing and concentrating on doing our specific jobs – in my case it was trying to do my bit at right half-forward and keep Ger Henderson quiet – then it was just madness and mayhem.

In some ways it was bigger because there had been virtually nothing since 1946. There was the Oireachtas win over the great Wexford side in 1954, but everything about the Oireachtas was framed around the fact that the following year Clare flopped in the Munster final.

We were a coming team – being in the Munster finals of 1967, '72 and '74 – and knocking on the door and this was the culmination of that. It was a significant step in the graph that would ultimately and eventually lead to the success of 1995.

WE WERE PUT on a lorry when we got back to Ennis, but I had too much to drink in Thurles. It was back to the Anner straight after the game, where I met Michael Hegarty. We drank whiskey. I think he might have been on the run from something at the time and appeared out of nowhere.

I wasn't a whiskey drinker, but when it was produced, I knocked it back.

That's why I don't even know how I travelled back to Ennis. I remember being in Michael 'Nuggi' Nihill's bar in O'Connell Square and it was massive. There was a huge crowd around the place. It was like the crowds that were at Fleadh Cheoil na hÉireann there later in the year.

Then after making it home to Clarecastle, my mother was still up.

John Hanly, Dr Bill Loughnane, Aidan Tuttle and Dónal Carey were still in the bar. They were all raconteurs. I'm sure Dr Bill had his fiddle to give people a taste of the Tulla Céilí Band on tour, while everyone was talking and not listening. A lot of it passed me by.

I just knew something had changed.

We had won something.

PART FOUR

A Thin Slice
of Heaven

« CHAPTER 12 »

The league is only the stepping stone to what we really want,
which is an All-Ireland title.
– Fr Harry Bohan, 1977

JULY 10, 1977

WE MEET AT golf outings now. Social occasions over 18 holes, and a few pints as part of the Hurlers Golf Society that was established back in the 70s by people like Pat Stakelum and Dermot Kelly as a way of building friendship and fraternity among former players from competing counties.

It's also a chance to trade a few blows – friendly fire and banter, but sometimes there's an edge to the slagging. It's definitely true where the 1977 Munster final is concerned. Craic over 40 years on, but craic that's still serious and sometimes hurts.

'Tell Jim Power that Ray Cummins is asking for him.'

Seanie O'Leary says that to me every time. First thing when we meet. The golf outing wouldn't be the same if he didn't say it. It's a ball-hop, but of course, he's having a rub. However, it's a gag too. because that's Seanie. I like Seanie.

'Feck off.'

I say that to Seanie every time. Still, he says it, even when Cummins could be around the corner from us in the clubhouse and almost within ear shot.

'Let it go… please let it go!'

But, all the time, in what he's saying there's that element of… 'We caught ye and ye know it… ye didn't know how to handle it'. It's no great credit to Cork.

I was tempted to ask Cummins once as to what really happened a couple of minutes before half-time in that Munster final in 1977. He'd just laugh at me though, so my attitude then and now was to move on because when you're beaten you maintain your dignity. You have to do that after the game is over and stick with that. All the time.

Still, it's one of the most infamous Munster final incidents of them all. It provokes debate even now, but when it happened it stoked a controversy that stalked everyone, most of all Jim Power who was put off before half-time.

We never recovered after that and the Munster final was lost, but maybe we wouldn't have been good enough for them anyway in the second-half. The sending off was the first real set-back the team had encountered all year.

IMMEDIATELY AFTER THE league final, and especially after all the drink had been run out of us, the focus was on the championship. Winning Munster and winning the All-Ireland.

We felt we were the best team in Ireland, but it was going to be very hard. To win Munster we had to beat Tipperary, Limerick and Cork – the big three.

Tipperary hadn't won a game in the championship since 1973 and during the 70s I never feared them; we could always beat them, but it took everything we had to get over them in the quarter-final.

Maybe it was a hangover from the league win.

We were very bad the first day. In the first-half we went 0-11 to 0-2 down. Tipp were all over us, but we got a goal before half-time that was badly needed.

Noel Casey cut in from the right wing after Tom Crowe fed him and slammed home to the net for a vital score. It was our first score in 28 minutes. We had the wind in the second-half, but despite dominating we hit 13 wides, including three in the last few minutes when the sides were level. I hit one of those wides, but by then I probably shouldn't have been on the field.

That game is the reason I have a moustache, to cover a scar I have.

Earlier in the game, Loughnane was taken off after he got a belt into the groin, but he was brought back on again. It meant there were two subs gone. Then Pat Morey was brought on for Tom Crowe, which meant all our subs were used.

After that, I got injured.

We were on the attack and I had the ball, and as I struck it Pat Fitzelle came across and accidently hit me with the point of the hurley into the mouth. I had lost my front teeth as a 13 year-old, but if I hadn't I probably would have lost them then!

I was cut from the corner of my nose down to my lip. It was a cut rather than a belt, because Pat Fitzelle wasn't a dirty player. He was just reaching and he connected.

The two St John's Ambulance guys came out to me on the Clare side of the Gaelic Grounds. I was bleeding profusely. They had me by each arm and were taking me off. Colm Flynn then arrived on the scene and jumped in between the three of us and pulled them off me.

The boys were still pulling me away and Colm gave one a back-hander – the shock one of them got. I was conscious that three subs had been used. There wasn't an awful lot of time left. Colm stopped the bleeding and I went back into position and suddenly I got a ball and managed to get the equaliser, before then missing another late chance to win it.

THE REPLAY WAS just as tense, but we survived.

Tipperary had a couple of chances to get a levelling goal in the last minute. Noel O'Dwyer's penalty was brilliantly saved by Seamus Durack for a '70'. Then, after it was lobbed in towards the goalmouth, another chance fell to O'Dwyer but when he was about to pull the trigger I poked in my hurley and pushed the ball away. Neither match was ever going to be commemorated in the annals of hurling folklore.

The semi-final against Limerick was more of the same. Again we didn't fire but we got over the line. I always loved playing Limerick. It was like Clarecastle playing Éire Óg – there was an extra edge to it.

Noel Dalton was refereeing that one and we got him again for the final. It was a much cagier game than the previous year, but we produced a strong defensive display. It wasn't about performance; it was about winning and we had three championship matches behind us going into the final.

That was a huge advantage, because Cork had only one. A semi-final against Waterford, while before that their last competitive game was in the National League way back in February. We had to have the edge on them in terms of game-time and big games, that's what I thought.

I can remember visiting Ennis on the occasion of Clare's last Munster final appearance three years ago, wrote *The Cork Examiner's* Jim O'Sullivan. *News had just broken that very day of injuries to John Callinan and Sean Stack and hope was replaced by near despair.*

Now there is a new air of confidence prevailing within the Clare camp that has long been apparent. To put it in a nutshell, Clare don't want to even hear of defeat; it's a dirty word.

WE HAD EVERY reason to be confident. Since the start of the 1975-76 season, we'd played 24 games between league and championship and lost only four of them. We felt we were the most consistent team in Ireland and would win that Munster championship.

Cork were reigning Munster and All-Ireland champions, but we were National League champions and were the form team in the country.

Forget the fact that we were taking on the red jersey.

My attitude to people who said we couldn't manage the red jersey is that I had no sense of that. There was no sense of it, individually or collectively. I'm not saying it didn't exist, but it wasn't in any way conscious.

Was it part of the subconscious? Justin McCarthy would later argue that it was and he argued it right up to 2018, when last I met him, but I still disagreed.

We did alright against Cork teams. You can only go by your own experience, while what I think happens is that people aggregate 30 years or more into a couple of games as the reason why we didn't beat Cork.

We were worried about Cork because they were a good team and had good players. What we were hoping was that we weren't going to give them anything soft. And the way we started that Munster final showed that we weren't afraid of them.

We were relaxed. The build-up to the big day was there and had to be contended with, but with the games coming one after another and one rolling into the next, it wasn't as intense as it might have been.

It was nothing like it was in 1978.

There were two weeks between the semi-final and the final; we had everyone fit, with Sean Hehir's first outing since the league semi-final against Offaly coming in the Limerick game. We thought it was set up for us.

My routine was to go for a run on the Saturday morning before the game, setting out from home and heading out towards Doora.

It was a nice 20-minute run. The whole exercise took about an hour, by the time I'd tog out, stretch, do the run, do a bit of stretching after finishing and get dressed again. There used to be people talking about me… 'Jesus he's running the roads'.

I was conscious of it, but it's something I felt I had to do.

I felt I couldn't play if I didn't have that run.

Then I would relax at home before the following day. Laze around, watch television. Being a rugby fan, I was aware that The Lions were playing the All Blacks that morning, and it was on RTÉ. I watched that and saw them cause a surprise and win that test match – maybe we could do the same and beat the favourites. The famous British Open duel between Tom Watson and Jack Nicklaus was also on the television that day, when the underdog also came out on top and Watson won.

If I was feeling superstitious, everything pointed to us doing the same the following day. We certainly believed we could. Then again, if we were superstitious the game was also on July 10 – the same date as the 1955 final, the last time there'd been such hype and expectation about Clare in a Munster final.

THEY GOT A goal from a Timmy Crowley penalty in the first minute. But we were soon hurling away and playing with a real freedom.

Enda O'Connor got a great goal after five minutes. Noel Casey got another, and we were five points up midway through the first-half. Casey was doing really well against Martin O'Doherty and the match was ebbing and flowing. But Cummins and Jimmy Barry Murphy got goals to put them 3-4 to 2-6 up two minutes before half-time.

Then, whatever happened… *happened.*

I was a good bit away from it, but I saw something inside and the next thing Jim Power was being put off by Noel Dalton. As to the rights and the wrongs of it, I had no clue in real time what had actually occurred.

My complaint always with Jim Power was that he wasn't tough enough, or dirty enough, or mean enough. He wasn't that type of player. For Jim to be put off... *what happened? What could have happened?* That was my immediate reaction to the whole thing.

Something had gone on over in the corner where Jackie O'Gorman was marking Charlie McCarthy, with Power getting a flaking around the knees in an incident that went unpunished. Cummins stuck his head into the argument and Jim just hit him. Cummins collapsed on the ground.

At half-time the whole thing was about trying to get organised. We battled away in the second-half, but were never going to win it, even though we kept plugging away and played well.

We had gone toe-to-toe with Cork up to a certain point. They went on to win the All-Ireland again. They were a top team and we knew there was no one better than them. We could manage the Leinster teams as we proved in the National League. We could manage Tipperary always, Waterford too, while we always fancied our chances of beating Limerick. Galway weren't really a factor.

We knew it was Cork!

It was all about Cork, and most people considered us the two best teams in the country for those few years. The thing was to be the number one, to beat them... and 1977 was our first chance. The sending off ruined it.

Was I devastatingly disappointed afterwards? Probably not, if you can have a pecking order when it comes to disappointments. But then the furore began in the dressing-room straight after the game. It all kicked off from there.

The rumour mill and the whispering about what Ray Cummins said or what Charlie McCarthy said, and what had *happened* began. I'm sure the drink that night helped it gain legs as the narrative moved forward, going from a situation where it was a surprise that Jim was put off – even though he wouldn't have been the first to get marched – to the man being absolutely wronged.

The same day, half the Munster final takings from an attendance of 44,586 were stolen, with the theft fitting with a storyline latched onto by some in the media that something had been stolen from Clare as well.

Clare can cry we wuz robbed, said an *Evening Herald* headline the following day, adding beneath it... *The £25,000 raid at Semple Stadium yesterday may to a large extent have overshadowed equally sensational proceedings on the field of play there, but the GAA officials, who were held at gunpoint, were not the only ones feeling cheated.*

We did feel cheated.

The whole thing built up into a real head of steam, and we were feeling more and more resentful as the days went by. So much so, that the storyline was that we were cheated out of the Munster title.

I resisted this as far as I could, fought against the victimhood of it – Clarecastle used to fall into this trap or this sanctuary in some of the games they were beaten in, too. I was against it at the time, and will disagree with Fr Harry and Durack to this day.

Fr Harry felt that an injustice was done to the lesser county in terms of hurling tradition.

'I was so sickened by it. I know for certain it was a massive mistake. It cost us a Munster final and I know for certain that we would have won the All-Ireland,' he said at the time.

'The general quality of refereeing has been dropping for some years. I have never before spoken out but this game was the culmination of so many bad refereeing performances that the time has come for the matter to be brought out into the open. It has become so bad that everybody connected with the game, including the public, will grow disenchanted and lose interest,' he added.

There were calls for an inquiry; we were in effect trying to get something overturned. The words that were used over those few weeks – outrage, injustice, human rights. Intense and all as I was about my hurling, my gut reaction was... *Wrong words lads.*

I never said things like... 'It's only a game'.

And I never thought like that but in my subconscious, I was saying... *Are we going to get it over-turned?*

We're not!

Fr Harry was so articulate about it, so principled about it. It was as if the decades of frustration poured out. Everything was directed at the referee Noel Dalton. I didn't know the man at all, but I think we went over the top.

I wasn't that comfortable with it. Did I talk up against it? I didn't.

To this day, if you got Duke going on what happened in that incident, he'd work himself up into a lather about it – the injustice still burns after 40 years.

I know he was much closer to it and he saw what happened. I concede that.

But I always said, 'Let it go, we have to move on from this'. It was not healthy.

In saying that I'm almost feeling disloyal, because there's no denying where these men's hearts were. I know where they were – it started and stopped with Clare hurling. For me though, I think I was a bad loser and it's important that you're a bad loser. However, we should have let things be. But, because of what happened and the furore after it, it's still there.

FR HARRY TOLD me years later that Jim Power was going to emigrate after it, that there were letters written by people giving out that it had cost us a Munster final. These weren't supporters. It was very wrong.

Jim was and is a very quiet fella, an absolute gent.

Everyone was devastated and sorry for him, because no one believed that this was Jim Power. It was very different to, say, if Vincent Loftus was sent off because he was tough man and you might be expecting that he'd be playing the game right on the edge.

But not with Jim. He wasn't that type of player. And, we wouldn't have been in the Munster final without him – he had two very strong games on Roger Ryan when we played Tipperary in the quarter-final, and then did the same against Éamonn Cregan in the semi-final.

Being beaten by five points in the Munster final, 4-15 to 4-10, after having played well with a man down for more than one half, we should have taken the positives out of it. We had competed and competed strongly, unlike 1972 and '74. We should have gone quietly and worked on coming back stronger and better.

In 1977 I was still only 22.

It's not like I was 32, so there were going to be other days, many other days. My feeling was that to get as embroiled as we did in controversy at that time was a bit similar to what happened with the Clare team in 1998.

There was no need for it.

We had to move on. And we had to do that straight away.

« CHAPTER 13 »

As our president, Dr Hillery, said afterwards in the dressing-room, this team did the county proud in 1977 by winning the National league title and by their fine hurling since. And though muted by the pangs of defeat, there was a great deal of pride in the heroic battle. Now the character of the team will be tested to the full as they regroup to complete the unfinished business.

— Gaelic Forum, 1977

1977 WAS A big year, even without any of the hurling.

I finally put my student days behind me after five years studying, between doing my law degree in UCD and my apprenticeship before getting my wings as a solicitor.

Qualifying meant being back in the mid-west permanently – first when being apprenticed to Kerin, Hickman and O'Donnell in Ennis, before moving into Limerick and to Leahy and O'Sullivan for better money.

Fr Harry got me that job in Limerick.

Fr Harry got jobs for loads of hurlers… teaching jobs, jobs in Shannon Airport, jobs in Shannon Development, jobs in the Shannon Free Zone… jobs everywhere.

This work, making connections and setting lads up in careers was something that went back to the genuine interest that Fr Harry took in players' lives. It was all about the hurling and trying to win National Leagues, Munsters and All-Irelands, but it was not just about the hurling.

Leahy and O'Sullivan were the firm of solicitors used by the Rural Housing Organisation – the body that had been founded by Fr Harry in 1969 after he came back to Ireland after doing post-graduate study in Cardiff University and then working with Irish communities in England for a few years.

RHO's aim was to secure the survival and development of countryside life in Ireland by having housing schemes in selected villages in rural areas. The first was in Fr Harry's native Feakle, where 20 houses were completed in 1972.

After qualifying, I could have stayed working in Ennis, but there was an opportunity in Leahy and O'Sullivan where the pay was good and Fr Harry did the rest. I went for an interview. It was a fairly cursory affair, and I had the job.

After I told my boss in Ennis, Jim MacClancy, that I was moving he said he'd immediately double my wages, but it was too late. I'd gone to him before looking for exactly that, but they didn't give it to me. It was time to move – when going there in the first place for my apprenticeship I was charged a premium of £200, which my mother paid in £20 notes on the signing of the articles when I became a solicitor's apprentice.

LIMERICK SUITED ME perfectly as Siobhán had been working in the bank in Dublin and she got transferred down there too. We were getting married the following year.

From a hurling point of view, being back in the region was a big help for training, but on the flip side the end of student life meant that my Fitzgibbon days, which were as much a part of my college life as studying, were finally behind me.

I had been captain of the team in 1976 and that meant I was also training the team. We were defending our title and had a strong team, but UCC beat us in the semi-final in the Mardyke.

I was determined to have another go at it in 1977. I had done a diploma in European Law in 1976 but they wouldn't allow me repeat in '77 and I got turfed out of the course. It was my lack of attendance at tutorials that cost me and it meant that I couldn't play Fitzgibbon that year in '77.

Instead, I was the trainer-coach of the team. That UCD team created a bit of

Fitzgibbon Cup history that year when we played Trinity College in the quarter-final in O'Toole Park, beating them by 51 points, 11-18 to 0-1. I don't know if it was the biggest win in Fitzgibbon Cup history, but it must be up there.

We could have shown them some mercy – we didn't, but we did give them a point in the first-half. A few weeks later we played hosts Maynooth in the semi-final. This time we certainly felt there was some mercy shown, but it was at UCD's expense, after which I had a huge run in with Frank Murphy who was refereeing the game.

We were nine points up with about 10 minutes to go and to us it seemed as if Frank just decided to make a match of it. It was a disaster and we were beaten.

They got three goals to beat us.

The sequence was a soft penalty, then another soft penalty and finally a soft goal in the last minute when the ball went in off the goalie's hand. We ended up being beaten by that goal.

Sean Stack said afterwards the UCD team that Maynooth had just ambushed was the best Fitzgibbon team he had ever seen. Matt Ruth was brilliant that day for us.

We were in the dressing-room afterwards and we were fuming, but one of the team was more animated than anyone else. Dave Billings was going crazy. He was corner-back on that Fitzgibbon team, but even though he had an All-Ireland football medal won with Dublin at that stage he didn't play any Sigerson Cup football with UCD. This was because he would have been playing against UCD, and for St Vincent's, in the Dublin championship and Eugene McGee's rule was that if you didn't play in the Dublin championship with the college, you didn't play Sigerson.

There were no exceptions.

Billings was tough and could have been put off in the match, but now at the height of our disappointment he was on his way out the door to visit Frank.

Everyone else in the room felt the same way. But Billings was determined to do something about it. I stopped him from going out because he might have hit Frank. But the only way I could prevent him from kicking the door down was to appease him by saying I'd go out myself.

'YOU BETTER HIT HIM!' he roared.

'I'm not hitting anyone.'

FRANK, I REMEMBER, was showered and was combing the hair over. It's still vivid with me – the hair was still wet and it was lank, and sticking out. It was almost in a cartoon-like position. For me this was a big deal.

'I'm trainer of the UCD team and I think you did us an awful injustice out there today… you blackguarded us.'

'Do you think so?'

'We were clearly the better team and you decided to make a match of it.'

'That's your opinion. I made my decision.'

I wasn't finished.

'It is no business of yours whether a match is won by nine points or one point… or 19 points. That's not a referee's job. Our dressing-room is very angry.'

'Are you threatening me?' he asked.

'I am not threatening you!'

It was a bit of a pointless exercise really, because the result wasn't going to be changed. We had lost, we had to suck it up, but it was terrible.

Making it worse for me was that all the goals that Maynooth got to beat us by 4-12 to 3-12 came from my own Clare teammates. Con Woods got one in the first-half. Then came the two penalties he scored near the end, before Stack finally killed us.

I REMEMBER WHEN Dave Billings died suddenly back in 2015, I was talking to a journalist who said I would have changed the course of GAA history if I had let him out of the dressing-room that day to have a go at Frank.

Instead, when the whole incident happened, I thought it would change the course of hurling history – my own. Munster were playing Leinster in the Railway Cup final in Croke Park just under two weeks later. Frank Murphy was a selector on the team and I was afraid that he'd take it out on me.

Fr Harry was also involved with the team in those years and when the team appeared in the paper, I automatically assumed that he had insisted on me being there at left-half-forward. I rang him to say thanks for going out on a limb when it came to my selection.

'Any issue with Frank Murphy about my selection?' I enquired.

'No, no… he might even have proposed that you be on the team.'

It was only then that I told Fr Harry what had happened the at the Fitzgibbon weekend, so credit where credit was due to Frank. He hadn't held it against me. Maybe he realised it was better to be facing me than Dave Billings, and he was thanking me for my interrogation in a roundabout way by selecting me on the team.

I loved playing in the Railway Cup, ever since being thrown in as a 17 year-old for the Combined Universities. I always looked on it as a great opportunity.

I have four Railway Cup medals.

It wasn't so much the medals, but a competitor wants to play at the highest level and when you're asked to play for your province it's an honour. I would also have been conscious of watching Railway Cups on St Patrick's Day on television. That it was a big thing. I never heard anyone from Clare saying, 'F**k that... why would I play in that?' Cork players all togged, so did Limerick, Tipperary and Waterford fellas. It wasn't taken ferociously seriously but we wanted to play.

They brought the finals to Ennis on a few occasions and that was an attempt it bring it to the provinces and give it a new bit of life. Centenary Year was one of those occasions, and I had one of the best games I ever had.

I hadn't been going that well in the National League matches coming up to it, but I didn't think anyone noticed. Micheál Ó Muircheartaigh confronted me about it after the match when interviewing both myself and Mossy Walsh from Waterford.

'Johnny, you were going really well today – you hadn't been going so well for Clare. What would you put that down to?'

I was thinking to myself... *Maybe I'm playing with better players...* but I just looked at him and he stonewalled me. It was live on the radio, so what was I to say, that... 'I'm normally playing with those Clare players and they're shite'.

I fecked him afterwards.

MY FIRST EXPERIENCE of a Railway Cup final was in 1975 (having played against Leinster and Munster in the two previous years), but I missed out on playing due to injury. That was the day Jimmy Barry Murphy scored 4-1 from about six touches in the football final, and then turned around to play for the hurlers straight afterwards. He came into the dressing-room after the football game and he was shaking with the cold.

Jimmy Barry could have done the famous double like Des Foley did in the '60s, but a late goal from Martin Quigley beat us. The following year I got my first medal, starting in the final, while Ger Loughnane came on and Colm Honan and Noel Casey were unused subs.

That year we had seven All Star nominations, with Johnny McMahon getting our only reward. He was a great corner-back. A very quiet fella but a real cornerstone of the team.

In 1977 after winning the league and contesting the Munster final we won four All Stars – Johnny McMahon and Ger Loughnane got their second awards, with Seamus Durack and Mick Moroney getting their first.

That was a big statement by the team and illustrated the esteem in which we were now held. We had made huge progress and by the time the All Stars banquet took place in The Burlington Hotel that December we'd well and truly put the disappointment of the Munster final defeat to Cork behind us.

What happened in 1977 didn't carry over into '78.

The controversy in the aftermath of the Munster final had finally blown itself out by the time the league started, and the positive things that had happened in the previous year were finally brought to the surface.

The winning of the league was looked on in its proper light. It was a brilliant achievement and in the Munster final, despite being completely overshadowed as a game because of what happened to Jim Power, we had definitely given as good as we got in a high scoring game.

Still, even then we were being boxed into being a winter team that didn't do it in the summer time. Journalist Kevin Cashman was one man who held that view. We didn't believe that, and were determined to prove this perception wrong in 1978.

◄ ◄ ◆ ▷ ▶

I'm going home a happy man tonight. We have a great team
at the moment, but Clare have a better one.
– Paddy Grace, Kilkenny County Secretary

THERE WAS NO inquiry or investigation into the Munster final. The only fallout was that Noel Dalton temporarily resigned from the inter-county panel a few months later in retaliation at being downgraded from an A to B standard referee by the powers-that-be.

For us it was back to Tulla in October to start the National League with a home game against Galway. We had Martin McKeogh back for his first game since the 1976 league final defeat. It was a huge boost to the squad.

He'd started corner-back in that league final; he was now at midfield with me on his return, while he later ended up as our full-forward for the year with Noel Casey coming out to centre-forward. Martin would have been a great player for Clare only for his bad knee. He could have been centre-back for a decade, releasing Stack to go midfield.

We recorded our 14th successive win in Tulla with a nine-point win, but this great record was interrupted in the next game when Tipperary held us to a draw, while Wexford finally brought the unbeaten run to an end when they beat us in the last game before Christmas.

We should have won that game.

I got a goal in the first-half, but after the green flag was raised the referee disallowed it; while we were three points up with two minutes to go after Pat Morey got a goal, only to concede 1-2 in the closing minutes.

All good things must come to an end, declared one headline afterwards, but it didn't bother me. Tulla was great, but at the same time I would have been one to challenge that whole myth around Tulla. It wasn't just because of Tulla that we beat teams.

We were a bloody good team to start with.

Dropping those three points at home meant that we had to 'do it' away from home to advance in that year's league. Beating Offaly in Birr was no big deal, but in our last game we had to go to Nowlan Park and beat Kilkenny. The last time we'd been there they'd hammered us by 11 points – this time we won by three to reach a fourth successive semi-final. I think I may have got a goal.

Beating Limerick comfortably by seven points in that semi-final set up a rematch in the final against Kilkenny, once they edged out Wexford after extra-time thanks once again to the scoring exploits of my old friend Matt Ruth.

IN THE FINAL the Clare team gave one of its best performances – all 3-10 coming from play, 3-7 of it in the second-half when Kilkenny were really blitzed.

For me, however, it was one of my worst displays in a big game. I didn't get a puck of the ball with Ger Henderson around me and was lucky to be left on the field. I had to unravel myself from that.

We had been poor in the first-half, trailing by 0-7 to 0-3 but the floodgates opened in the second half. Noel Casey got a goal inside a minute, then Martin McKeogh got two by the 50th minute and we were away.

I tried to enjoy the success a bit more and made sure not to drink whiskey this time. It wasn't anything like the breakthrough of the previous year in terms of the public reaction or the celebrations. This time it was viewed as just another step along the way.

Afterwards, in the *Irish Independent* Dónal Carroll wrote, *Harry Bohan's boys rapped out a warning to all that they will be the team to beat in the knockout series.*

That's what we believed would happen, a feeling that would have grown again in all of us when we had a comfortable victory over Limerick in the Munster semi-final.

Willie Fitzmaurice got three goals that day for Limerick, but it was another big display by us. We played really well in the middle of the field and in attack. Limerick took Eámonn Cregan off Jackie O'Gorman and Fitzmaurice, who had got nothing out of Sean Hehir for the first 50 minutes, went into the corner and got a hat-trick in 10 minutes.

If you meet Canon Willie to this day he'll say, 'I missed one, it should have been four'.

When we survived that onslaught to win by seven, we didn't have any doubts. We were good enough to win the Munster and All-Ireland titles. And the pressure was coming on, but it was pressure that we were putting on ourselves, never mind the pressure from the expectation of the public.

This was the game we wanted and had been waiting for.

Everyone in hurling wanted it too.

« CHAPTER 14 »

Our luck must change and despite our failings in the past there isn't a Clareman who believes we will fail to Cork this time. I think the time is ripe for us to reap our due reward. It must be agreed we are the most improved team in the land. And what better way to prove it than by winning Munster and All-Ireland honours.

— John Callinan, July 1978

JULY 30, 1978

LIKE GOOD CREATURES of habit we were meeting up at the Anner Hotel.

It's where we always went before big games in Thurles – league semi-finals and finals, every championship game. Sit down, chat things over… a cup of tea and sandwich if you wanted it. Then out the road to Semple.

I'll never forget the journey there that day.

Enda O'Connor's uncle, the famous Dónal O'Grady from the 1955 Munster final, drove us to Thurles in Enda's blue Mercedes. Enda, Pat, Mick Moroney and myself were in the car. We left in plenty of time after I was the last one picked up in Clarecastle.

We made good speed down the road, but next thing on the outskirts of Thurles the cars were all backed up. We were five miles from the town and nothing was moving. Gradually, we moved along a bit, but we were fecked – in an era of no mobile phones and no communication we were stranded in this gridlock.

We had to get right through the town to the other side of it. We didn't know what to do, as we weren't sure of any alternative route if we doubled back. We decided to walk two or three miles, while Dónal went straight to the field with our gear and hurleys.

IT WAS NO big deal to make the walk. There's no way we would have made it in the car.

Walking through the crowds on Munster final day wasn't a great look, of course. We were recognized, and were observing the bedlam in the town.

Meanwhile, the rest of the team was in the Anner.

Argentina had won the World Cup the previous week. Apart from the football, one of the most memorable things about the competition was the chain-smoking César Menotti. Fr Harry was like the Argentinian manager in the Anner, going through a packet of cigarettes as he waited and waited for us to arrive.

We knew it was a huge game – the biggest of our lives but as we waded through the crowds of people to get to the hotel for that team meeting, we saw just how huge an occasion it was.

This was *the* game.

It brought the magnitude of it home. It was bigger than an All-Ireland final. It was bigger than Tipperary Vs Cork… it was bigger than Limerick Vs Cork, or Limerick Vs Tipperary. It was bigger because it was Clare trying to make the great breakthrough.

Cork were the two in-a-row All-Ireland champions, but there was this thing about Clare. We were the sexy team and Clare was sexy anyway – the traditional music, the first Lisdoonvarna Music Festival that blazed a trail for the whole country just two weeks earlier, the Burren, and much more. Clare had a lot of things going for it in the minds of people outside the county.

And, just like 1995, that Clare team was taken into people's hearts. If you were interested in Gaelic Games, you knew about this Clare team that had penetrated beyond the public consciousness of their own people. That was because of Fr Harry's personality; Justin McCarthy's too, but also the players that we had.

On the day itself RTÉ even got in on the excitement and sense of expectation around the team – that feeling we were going to do it. Finally.

Doireann Ní Bhriain was a young reporter working for *PM*, a magazine programme sandwiched between *The Sullivans* and *Welcome to the Ceilidh* that went out on television every Tuesday night. A big chunk of the programme was dedicated to Clare and the Munster final voyage that we were on.

The special trains from Ennis. The crowds in Liberty Square.

In the dressing room… coming out onto the field… and the heartbreak and the devastation afterwards. Instead of being heroes forever and a day.

It was all there.

The whole roller coaster.

THE MUNSTER FINAL and all about it was there for what seemed like an eternity. After the semi-final there was a month of a lead in before the final. It was far too long.

There was a massive build up. Cork had qualified by beating Waterford the week before we did, so even prior to the Limerick game the build up towards another final against Cork was taking root in our minds, and everyone else's too.

We knew that this would decide everything. What Loughnane said about it being the 'Shoot-out at the O.K. Corral' was right. Cork had won the previous two All-Irelands, we'd won the previous two National Leagues.

It was everything.

It would define us. Yes, I was still only 23 and I didn't want to have my whole career, everything that was to come afterwards, defined by one 70 minutes of hurling at this stage of my life. But the sense that such was the case had been building for four weeks.

The media attention mightn't have been as massive then as it is now, but it was still big and seemed huge for this game. It was built up by everyone. Everywhere.

Tom O'Riordan summed it up in the *Irish Independent*.

A quiet passion has been reaching boiling point throughout Clare over the last few weeks. People have attempted to go about their daily routine without trying to show much concern about the joy and ecstasy which will be rife if the Banner triumph.

The hay may be saved but who cares about the harvest just yet. Beat Cork tomorrow and the 46 years' wait would feel like only yesterday. There would be no tomorrow and September 3 and the All-Ireland final would still be a long way away.

Elderly people who had forgotten what it was like to see Clare win something cheered themselves hoarse as the county took home the last two National League titles. Victory and an opportunity to see their heroes on All-Ireland final day, and many of these would die happy.

All neutrals will want Clare to win, because of what it would mean for the game of hurling, said Raymond Smith in the same paper. *They will celebrate for a week if they triumph and the traditional musicians and ballad singers will be at the heart of the festivities. It all rests on the 15 men and seldom has a band of Clare hurlers gone into a match with such high hopes resting on them.*

They used to do a preview of the big games on the eve of the match on RTÉ's *Sports Stadium*. Mick Dunne travelled to Tubber to interview Enda and Pat O'Connor. It was done on the Tuesday or Wednesday beforehand, but when it came out on the Saturday afternoon you had fellas thinking it was a live broadcast.

Mick Dunne was pressing the two lads, putting it out there that this was the defining 70 minutes for this Clare team. Enda and Pat did their best to deflect that narrative, yet that was the perception cloaked around the game.

It was make-or-break… do-or-die… all over for Clare if they don't win!

The game went from the back pages of every newspaper right to the front. It was news. We were *the* news. Big news. Clare Vs Cork. The country had a Clare President and a Cork Taoiseach – Paddy Hillery Vs Jack Lynch was Clare Vs Cork.

President Hillery was a regular visitor to our dressing-room. He was there after we won the first National league, toasting the victory and at the same time looking forward to the Munster and All-Ireland titles to be won, just as we were.

Michael O'Hehir also called in, not as a commentator but as the son of Clareman, Jim O'Hehir from Ballynacally, who had coached the last Clare team to win an All-Ireland title in 1914. We would be the next? It wasn't a question though – it was going to happen. He even brought the sliotar that was used in the 1914 final on one of his visits.

Fr Harry encouraged all of this. It was pretty open season in the Clare dressing-room. Jackie O'Gorman used to say that it was much easier to put on your trousers after you were beaten than after you won. The dressing-room wasn't structured or organised.

I'd say that Fr Harry was flattered by all the attention as well. I don't mean he was flattered by the attention being on him, but rather the attention being on the team. He looked on all of that very positively.

How could this do any harm once you perform inside the white lines?

We were ready to perform, too.

We were as ready as we ever could be. We'd answered every question, but this was the biggest one we'd ever faced.

◄◄◆►►

One is forced to the conclusion that while Clare were physically primed for the occasion, they were less than right mentally.
– Dónal Carroll, *Irish Independent*

DECEMBER 6, 1995

SEVENTEEN YEARS HAD gone by, and Clare had finally won the Munster and All-Ireland titles that we so badly wanted in my playing days and had threatened to win on so many different occasions.

In celebration of those triumphs, the Clare team, management and their partners were brought to Boston and New York for a beer-up in early December of 1995 that was every bit as memorable as the one we as players had back in 1976.

As a member of the Clare Hurlers Supporters Group, I got to go – I even had my seat upgraded from economy to business class by Aer Lingus' head of operations in Shannon, Tom McInerney. It meant I was with members of the management on our transatlantic journey and ended up sitting beside Ger Loughnane for the trip.

We were together in the middle aisle.

We drank a lot of red wine and a lot of water, and we had lovely food, but all the way we were talking about the Munster finals. The games we lost.

The heartbreak we endured along the way.

The 1978 Munster final was the big one – the conversation between the pair of us went on for the greatest portion of our journey across the Atlantic.

WE'D NEVER TALKED about it before.

It took us 17 years to have that conversation. We went through it, minute-by-minute, puck-by-puck as if we had a video of the match in front of us. Even allowing for the passage of time, it was forensic in our own minds.

What happened?

Could we have done better?

Why didn't we do better?

Why didn't I stick to the plan?

It was still very raw. Even after 17 years it was like an open wound, because that was our big opportunity. The game we were supposed to win.

Tactically we got it wrong, very wrong when it had been planned down to the last. Even down to our hurleys, their weight, their size… their everything, because that's what Justin McCarthy did.

Jackie O'Gorman's with a flat handle because he had damaged fingers; Noel Casey was a big, strong man, but liked to have a light hurley; Colm Honan's was heavy; Seamus Durack's was two inches longer than normal for long puck outs… on it went.

There was more! One year, the Adidas factory in Cork brought out a special boot with a canvas upper on it and Justin got permission from the county board to get a pair for everyone on the panel. They were much lighter and he felt that's what we needed for summer hurling.

There was the same precision in planning for Cork and how to beat them. Justin was the best man I ever saw on a training pitch. I really believe that, but…

I think it all got to him and I've said it to him, though he denies it. We agree to differ and move on, but I thought he prepared us to stop Cork, rather than to play ourselves.

He had me on Tom Cashman, while he gave Noel Casey the job of breaking the ball past Johnny Crowley. I couldn't understand that – Crowley was only a young fella in 1978, while in our eyes 'The Case' was the equivalent of the West German football ace, Gerd Muller; he was that good, a striker who could win the game for us.

It just seemed strange. He had a whole series of plans on how we would limit Cork from playing, without placing enough emphasis on how we would play to win the game. And given how he believed that our self-esteem was less than

Cork's, this was almost re-enforcing that stereotype for us and laying it out that...
Ye're not really better than Cork... so we have to find a way to stop them.

Maybe that was realistic. The right thing to do?

They were two-time All-Ireland champions and had done it on the big
championship days. We hadn't done it. Cork had the tradition of winning Munster
titles and All-Irelands, Clare didn't. Justin believed that and wanted to put a plan
together to override it and beat it. He said as much the week of the game.

'When you are a Cork player you are very conscious that you are following
in the footsteps of men who have brought honour and glory to the county. So,
when you are wearing that red jersey it gives you a sense of stature, a feeling of
confidence, as well as an incentive to live up to the responsibility of maintaining
that winning tradition.

'Opponents who have not a tradition of success are inclined to be overawed –
to have an inferiority complex, feeling that all the other fellows are supermen and
looking up to their opponents when they should be taking the field on equal terms.

'It takes a lot of hard work to convince players they can be as good as those
of the great traditions. But when they see what Argentina did in the World Cup
and what they themselves did in winning and retaining the National League
title, they realise they don't have to play second fiddle to anybody.'

That was his thought process.

That was the plan, but I still think it was the wrong tack.

I'm not saying we didn't need to be mindful of Cork and their strengths and
how we were going to handle Charlie McCarthy, Ray Cummins, Jimmy Barry
Murphy and so on, but I felt there was tension at training sessions that I hadn't
sensed before in the lead up to the match. As well as that, there was a lot of back-
slapping, with more fellas in the dressing-room than usual.

I remember a surge of sound when we ran out onto the field that day. It was
physical, other worldly almost. It was a crash. This was a field where there was
only one stand, so the noise generated could get lost and go in towards town
and disappear into the air. But the 58,000 people made it seem like there were
580,000 there.

We were nearly thrown back by the noise

Did it affect us? Not in the first-half, I'd say. Cork's only score from play came
in the 22nd minute through Tom Cashman, but John Horgan landed four frees.

Mick Moroney got our first point from a sideline cut, while Colm Honan and Noel Casey got the others as we trailed 0-5 to 0-3 at the break. Casey's could have been a goal that would have had us level. But it was still set up for us in the second 35 minutes.

When Seamus Durack saved a penalty before half-time there were chants of… 'CLARE… CLARE… CLARE!' as we left the field. The feeling at half-time was that we were going to win, but I thought that the dressing-room was far too full.

LOOK AT A professional dressing-room now and you see how structured the whole thing is. I have this memory that there was just mayhem in our dressing-room. There was a television camera that was there before the match, and was there at half-time as well.

I'm loathe to blame any of the fanfare in the dressing-room for what happened after.

But was it appropriate? Could we have been shielded from that? The bottom line was that we didn't perform in the second-half. It was a disaster.

Justin wanted me to mark Cashman, but Cork didn't want that, so they just wouldn't fall into step and allow it to happen. The result was that we had a very confused situation where both myself and Mick Moroney were running around after Tom Cashman.

Mick was getting sick of it, before he eventually said, 'You take this side… I'll take that side!' I ended up on Tim Crowley and did alright on him.

Cashman had a good game and to this day Loughnane hasn't forgiven me for not sticking to the plan. That's what we talked about most on the trip to Boston.

Durack and Loughnane were the only two players who really performed on the day. We knew that we tried and we left everything out there, but ultimately we let ourselves down.

It was July 30 – it was Reek Sunday up in Croagh Patrick. We could see the mountaintop in Thurles, but couldn't reach it.

Clare's great hopes were nearing the rocks - their forwards found their purse was empty, wrote Con Houlihan in the *Evening Press*… *Clare had failed to play what could be called their normal game. Sometimes, you fail because you try too hard. That would seem to be the lesson learned from Thurles.*

We failed to produce.

Loughnane and Durack played well because they were defiant. The rest of us lacked defiance, the defiance we had to have to win the game. That's what I would be annoyed with about myself. We didn't show enough, not nearly enough.

Individually or collectively.

But leaving aside the team, as individuals through the team we believed the exact same thing... *We didn't play... we didn't f**king perform... the f**kers had to do nothing to beat us.*

We had stopped them. Tactically, from Justin's point of view, things had worked as we limited them to five points in the first 35 minutes of hurling. The plan worked. We were there, but it was hard to switch from that negative play to the positive when we needed to.

We needed to change to win the game.

But positioning on the field was quite rigid then. It was suggested later that Loughnane could have been switched out to Tom Cashman, but that was never considered – no more than Jackie coming out on his future brother-in-law, Richie Bennis in the 1973 semi-final. I believe that if Mick Moroney and myself hadn't been given such rigid instructions that either of us could have done a good job on Tom Cashman. Extravagant switches are often for the ego of the manager or coach, and are discussed past the post.

Loughnane said years later that the defeat was the end of that Clare team, but he didn't say it in the dressing-room after the game when Doireann Ní Bhriain interviewed him for the *PM* programme.

Instead, he was defiant.

And rightly so, he was only 25 years of age.

WHEN HE SAID subsequently that this defeat in the high summer of 1978 was the end of the Clare team, I wasn't sure whether he meant it took the heart out of the Clare team or the heart out of Clare – and there is a difference.

The madness that was in Ger Loughnane as a player – that tearaway madness, when he was manic almost – certainly dissipated after 1978. On reflection, he didn't play like he spoke after the 1978 Munster final when we were in the depths of our disappointment.

That Feakle madness had carried us a long way. They all had it. It was a glorious madness they had. The Duke, Fr Harry... Loughnane. They were the big drivers of the team on and off the field.

Loughnane continued to be a very good player for nine more years for Clare and because of that he had a defiance about him, but I think maybe he started to accept defeat more easily than before. Yes, he hated it, we all hated it, but that feeling that our time had passed was there amongst some players, even though we kept coming back and kept chasing it.

It broke our spirit and I think it might have broken Fr Harry's spirit.

It broke his unshakable belief that we were going to do it. It shook that maniacal conviction that he had from the time he took over the team in September 1973, that we could do it and that we would win Munster and All-Ireland titles.

He was the first man that ever said in a Clare dressing-room that we were going to win an All-Ireland. This defeat knocked the Clare psyche; it knocked us back on an individual basis and collectively as well.

It was devastating.

We were awful. I said to the fella who gave me the tape of the match... 'You must really hate me?' I've looked at it once, but it was once too many.

Hearing Charlie McCarthy afterwards as he accepted the cup hit us even more.

'As the saying goes, there's only one team that can win... and that's Cork'.

We were crestfallen.

At the same time, I was never prepared to admit that this was the end of me as a county hurler, or the end for the team that I had played with.

I loved to play the game.

Would I go so far as to say that playing the game was more important than winning? I wouldn't say that, but it was still about playing the game, so that's why I wasn't bereft after that defeat; the positivity in me was looking to the next game.

It was always the next game.

« CHAPTER 15 »

Flaming tar barrels and blazing bonfires heralded Clarecastle senior hurlers' return to the summit of Clare hurling. It was a long time coming for the Magpies, but like all victories and after all the final defeats and disappointments it was worth waiting for.
— Seamus O'Reilly, *Clare GAA Club Scene*

OCTOBER 22, 1978

NO MATTER HOW hard every championship exit can be for a county player, there's always the sanctuary and safe haven of the club – your own. Always after those defeats, I returned home. Others might have come to terms with it by going away for a few days, but I always defaulted to Clarecastle.

The village. The pubs. The people.

When coming to terms with defeats, I got crosser and crosser as the years went on. Loughnane said in his memoir that I was too nice – I've always meant to ask what he meant by that? Was it that I wasn't dirty enough? Vicious enough?

I don't know.

Still, I always faced my own people after games. There was always the club and the next match – the championship and the chance to win one of those. By 1978 I'd been chasing a senior championship medal a long time, since Clarecastle had last won the Canon Hamilton trophy in 1970.

That year I wasn't the young fella up on the roof anymore being kept out of harm's way, but I wasn't a member of the team either. There was just relief to finally win it when we beat Crusheen in the final. However, the big thing was beating Newmarket in the semi-final. That was our real county final, because that dominance of Newmarket over Clarecastle did leave a mark.

We beat them dramatically, after another testy hour. They had Paddy McNamara and Jimmy Cullinan sent off, while Michael Donnelly was marched for us, but despite having an extra man we looked beaten when a Jim Woods goal left us five behind with time almost up.

Then we just exploded.

Our captain Christy 'Wax' Guinnane blasted home a goal and then added a point, before an 80-yard free from Tom Slattery went all the way to the net to give us a remarkable victory.

It was no wonder that the final itself was an anti-climax. The expectation was that if you could beat Newmarket, you could beat anyone, but Crusheen hadn't read that script and it took us a replay to finally beat them.

We thought we had won the first day when Patsy Condon fired over a point in the last seconds, but referee Frank Murphy ruled it out by saying he had blown his final whistle before Patsy gathered Tom Slattery's pass and had his shot.

We made no mistake in the replay and won by five points. The fact that we had to go back to 1949 for the last county title meant nothing to me, but it meant everything to the club.

Paul Higgins was wing-back on the team and made the song *21 Years is a Mighty Long Time* famous in the village afterwards – that was the recording of Dermot Hegarty and The Plainsmen, as opposed to Woody Guthrie's version.

After that the Munster club was very exciting. We played Patrickswell and beat them in a replay, and then beat UCC after another replay. I was on the panel for the final against Roscrea that wasn't played until well into 1971.

I was only being brought along for the experience and was never going to be played. They were a good team with the likes of Tadhg O'Connor, Roger Ryan and Francis Loughnane. We didn't raise a gallop against them.

That time, whoever turned up was on the panel and there was no panel announced. You arrived to the field and you trained away, and then you went to the match. That's how I fell in with the senior panel first, having first started by playing a bit of Junior B.

MY FIRST SENIOR game was in the 1971 championship against Sixmilebridge in Newmarket. The 'Bridge were only an intermediate team and had the assistance of Clonlara, Meelick and Parteen. I was played for 20 minutes.

I asked John Hanly about it years later and he told me the only reason I was thrown in was because they wanted to disqualify me from playing Junior B.

The fact that I played shows you how poor the 'Bridge were then – that I could be put in corner-forward, not expected to do anything, and then be whisked off after 20 minutes, told you how little we rated the 'Bridge then. After starting I was livid that I was taken off because I thought I was going well, but I was angry also that I couldn't play Junior B anymore.

It meant that I got no more adult game time until the replay of the county senior final. In the arrogance of youth, I felt I should have been playing in every game.

When we won in 1970, Haulie Daly, Gerry Murphy and Pat Joe McMahon were also over the team, but Fr Pat Loughnane gave them dog's abuse at the AGM the following year because they hadn't made the switches in that final against Newmarket in '71. There was even the implication in Fr Loughnane's criticism that I should have been brought onto the team in the drawn game. Of course, I agreed with Fr Loughnane's assessment and thought I should have been introduced in the drawn game. But I was left on the sideline.

I should have come on that day for Michael Slattery as he was getting a tough time of it from county player, DJ Meehan, but maybe I was as well off that I was left on the sideline because DJ was a good player.

Then between the draw and replay, I felt I was flying it. Again, I had myself convinced that I'd be playing, but again I was left off. This time I came on after about 20 minutes for Tom Cullinan, Jimmy 'Puddin' Cullinan's brother.

It was a real eye-opener for me – from being the kid watching the Newmarket lads come into the my mother's bar with the Canon Hamilton Cup on their way home, to now playing against them. It was a big deal for me.

FOR A COUPLE of years, I went for my summer holidays down to my mother's cousins in Newmarket. The greatest hurlers I had ever seen were from Newmarket – Jimmy 'Puddin' Cullinan, Liam Danagher and Pat Cronin.

You couldn't but say they were three superstars, and not only in Clare club hurling, but by playing for Clare and Munster too. They were absolutely brilliant and I really looked up to them.

They were like Seanie McMahon, Ollie Baker and Jamesie O'Connor from St Joseph's Doora-Barefield. All from the same club. Puddin was 5'5", but still a brilliant centre-back. How could you play centre-back and be that size? I couldn't figure it out, but he could, because he was gifted, he was bold and cheeky, and he could do brilliant things.

Those Newmarket lads were my heroes.

The first time I got a chance, when I got on a county panel, to train with these guys, I remember I went over to Puddin and did the drills with him.

There might be people in Clarecastle saying this was treachery. that you couldn't respect, like and be in awe of the enemy. I went against that, we just had to recognise how good they were.

Liam Danaher was nicknamed 'Cass' after Cassius Clay, because he was considered Newmarket's *Greatest*. He was my favourite of the three, because he was a runner. To me he never touched the ground, he just glided and floated around the field effortlessly. He was like a young Ryan Giggs with Manchester United – both legs seemed to be in the air all the time. He covered the ground so easily and was a great stickman. Tony Kelly is the modern version.

Then you had Pat 'Fagin' Cronin at wing or corner-forward. He was a drink of water – 5'9", pulling the hurley as if it was a load on his back, but give him half a chance, left or right, and he'd bury a score.

Cronin won three *Gaelic Weekly* All Stars in the 60s. Puddin also got one, while Danaher should definitely have been honoured as well.

No one in Clarecastle would say how good they were, but we knew. They were incredible and in some sense for Clarecastle to be getting as close to them as we did was no mean achievement.

IN 1973, WE definitely should have beaten them in the final. From midfield up, it was one of the best displays a group of eight Clarecastle players ever gave. In that final we scored 4-16, with 3-13 of it coming from play and were still beaten.

They hit 7-10 to do us in again; the sixth time since 1964 that they had beaten us in the final.

That was a huge disappointment. Paschal Russell, who scored six points, had a great game at centre-forward and I was midfield. Michael Slattery changed us at one stage for no real reason. He was the main man that time, playing on the team and selecting the side.

We left it behind us. It would have been a great win for the club – the previous Sunday, Slattery had refereed the All-Ireland final between Limerick and Kilkenny, with four Clarecastle umpires in John Scanlan, Michael Keane, Tom Slattery and John Hanly with him. And the umpires broke the mould in Croke Park that day by wearing white tracksuits instead of the traditional trench coats.

Us beating Newmarket in the county final would have shattered the mould. You can sometimes leave a match behind you when not playing well, but we really played well that day and yet we still lost.

Dermot Fitzgerald scored 3-1, and Eugene Moylan got another goal. Frankie McNamara and myself played well at midfield and we knew we had them on the rack and should have killed them off, but then some terrible goals went in down the other end. Paddy McNamara drove the final nail home in the last minute when he got the winning goal.

After those finals in 1971 and '73 that I played in, the Newmarket lads still stopped in the pub on their way home. It was hard. I kept myself scarce. I certainly wouldn't have been in the pub pulling pints for them.

They had no regard for my sensitivities.

It was their tradition, and the fact that I was playing for Clarecastle wasn't going to come between them and that tradition of a lifetime. Tom Hayes' pub was there as long as they were winning county titles and they never passed it by.

That team more or less broke up after that 1973 county final defeat. Tom Slattery, Michael Slattery, Chris Hanrahan and Christy 'Wax' Guinnane stepped away soon afterwards.

The elder fellas left then were Oliver Plunkett, Paschal Russell, Dermot Fitzgerald and Johnny Scanlan. I was in the next generation again.

It took us five years to get back to another county final, but before that there was the very important matter of getting married. Like any hurler or footballer with aspirations of winning an All-Ireland, it was a September wedding, fixed for a few weeks after Cork, instead of us, beat Kilkenny and claimed their three in-a-row.

I MET SIOBHÁN in a Dublin pub, Kennedy's at Kelly's Corner, managed by a life-long friend, Jack Rea, Ned's brother. She was working in AIB on South Richmond Street, near Kelly's Corner. Tom Quinn lived in a flat in Lennox Street where I also lived for a year, and we used to go to the same pub, so that's what brought me there.

I was the real old romantic. I believe I may have brought her home on the bar of the bike after meeting her – not quite *Butch Cassidy and the Sundance Kid* in the Paul Newman and Katharine Ross scene from that movie, but that was it and we were married a few years later.

It was a hurling wedding.

There was the guard of honour, with the hurleys held aloft and all that, coming out of the church, while Enda O'Connor's mercedes that had brought me to the Munster final was the wedding car. I myself had a blue ford escort then and it got us all the way to Stuttgart for our honeymoon. But for the main business, the county championship, I was back home in time.

Newmarket-on-Fergus was that business, because they had dominated the championship like no other team before or after. The year after I went to the All-Ireland with my father, they won their first title in eight years when beating Whitegate in the final. Then they won 11 of the next 14, and most of them were at our expense.

Getting to the county final 1978 came a little bit out of the blue, but it was a huge opportunity for us because we were going in against an ageing Newmarket team. That opportunity turned into another nightmare, one that nearly broke our club.

◄ ◄ ◆ ▷ ►

*He was punched and as he fell to the ground, he was kicked
on the head and struck with a hurley. He seemed to be a bit
shaken but managed to get up and walk off the field.*
– Ray McManus, *Evening Press*

WE HAD THIS sense that Newmarket just couldn't keep it up; they couldn't keep winning. We knew they were coming to the end and that they had grown old together.

Still, they had to be pushed over the edge.

For vast tracts of this county final, we were just doing that. We'd made the best possible start, with a great goal by Dermot Fitzgerald in the 15th minute, after he was set up by Eugene Considine, putting us in control. When Dermot got a second goal early in the second-half we had the match for the taking.

We were leading by double scores – 2-6 to 1-3 – but back came Newmarket thanks to goals from Jimmy and Paddy McNamara.

They went ahead, but we still weren't beaten.

We were playing into the road goal. I was running with the ball and I knew Gus Lohan was behind me. He was a great man to hook and had a great reach. I was never confident that I was away from him to strike, so I didn't shoot until I was about 25 yards out.

He eventually got the hurley in and I only got half a hit on it.

The ball ran along the ground towards the end line. I ran as hard as I could and got to the ball at the end line and pulled on it off my left. It was a bit like in soccer when you pull it back from the end-line.

Immediately, the umpire Jim Corr took a step away from the post and waved the ball wide. I didn't know then and don't know now whether it was wide or not. All I know is that there was lime on the bands of the hurley. That's all I can say.

He made a decision, I have no doubt, in the best of faith.

To myself I said… *F**k it*, turned around and then realised they were hurling away and tussling for the ball in the square. And the next thing the ball was flashed into the net for another Dermot Fitzgerald goal.

Newmarket selector Jim Woods was placed where he nearly always was, 20 yards to the left of the goals and he started roaring at the referee, Kevin Walsh.

There was this crazy situation where most people saw the ball in the net, yet the umpire was waving the ball wide because he kept his hands up. Kevin Walsh then came in and consulted with his umpires, and disallowed the goal.

That was it.

They went down the field and got a few more scores.

Another defeat, when it could have been won. We were all traipsing down to the corner – all players funnelling down into the one corner. Apparently, something was said on the way and Dermot Fitzgerald punched Jim Corr in the throat and knocked him. Then Eugene Considine came along and kicked him.

I was back in the dressing-room and wasn't aware of what had gone on at all. Someone said the Gardai were coming so immediately I told everyone to take off their jerseys.

As it turned out the Gardai didn't come in, but it was another cloud on top of a storm of disappointment. Still, that night it wasn't a big issue for us, because we thought it would pass. The bigger issue was the disallowed goal.

I WAS BEING asked about what happened, with people telling me it was never wide – people that were 80 yards away swearing by this. My answer was, 'I hit it, I was the closest to it and even I don't know whether it was wide or not'.

The following day's *Evening Press* changed everything.

It was on the front page of the country edition of the paper and on the inside of Dublin city editions – all the details of what happened were there with the testimony from Ray McManus, his photographs and his words.

Hurley attack by players on umpire, said one of the headlines. Then *The Clare Champion* waded in… *The game was brought into disrepute, of that there can be no doubt*, it said. *The response must be strict. The time for soft talk and leniency is now gone. It's a pity that it took an assault of an innocent official for this to be realised.*

County Board chairman Brendan Vaughan then entered into the dispute in his *Gaelic Forum* column in the newspaper. He turned on the Clarecastle club as a whole. *A club which fields indisciplined players whether their indiscipline hurt other players or officials, is lacking in the real understanding of the attributes of what makes a truly great club. Even if victory were won by this wretched behaviour, and all the evidence is that the exact opposite is the case, nine times out of ten, it would be bought too dearly. A sense of sportsmanship, which can take defeat as well as victory must and should be insisted on by clubs and their officials.*

It was awful and the whole thing became a huge issue. Still, it was an issue that should have been dealt with there and then, but instead was allowed fester and grow.

No one grabbed it and I'd include myself in that.

Paddy Kelly was chairman of the club and he got a lot of stick afterwards, with people saying that it should have been sorted out. This was unfair on him.

Jim Corr made a statement, but it was not an aggressive statement. He didn't say anything other than what had happened. The local Garda was the complainant – he was the one who pushed this.

When we ended up in court and jail sentences were handed out there was a lot of recrimination… 'This should have been done… and that should have been done'.

However, the club didn't 'do this' and the club didn't 'do that'.

Families were divided over it.

I WAS THE defending solicitor; the madness of that. I was only a year qualified and I was just 23. I hadn't the experience to handle it and even said to the lads, 'You might be calling me as a witness'.

The compromise was reached that we would engage the services of Brendan Nix, who went on to become a prominent criminal barrister.

The lads pleaded guilty and although it was in the heat of the moment, Mr Justice Hurley said it was a 'blackguardly act' and he imposed three months on Eugene and one month on Dermot.

The few of us that were there in Tulla Courthouse were shocked. Local publican John Minogue happened to be in the court and only that he agreed to go surety, the lads would have been taken away there and then.

It went on appeal to the Circuit Court and we separated the cases.

Dermot's case went before Judge Thomas Desmond who actually considered increasing his sentence, notwithstanding that he had an unblemished record, was a married man and was working for the ESB. It was very harsh. Before Judge Johnny Gleeson a suspended sentence was given to Eugene.

Because of the whole affair I considered giving up the law – it had that much of an effect on me, personally and professionally.

« CHAPTER 16 »

This extended and complicated programme, allied to collective training since last October, would seem to have taken a vital edge off the players. All the symptoms are there to see with players like Hehir, Callinan, McNamara, McMahon and even Durack not performing at the level we know they can. They appeared to have passed their peak and experienced some degree of mental staleness. Were some of the players at their peak for the league final and over the top for this final?

– Gaelic Forum, 1978

IT STARTED WITH a letter, just because writing letters is what solicitors do. In this case, it was the beginning of a series of correspondence to and fro over a few years that I had with the chairman of the Clare County Board, Brendan Vaughan.

He was an enlightened man in many ways – he was the driving force in the redevelopment of Cusack Park, a huge infrastructural project he initiated after coming in as chairman in 1976. Before that he had been a staunch advocate for ending the Ban, campaigning as a club delegate at county board level long before its abolition in 1971.

However, when it came to the county hurling team we were at loggerheads, mainly because of the column he wrote in *The Clare Champion* under the nom-de-plume of *Gaelic Forum*.

It was his forum, his platform to have a go. That's the way I looked at it. To me, it was the Clare County Board speaking and while there was praise for the team when things were going well, there was a lot of questions and criticism directed at us when we didn't win.

Criticism is fine, but not under cover.

I wrote to him on five or six occasions. They weren't Samuel Beckett letters or anything like that, but I was comfortable in engaging with him in this way. I didn't ring him, confront him and have it out with him – writing letters was my way of doing it.

Statements he made jarred with me.

Maybe we should have a rethink on training, he said in 1978 after we lost the Munster final. *A degree of mental staleness has set in*, he wrote on another occasion, adding… *the future is still there for this team, provided the right policies are followed*.

I decided to take him on.

I wanted him to 'out' himself as the chairman of the county board who was making these comments. The implication was that we were just a winter team and were over-training during the National League, and that's why we weren't doing it in the summer.

That was a common enough complaint about us. Because we were having success in the league and not delivering the championship, people were working backwards from that.

There might have been an element of truth in it, but as I was reading it I felt it was a way of saving money for the county board; that they wanted to cut down on training sessions in the winter to save some money. Not that we were costing the board very much, because they weren't giving us much food.

One of the things he said at the time was that the *Corks and Kilkennys* didn't winter train. He said he was told this. I remember writing to him and asking, 'Why do you think the Corks and Kilkennys would tell you the secret of their success?'

I ALWAYS USED the *Superstars* competition on RTÉ to illustrate my point. Cork's John Fenton competed in the competition one year and ran the 800m in a remarkably fast time; he was only a couple of seconds outside the European

Championship qualifying standard that was in place at the time.

And there were people telling me that John Fenton didn't train in the winter – that he just rocked up every summer and was this brilliant athlete. You just couldn't do that.

Maybe it's just that John Fenton was training by himself and that they weren't collectively training, but this myth and narrative that the big teams – the teams that won All-Irelands – didn't winter train was rubbish. It couldn't have been true.

The obvious place for all teams to improve is in physical fitness. We concentrated on that and I wouldn't apologise to anyone for that – maybe we didn't do enough of it. Maybe we needed to do more.

Brendan would have been a critic of that and the way we were doing it. I didn't like the criticism, but I really didn't like the nom-de-plume part of it. He was exerting influence by his writing, in my opinion.

He responded and argued his case, and he was always very eloquent and measured in putting his point of view across, but he never addressed the fact that he wrote the column. This was the start of my activism within the GAA, even though I never thought of myself as an activist.

As a county player I had seen the injustices that were there – expenses and the fight for them, and the treatment in general by the county board.

Aidan Tuttle called the county board the cloth cap brigade, his description of the average GAA official; cloth caps instead of hats, indicating that they were without ambition or style.

Aidan was a great fella to have around 'The Scene', a phrase that Seamus Durack coined to describe what it was like being a Clare hurler at that time. He was great, not just because he was disrespectful of the county board; he was always quick witted and was of the world. And he was on our side – and there were two sides.

We almost felt that the better we got and the more we achieved, the feeling at board level was that we were getting above our station.

There would be issues after matches.

Issues about wives and girlfriends, and team meals which excluded them. We might be in Thurles, eating in the Anner, and there'd be issues about wives and girlfriends joining us for a meal. It was a big deal.

Most of the women themselves said they wouldn't lower themselves to come in and join the team. It was terrible. We'd play the game. Our wives and girlfriends would be there to meet us after the game, but we'd have to say to them, 'Wait there… while we go in for the meal'.

I remember we were agitating for food after training in Tulla. This was when all the money was coming in during the great run of success that we had in Dr Daly Park.

We went to the Clare Hurling Board at the time. Hehir, Loughnane and myself – which was no surprise, but a bigger surprise was that Durack wasn't doing it – went looking for food.

Sean Hehir was very vocal that night. 'We have to sustain ourselves' he said, with his head nodding persistently as he spoke. 'We're coming to training and fellas are coming from work.'

We were asked, 'Does that mean ye'd get two dinners?'

The speaker was serious. Our mouths were open. We just looked at each other. The man thought that we were finishing work at 5pm, having a dinner at home, going to training and then wanting another dinner after it. Hehir went to grab him.

It illustrated the gap that was there between us as players, who were trying to be as 'professional' as we possibly could, and administrators. I insulted the county board at one stage when I said I had never met a Clare administrator who had the same ambition as I had, which was to win Munster and an All-Ireland titles. Afterwards I rang Seamus Gardiner, who was PRO at the time, to tell him that I excused him from that list.

Not paying expenses was real for fellas. It was real for me.

I needed that money. When I was in Dublin, myself and Stack were students, while Hehir and Loughnane were newly qualified teachers. It didn't matter to the two boys if it ran to three or four trips before they got paid by the board, but to Stack and myself, it was a problem. We needed the money.

To pay a fiver for the train from Dublin to training was a difficulty. We needed to get that back quickly, but we never did. Only for Enda O'Connor slipping me a few quid as we went into Minogue's after those matches in Tulla, I wouldn't have had the price of a drink.

That sounds poor-mouthing it, because students are penniless while never being penniless and always gather a few quid for the important things, like pints. But the county board – they just didn't want to part with their money, even when it was due to us.

I wouldn't say a word about Flan Hynes, who was a great man, but with all his gate-checkers he went straight to the Queen's Hotel after matches to get their meal. That was right, but it was wrong that players were left hanging and hanging for expenses.

Fr Harry possibly could have done more, by telling the board how badly we needed the money. But at the same time, he shouldn't have had to do that. It irritates me to this day. It sounds petty but when your grant for the college term was £30 and you paid a fiver for your train ticket, you wouldn't be long going through that coming back home for training and matches.

Stack would come in from Maynooth on the 66 bus and I'd meet him at Heuston Station, and we'd get the train down to Limerick and then hitch home from there. It was £4.20 return for a student fare on the train and we used to get a fiver – we were 'doing' the county board for 80p.

We were not mercenaries by any stretch. We resented being made to chase our own money, that was the part that irritated us most. It was the lack of respect, the lack of recognition that this was essential for fellas.

I needed financial help while I was in college – from my mother, and my sister, Mary. The County Council grant was £90 a year, so I needed to get the expenses that were due to me.

When I was living in Broadford after getting married, money was still very tight. I hadn't a bob, still repaying my college fees. We knew the mileage from Broadford to Ennis, and Siobhán being a bookkeeper and a banker kept the records meticulously. I'd put in my expenses but there was no sign of them being paid.

Chasing money wouldn't be a strong point of mine, and it left too many players feeling undignified. I had a great relationship with the treasurer of Clarecastle, John 'Ronnie' McInerney, who came to me any time I came from Dublin to play for Clarecastle. Straight away he'd be on to me, 'How are you fixed Cal?'

That's how it should be done. Most of the time I would have caught a lift down. But, win or lose, whatever match it was, I'd be asked by Ronnie if I had incurred any expenses?

With the county board it was different.

WHEN I GOT my first All Star, the county board invited me to the West County Hotel in Ennis because they wanted to give me some money going to America.

I said to them, 'Pay my fecking expenses' and they did. My expenses came to £110, I remember, and they sent me a cheque for £100.

'Send it back!' Siobhán urged me.

I was reluctant to do that, but in the end I did. Next thing I was getting my photograph taken for *The Clare Champion* and they handed me a cheque of £100 for the All Star trip. They wouldn't pay me the expenses that I had incurred.

In the end they eventually gave it to me, but the vividness of the whole incident, the tug-o-war over trying to get what was due to me, was degrading.

This tug-o-war extended down to the level of keeping a jersey. I finished my career that lasted 16 seasons with only a few jerseys. I wouldn't get into the row and the confrontation that would present itself if we dared swap a jersey with the opposition, or keep a Clare jersey. I remember Barry Smythe and Deccie Coote got into bother over jerseys on a trip we had to Amsterdam in 1981 when we played Wexford in a challenge game as guests of the Hurley Club of Amsterdam.

Myself, Colm Honan and Michael O'Connor from Parteen, when we were there, went to Rotterdam from Amsterdam for the Ireland V's Holland World Cup qualifier. It was a famous game. They talk about atmosphere at games – it was incredible that night under lights. It was a 2-2 draw with Frank Stapleton getting the equalising goal at our end, where all the Irish supporters were crowded.

The players came down afterwards, with Liam Brady climbing up the webbing between them and us on the terrace. He was up about 20 feet in the air and he threw his jersey into the crowd in celebration. We were as high as kites afterwards.

I'm sure, even the FAI, for all its faults, didn't give out to Brady about throwing away his jersey – unlike the Clare County Board on that trip, as we found out a few days later when we played our game.

It was a great trip, but the trouble and penny-pinching started even before we left. To ensure that all members of the squad that contested the Munster final that year could go on the trip we had to fundraise ourselves, selling lines in a draw for 10 All-Ireland tickets, while Dan McInerney chipped in a sizeable contribution to the fund.

Wexford had a brand new set of jerseys, while Clare had this 'mix em-gather-em' collection of jerseys. Sean Hehir was wearing No. 7, but it was actually 17 with the one taken off.

It was a terrible insult really, because the event was brilliantly organised and run. We played on three grass hockey pitches – definitely the best surface I have ever played on. It got coverage on the television over there in what was the equivalent of Match of the Day. There were over 7,000 people at the match.

We copped what the crowd wanted and gave them a few good clashes to get them going. Afterwards some of the lads started to swap jerseys. It was something I never got into – maybe I was too good and didn't want to cause offence – but Smythe and Coote had no problem.

There was war.

The line from the secretary of the Clare Hurling Board, was, 'The Wexford boys are going mad in their dressing-room, they want their jerseys back, we have to do it'.

Apparently in the Wexford dressing-room they were saying that it's the Clare officials that were going mad. Wexford's Jack Russell, who I knew in UCD, told me there was no hassle in their dressing-room and they didn't want them back at all.

The county board never got the jerseys back, but to rub salt into the board's wounds, Smythe and Coote would turn up to training wearing the Wexford jerseys. It drove the county board officials mad.

THE MOST DAMNING incident was in 1980 and Jackie O'Gorman's last year playing for Clare. We were beaten in the Munster semi-final at the Gaelic Grounds and the jerseys were being collected.

Everyone knew that defeat meant it was Jackie's last day – this was a man who had played championship for Clare in three decades and was the last survivor from the squad that contested the 1967 Munster final and first wore a Clare jersey in the early 60s.

We were sitting in the dressing-room afterwards.

Loughnane was to Jackie's left and I was to his right. Jackie had the jersey in his hand and just said, 'Jesus, leave it with me… it's my last one!'

The secretary said, 'I can't'.

Loughnane grabbed the jersey and pushed it into Jackie's bag. That should have been it, he deserved that jersey after all he'd given to Clare hurling. In the end I think he gave it back, because the pressure came on again.

I remember feeling really sorry for Jackie that day – Jackie was more than a cult hero for Clare hurling in the 70s.

He was my hero.

There was a strut about Jackie. He had a bravado, and a fearlessness that he didn't give a damn. He was the man. Everyone loved him because of what he was on the field – tough and uncompromising, and with the big head of hair, almost like an afro. It made him look like the great Cuban middle distance runner, Alberto Juantorena, though he wasn't as fast!

An feirmeoir leis an gruaig fhada, as Michéal Ó Muircheartaigh used to describe him.

And this image of him wasn't just with fellow players or supporters. The Clare County Board knew the value of Jackie's popularity and the power of his charismatic personality too. When the board, under Brendan Vaughan's chairmanship, were driving the redevelopment of Cusack Park they used Jackie as part of their charm offensive to get financial backing from the public.

'Let's Back Jack for the Park,' was one of the slogans the board used. He was a poster boy for that development, with the wording being a play on the one Fianna Fáil built around Jack Lynch in the 1977 General Election.

The day after we won the Nationa League that year the redevelopment of the Park was officially unveiled by Vaughan, with the goodwill generated by our success and the feel-good factor in the county a major selling point for the board in its fundraising activities.

Still, after all that, the same county board didn't want to give Jackie a jersey after his last ever game representing Clare. It didn't say much for them and what they really thought of the players representing Clare.

I always remembered what my Clarecastle clubmate, Michael Hegarty said to me. 'Whatever you do Cal, don't take your own jersey… because if you do, you'll be found out and have to give it back. Always take a jersey belonging to someone else'.

It was good advice.

« CHAPTER 17 »

This week Cumann na nImreoirí will be properly constituted when the 500-member organisation holds its first AGM. It is probably an exaggeration to say that shudders of fear will be felt in Croke Park. This is a body the GAA hopes will fade away. For almost 100 years GAA players have served a role akin to subservience. Officialdom has dictated and players have dutifully obeyed. The notion that players acting in concert would actually want their voice heard is greeted with suspicion at best and a degree of hostility at worst.

– Liam Kelly, *The Irish Press*

EXPERIENCING HURLING LIFE as it was in Clare, and seeing at first hand the struggles players had to put up with in their relationship with the county board, made me wonder what life was like in other counties. Did the gilded hurlers from Cork, Kilkenny, Limerick and Tipperary want for nothing?

In Clare we always had this image of Cork, since seeing their underage teams arrive in a string of limousines. We were jealous, but we only learned afterwards that it was a cover and just a show they put on for the opposition.

They were treated really badly, whereas we would have assumed we were a lot worse.

From talking to the Kilkenny lads, they seemed to be doing fairly okay and were not overly vocal about how the county board treated them. I heard afterwards that their secretary, Paddy Grace would go around the county before Christmas to check in with players and, if they needed a dig out, he'd give them some money.

The All Stars tours were a great way to gauge what it was like for players in other counties. I was lucky to go on a couple of tours after winning awards in 1979 and '81 – I was the only one from Clare the first year, but Sean Stack and Seamus Durack were with me the second time around.

Before the first tour I had a sense we were different in Clare. When initially nominated for the All Stars team, the sponsors, Bank of Ireland always sent someone down to take the player's photograph. When the photographer came to me, he asked, 'Will you put on a Clare jersey?'

'I would if I had one!' I replied.

That was the level of it. I had no Clare jersey I could wear.

WHAT'S WORSE IS that we were so cowed in Clare that we didn't even look to keep our jerseys after winning those National League titles in 1977 and '78.

At that time it was common place to only have one set of jerseys – a set that might have to do a number of different county teams.

The photographer couldn't believe it.

In 1979 when I won my first All Star, all I had for the photograph was a yellow tracksuit, with no jersey inside it. In the poster that was produced by the sponsors – posters that are collectors' items now – it's noticeable that I'm the only player of the 30 in the hurling and football teams not wearing a county jersey. It looked bad, and it still does.

Two years later, when I was nominated once more, they didn't bother to send a photographer. They probably figured I still wouldn't have a Clare jersey so they just used the image they had from '79. It looked even worse.

Meanwhile, the tours themselves also highlighted the difference between then and now in terms of the way players are treated. Siobhán came with me on the first trip, but we had no room in the hotel. She paid for her own flights, but we kept it under the radar in case she'd be stopped and wouldn't be allowed go.

We ended up in a room with Ollie O'Connor and Mossy Carroll from Limerick, but we didn't all have beds, with a few of us on the floor.

I remember waking up in the hotel in New York, and Ollie and Siobhán were watching the television, with something like *The Flinstones* on. That was the level of it, things like having television early in the morning was a novelty for us.

Still, those trips were great craic.

They were three-week trips. The first time was to New York and Chicago and we were in hotels, while in San Francisco and Los Angeles we were in people's homes.

There was a lot of drinking on those trips, because there was a drinking culture. We still went and saw the sights, but it wasn't hard to be persuaded to go for a drink.

The All-Ireland winning teams that went on those tours didn't really mix with the players from other counties – their own mates were there, so they had each other and they didn't need to reach out. But I got to know lads like Pat Lawlor, Joe Hennessy, Liam 'Chunky' O'Brien and Billy Fitzpatrick. There was a tendency for hurling people to stay with hurling people.

AT THAT TIME in the earlier 80s, Brian Mullins, the great Dublin footballer, was in New York studying for his Masters, while on the side he was working as a barman in Rosie O'Grady's on Seventh Avenue. A lot of us ended up there one night.

Bomber Liston and Ogie Moran arrived in after a Kerrymen function downtown, and they had their Kerry blazers on. It was about 1am in the morning. I knew Ogie from UCD. He was a proper hurler and we tried to get him to put his hand up and try out for the Fitzgibbon team, or at least play intermediate. We also went training together in Belfield. We'd go pucking and then kicking. Barry Walsh was also in UCD and through them I got to know the Bomber.

'See what's in there… see what's in there!' said Ogie when he arrived in Rosie's that night. He had nearly $400 in his breast pocket, from fellas coming up to him and pushing the notes on him. I'm sure that Bomber had the same. One thing for sure, they were buying the drink. Gerry McEntee from Meath joined us, so there was a bit of a UCD thing going on, as he had also gone to college there.

Of course, McEntee and Mullins were arguing over football, over Dublin and Meath, and they may as well have been butting heads. Mullins was behind the bar and you could see he was still suffering from the effects of the car accident he'd had a few years before that. He couldn't walk properly, or very easily anyway.

He needed the counter and shelf as a prop to navigate his way around. They were arguing away and the next thing, at around 2am or 3am, this florally dressed pimp with two or three women in tow, landed at the bar.

Mullins had us all talking Irish. He was a fluent speaker, as was Ogie, so the rest of us were desperately trying to stay with them in the conversation.

We ended up out on the street at 4am.

Mullins hadn't any drink taken at all and for the fun of it he started mock-sparring with McEntee. He had only one good leg but he was tipping away at McEntee, saying, 'I'll be back... I shall return'.

He was like Muhammad Ali with Joe Frazier or George Foreman, just winding him up for the craic, only that McEntee was minded to punch him. For sure, he'd have done it, because the fun was gone out of it for him.

The rest of us were loving it, looking on and laughing.

Next thing a cop came along.

'HEY MULLINS... move 'em on, get 'em... OUTTA HERE!'

The gun was in the holster and only for the fact that he knew Mullins well you'd be thinking... *What's he going to do here, are we in trouble?*

'Where the f**k do you think this is... O'CONNELL STREET?' the cop roared. We moved off in a set of cabs and ended a memorable night fast.

THOSE TRIPS WERE great, because we didn't meet lads from other counties regularly. But when we did, we made a great connection.

Away from home and meeting our peers from other counties, we'd openly complain about the Clare County Board, but then we'd hear that the Cork County Board or the Limerick County Board was just as bad, if not worse. And we thought we were the only ones.

The complaints that were being brought up again and again were common to all counties and this sharing of information certainly gave a huge impetus towards the foundation of the first GPA.

I got involved in the new organisation through Éamonn Cregan.

He was auctioneering at the time and I had gotten to know him well in Limerick – he told me about the first exploratory meeting that was coming up in Portlaoise, so I went along and got involved straight away.

I started talking and couldn't shut up.

The next thing, Cregan proposed me as chairman. I took it and was comfortable stepping into that role even if there was concern that if you were still playing that you might be blacklisted for being involved in what was essentially a renegade organisation that aimed to take on the GAA.

We were like a union. I was confident that there wouldn't be repercussions from my involvement, but if there was, someone was going to have to pay for it. That was my attitude and I was gung-ho and bullish about it.

After that first meeting we had our next gathering in Dublin, meeting unofficially as a group first in The Oval, that small pub beside the old *Irish Independent* offices on Abbey Street, before then being officially launched.

Former Roscommon footballer Tom Heneghan was elected vice-chairman. Dublin's Robbie Kelleher became secretary, while Jimmy Keaveny was the PRO and Seanie Moloney, the Clare footballer, was treasurer. The committee included Mick O'Dwyer, Paddy Cullen, Noel Skehan, Colm O'Rourke, Joe McKenna, Pat Spillane, Eámonn Cregan and Iggy Clarke.

The aims set out that first day included the, 'creation of great social contact between players, particularly at inter county level' and the 'improvement of the GAA at all levels'.

I had comfort in the fact that people around me were either retired or close to it. Kelleher was in his last season with Dublin, while Keaveney and Heneghan had stopped playing.

I was flattered to be asked and it was something I had a deep interest in.

There was a buzz from it. It was politics. In terms of ordinary politics, when campaigning over many years with Dónal Carey, I had seen what was necessary – the things he had to do to get elected I had no interest in. The dinners, the meetings, the funerals?

This was different. I was interested in being influential and having a say in what direction players wanted to go through the GPA. It was my half-way house.

I felt there was a gap in the inter-county game, that it could be developed more and had greater scope. We had the usual list of indignities that were irritating, with food and expenses being the obvious ones. But games at inter-county level, for a lot of county board officials, were a bit of a nuisance. Certainly, the games weren't at the top of the agenda. In becoming chairman of the GPA, it was that gap which I thought the new body could fill.

I saw county boards as fixtures committees, rather than them having any vision or blueprint for building up underage structures to help counties. I was there for three years. Liam Mulvihill was the man in Croke Park as Director General and they played us like a good salmon fisherman – they didn't break the strain and the line.

Meanwhile, we were grandiose and had notions about ourselves.

We had our AGM in The Shelbourne Hotel and after that it was decided that I'd ring Croke Park and tell them what the organisation was about.

Unfortunately, the only one I could get on the phone was Jimmy Smyth. Yeah, it was one Clareman talking to another, but I didn't have a great relationship with Jimmy, who had been in charge of Third Level GAA. In UCD we were not impressed with what he was doing for Third Level.

'What's all this about?'

'We're just giving you notice that this is going to happen… you might bring it to the Ard Stiúrathóir's attention.'

'I'll give ye two years!'

HE WASN'T FAR wrong.

He certainly wasn't wishing us the best of luck or anything like that.

We went on a recruitment drive and it was easy enough to get the membership of £1 a head. We issued membership cards to every paid-up player. To announce ourselves, we played a hurling match in Ballinasloe, with the Rest of Ireland taking on Galway. We got some lovely gear for that game – gear that was sponsored and we were allowed to keep.

Ned Buggy and Tony Doran drove all the way up from Wexford on a week night to play in this match and got a huge amount of abuse from the crowd. If it was nowadays, they would have walked off the field. This animosity towards them went back to the 1976 All-Ireland semi-final.

In Hayden's Hotel afterwards, I was talking to Doran and Buggy and they were looking at a five-hour drive back to Wexford on bad roads. They only had time for a cup of tea before they headed off.

The biggest issue that came up initially was a football one, after referees rigidly implemented the personal foul rule that was introduced for the 1982-83 season. The first man to fall foul of the rule was Wexford hurler George O'Connor, when lining out for the footballers. But when Seamus Aldridge sent off four players in an Ulster Vs Munster Railway Cup match everything came to a head.

Armagh's Fran McMahon and Derry's Joe Irwin were the Ulster players marched, as were Cork's Eoin O'Mahony and Kerry's John O'Keeffe. Sending off O'Keeffe was like sending off God. 'It's a lonely walk to the dugout, I can tell you,' he commented afterwards. 'It was very humiliating.'

Meanwhile, the newspapers had a field day.

What a game, what a ref, what a farce, said Tom O'Riordan in the *Independent*.

He acted in such an authoritarian manner that players were literally afraid to challenge for the ball long before the curtain fell on this dreadful spectacle, said the *Examiner's* Michael Ellard.

We had to act. We demanded a meeting.

They met us, but the GAA hierarchy's ploy always was that they would meet us on the second request or a third request, just when we were about to go public on an issue.

The word would come back, 'We'll see you, but it will be next week'.

By the time we got to meet them, the juice was gone out of the story. I ended up going into a meeting with Colm O'Rourke and Robbie Kelleher to meet Liam Mulvihill. I was there as chairman, but I was a hurler.

I remember Mulvihill looking at me when I was raising the implementation of some Gaelic Football rule, as if to say... *Why are you even here?*

Why that version of the GPA failed was simple. We didn't take the GAA on and they didn't take us on. That's what ultimately made the GPA irrelevant. We needed to be in the newspapers every three or four weeks with some kind of an issue. We didn't do that.

I can't point at too many GPA achievements, but I think by physically creating an organisation, we paved the way. That we existed for those few years showed that there was a need and room for such an organisation.

« CHAPTER 18 »

I think we might have over-prepared for this one in previous years when we were preparing for this Corkman and that Corkman. It's more important to concentrate on your own game. That's something I feel happened to us in 1978. I felt we didn't play as we were capable and there were only two points in it. The other night after training the secretary came in and said he had the team. All the lads thought it was the Clare team and when he started reading out the Cork side we just didn't care. They're only interested in their own team and their own game.

— John Callinan, 1981

BEING INVOLVED WITH the GPA while playing was never a problem, but there was one time when the two roles of player welfare and playing collided. We finally beat Cork in the championship in 1981 – the same year that the GPA was established – with the game's aftermath showing what players had to deal with when it came to officialdom.

That day in Thurles some players from both sides had the temerity to swap jerseys – I wasn't one of them, but those on the Cork side soon felt the wrath of their county board elders.

They were written to… 'Your jersey was not returned on Sunday, June 14, after the match with Clare. The County Board is taking a serious view of this recurring situation after a game, and requests you to make arrangements to have the jersey returned'.

Failing this, they were being asked to pay £6 for a new jersey.

That was the level of it.

Jerseys cost money; our money, and we want our money back.

I DON'T KNOW if the Cork County Board got their jerseys, or their money. The important thing was that we'd finally beaten them. Apart from the win in 1955, and a draw in '66, they'd beaten us in every championship game since the 1932 Munster final.

There had been such an empty feeling in everyone after being beaten by them in 1978. I think there's a big difference between playing well, giving your all and getting beaten – and playing terribly and getting beaten. We would have lived with playing terribly and winning, but the biggest disappointment was that as a group in '78 we didn't play our best.

By 1978, Cork had become a very crafty team; they were a team that knew how to win. They were in their fourth year on the go, winning Munster, and had got a bit of new life with Dermot MacCurtain, Johnny Crowley and Pat Horgan coming into the team. We were always going to have to play well to win, but the suffocation prevented us from performing, never mind winning. We didn't play with any kind of abandon or defiance. We were tight and negative.

Things were a lot different in 1981 though.

Cork were different. Charlie McCarthy was gone, Denis Coughlan was gone, Gerald McCarthy was gone... Ray Cummins had the flu and missed the game.

We had a good team and there was a real freshness about things. Tony Nugent and Deccie Coote were midfield, Barry Smythe, John Ryan and Tommy Keane were in defence, while up front we had Gerry McInerney, Noelie Ryan and Leo Quinlan.

And, while there was a newness about the team, there was still a core of players from the 1977 and '78 Munster finals. I was 26, and Loughnane, Stack, Hehir and Enda O'Connor were 28.

It was my best championship year. I felt that a lot of us we were of the right age and maturity to make the big breakthrough, even though we had all this baggage and defeats behind us. Plus, I think we had more flair than the 1977-78 side.

We produced that afternoon. A great goal by Enda before half-time, when he picked up a sideline from Tony Nugent, rode a few big tackles and blasted to the net, was a crucial score for us because it was so defiant.

Sean Stack had a huge game at centre-back. He played many majestic games for Clare. Centre-back, on the wing or midfield. He wasn't the quickest by any stretch, but he had a way of being in the right place, and he was good overhead and strong off both sides. That was his day. He hurled brilliantly, and so did Loughnane and Hehir on either side of him.

The winners struck a blow for youth and set a headline for other counties holding onto men clearly past their best, wrote Gerry McCarthy in *The Irish Press. Clare introduced new blood and can sit back, secure in the knowledge that whatever the future holds their bold policy has been vindicated. They took their courage in their hands, gave youth its chance and reaped the dividends.*

This turn towards youth wasn't the only change that the 1980-81 season brought. There was also Fr Harry's return as manager, after he'd called it a day following the Munster semi-final defeat to Limerick in 1979.

In his absence Justin McCarthy had stepped up, with Jimmy Cullinan and Robert Frost also involved for the 1980 championship, but after beating Waterford in a quarter-final we again went down to Limerick in the semi-final.

That whole 1979-80 season was overshadowed by the infamous row in Tulla at the end of our National League game against Offaly before Christmas. As we all funnelled out the gate at the end of the game it kicked off. Offaly's Pat Carroll was hit.

There was a huge bust up. It was not a good day.

Clare were in the dock, with Offaly chairman Fr Sean Heaney really giving it to us in his report to the county convention a few weeks later. 'The Offaly party genuinely were in a state of terror at the end of it all, partly because most of the players felt that the life of a teammate was in danger and partly because of the ugly and vicious hostility of the crowd around the Offaly dressing-room.'

He called on the Activities Committee of the GAA to investigate what happened. A couple of months later, I was one of those called to give evidence in Croke Park.

Before going into the meeting, we were all hanging around and Offaly secretary John Dowling, who became GAA president afterwards, called me over.

'What are ye going to say?'

'I saw nothing.' I genuinely hadn't.

So, it was agreed between John and myself that both sides would say nothing. I went into the meeting and was interrogated about the incident by the chairman of the committee, Peter Quinn.

My line was, 'It's absolutely extraordinary that in the second most important competition in the GAA you have games played in venues that are not secure from the sideline'.

He just looked at me and was perplexed.

'What has this got to do with the incident?

'You are asked in here to give your views on the incident,' he continued.

'Surely this committee will look into why this did happen,' I responded.

He wanted to keep me on track to talk about the incident, so my line was... 'Am I not needed here'?

'If you get hit with a hurl next week and no one sees it, will you be satisfied with that?' I was asked.

My answer was, 'Do you want players to become informers?'

I knew that saying something like that to someone from Ulster – Quinn was a Fermanaghman – would have an effect. It was bold to throw out the word 'informer' in 1980, and I was dismissed – my presence at the hearing was no longer required.

But I had a point to make. If the row had started between the players and there wasn't hundreds of supporters coming in from both sides, officials would have been able to identify the culprits. That was my point.

Still, if there was a low point from our Tulla experiences that was definitey it.

FOR THE FOLLOWING season, we wanted Fr Harry back. It came down to a choice between two different management systems put forward by a special county board committee that was chaired by Brendan Vaughan.

It was Fr Harry as manager, with Jackie O'Gorman and Mick Moroney as his selectors, or a three-man selection committee made up of Robert Frost, Jimmy Cullinan and Kevin Keane. Fr Harry won the vote decisively 34-6. It was like the members of the band getting back together.

This carried over into a solid enough National League campaign. The only set-back in the group stage was a two-point defeat to Kilkenny in Nowlan Park, but we crashed to a seven-point defeat to Waterford in the quarter-final.

The fact we then had Waterford in the Munster quarter-final was a good thing. We beat them by a goal with a team that included seven championship debutants. And with Cork in the semi-final, we were going in as underdogs, another thing that helped us.

To an extent, we were in the long grass.

Defeat would not be a disgrace; victory would be hailed as a great achievement. That's what *The Sunday Independent* said on the day of the game.

There was no pressure, whereas three years previously the pressure was overwhelming. It was such a big deal to finally beat them. We were beating everyone else in Munster, apart from Cork. It's the county game that sticks out above any other for me. I found county hurling very hard. There was no game I played, that I found easy.

I'm not too sure I did myself justice in bigger matches. It's as if I was trying too hard. That meant I didn't play as well as I felt I should have a lot of the time, unlike Loughnane and Durack who seemed to reserve their best for the big day. But I had a good game that day.

I started on Tom Cashman and got some sort of revenge for three years earlier, and played very well, but in the last 20 minutes they switched Dermot MacCurtain over on me and I didn't get as much change out of him.

It didn't matter, we had done enough and held on.

It was a famous win.

◄ ◄ ◆ ▷ ►

There is no way it is getting easier to take defeat, in fact it's getting harder and harder to take as the years go by. We played well today for a lot of the game, but Joe McKenna was just amazing for Limerick.
– John Callinan, 1981

LIMERICK IN THE final was another huge chance. Yes, they were more experienced – only seven of us had played in a Munster final before, while Limerick had 14 who played on the big day when they beat Cork in the previous year's final. That didn't bother us and we were confident going into it.

We were always confident going in against Limerick.

Losing that game was the most disappointing defeat of all for me. Even though 1978 was a crushing blow, I wouldn't let myself believe that at 23 I'd think we were never going to win anything, but at 26 it was different. We could have won that game.

It was very hard to take.

I am not certain we were better than Cork in those 1977 and '78 finals. If we had played better, would they have found more? They always said they would.

It was different in the 1981 final though. We put up a decent score and we played well, and with a small adjustment we would have won that Munster final.

It's not that we weren't warned where the danger lay.

People were literally screaming it.

The outcome could hinge, as it does in every game involving Limerick, on how the opposition can cope with Joe McKenna and his help-mate in destruction, Éamonn Cregan, stated Gerry McCarthy in *The Irish Press*. *Without this pair the Munster Champions' attack would present a sorry picture*, he concluded.

We could see that as well.

McKenna had scored 4-5 over the course of the two games it took to decide their semi-final against Tipperary, while Cregan, one of Limerick's greatest ever players, always had to be watched.

We knew exactly how they played it. It was a two-man full-forward line, where Cregan stood a little bit to the left of the left hand post and McKenna a little bit to the right of the right hand post – then Ollie O'Connor would go off roaming around the field.

THE FIRST BALL that Ollie got, he hit it in off his left to Cregan. Just as it arrived he got an elbow into the ear from Barry Smythe, who caught it, knocked Cregan sideways, took a step or two and barged McKenna out of his way and drove the ball long down the field. It was a real statement.

Straight away, it was as if Cregan thought… *To hell with this, I'll try something else.*

He went over and stood on the sideline, and Limerick ended up with a one-man full-forward line. Smythe continued to have a fine game, but to an extent he was taken away from where he could and should have been – where he could have dominated. It was unfair on John Ryan, because he was cruelly exposed in those circumstances, by the space that was created for McKenna.

After the semi-final, I had a pint with Cork's corner-forward, Eamon O'Donoghue. We used to go for pints the odd time and I had pints with him after the 1977 and '78 Munster finals as well. He was a likeable fella and we struck up a relationship and anytime we met we'd try to find a way to have a couple of pints.

We were down half way on the first pint and he said, 'Don't go into the Munster final with John Ryan as full-back'.

'You can't say that to me – he's my teammate,' I replied.

I gave him Jackie O'Gorman's number. I don't know if he ever rang him. We had options. Smythe would have loved Joe McKenna. He would have gloried in going in on McKenna; he was on an all-time great in Éamonn Cregan and had no respect for him. Jim Power could have come in at corner-back – Jim's biggest problem was Ray Cummins, and he wasn't playing

The team wasn't changed from the semi-final and I think it should have been. Colm Honan was injured for the semi-final and he should have been brought in. The boys made no change, because at that time you didn't change winning teams.

Still, despite conceding a goal to McKenna as early as the fifth minute we had the better of things in the first-half. Noelie Ryan responded with a goal inside a couple of minutes, while after Gerry McInerney fired home a penalty in the 23rd minute we were 2-3 to 1-2 ahead. And it could have been more.

I was upended in the square just before half-time, but McInerney's shot for goal flashed inches wide of the post. We were playing well, but what killed us in the end was that McKenna kept getting goals.

He managed to get 4-4 that day, with 1-1 of it disallowed.

Seamus Durack was at fault for one of them, but Duke had nearly lost it with McKenna at that stage, because once McKenna got the ball he always felt he was going to score. He might even have scored one off his right.

It was a crushing disappointment.

Yet again.

PART FIVE

Dying Happily

« CHAPTER 19 »

From everybody's point of view this was a disastrous result. On the day we did not play as a team with the conviction, fire and determination necessary to win a Munster championship match. We did not match Tipperary's hunger and spirit. Yet again we allowed a team with less ability to beat us.

— John Callinan, 1983

I WAS DRIVING from Ardnacrusha to Ennis, and a rendezvous in the Auburn Lodge Hotel for a team meeting, before heading to Cusack Park for our championship game against Tipperary. It was June 1985, and it was the first meeting between the sides in the championship in Ennis in 73 years.

I was grumpy and in bad form, and stuck in match traffic that was backed up as far as Clarecastle. It wasn't the snail's pace we were going at that had me in bad humour – it was hurling.

In front of me was a Tipperary car, and I just snapped.

I jumped out of my car. It's not that I had an urge to fight, even if like everyone else in the country I was now a boxing fan having watched Barry McGuigan beat Eusebio Pedrosa to win the world title the previous night.

But I was very mad.

Nothing wrong with the Tipp car, but just beyond where the entrance to the

Clarecastle club grounds are now, the car door opened and the driver tipped what looked like up to 200 cigarette butts onto the ground.

However, just after jumping out of my car, the line of traffic started to move. I was running up to the car roaring at him over what he did, an illustration of how angry I was.

It's not that I was a member of Clarecastle Tidy Towns Committee, but I was fuming – and something had been building up in me ever since the previous Thursday night in Cusack Park. We'd finished training, were in the dressing-room and the team for Sunday was read out by manager Fr Michael McNamara.

A good few of the hardy annuals I'd soldiered with for the previous decade were there. Sean Hehir at full-back, Sean Stack at centre-back, with Ger Loughnane on his right, while Enda O'Connor was top of the right. I wasn't there. Dropped.

Dropped for the first time in my senior career.

I was raging.

IT SEALED IT for me. I was 30, had been 13 years on the go and now I found myself surplus to requirements. It had been a depressing enough time to be a Clare hurler for a few years anyway, but this was the most depressing of all, just because it had never happened me before.

We were going badly and I couldn't make the team. It didn't say much for me.

You could say we had been going downhill since the 1981 Munster final. Ahead of that game, one comment that appeared in the newspaper coverage said, *Clare, whatever their fate can look to the future with a degree of confidence that has been foreign to them for the past couple of years.*

Of course, all of us hoped that it would be true – alas, it was a very bad wide and couldn't have been further from the truth as the Clare team soon went into a freefall that seemed to roll over from one year to the next.

We had some awful years.

The Cork game in 1982 down in Thurles, when they hammered us by 16 points. It was a nightmare and we weren't spared afterwards. *Even John Callinan, Sean Stack and Ger Loughnane, who figured for a while in the first-half, threw in the towel. It was a sad sight to see Clare beaten off the park and not even put up a token resistance,* stated Michael Ellard in *The Cork Examiner.*

We could have no complaints. What a difference a year had made.

Being beaten by a goal by Tipperary the following year in the championship mightn't seem as bad, but it was worse. It was their first win in the Munster championship in 10 years. They won because they wanted it more than us.

It wasn't much better in 1984 – which was a huge one for everyone because of it being the Centenary Year of the GAA.

You'd think it would have been more important to Clare than others, because there was a huge amount of activity in the county to mark 100 years of the GAA.

Those centenary celebrations had started in Clare and a centrepoint of the year's activities was all the living presidents of the GAA coming to Carron in North Clare that was the birthplace of the GAA founder Michael Cusack.

As a hurling team we were far from being the centrepoint.

Were we a bit of a shambles? One thing is certain, we were going nowhere.

We played Waterford in the first round in Thurles and we won, with just over 5,000 at the game. It was a far cry from when the gates of Thurles were broken down in expectation of Clare winning a Munster final. There was no buzz about Clare hurling. Far from it.

Then in the semi-final against Tipperary in Thurles we improved a good bit, but were beaten by a point. A goal from a 21-yard free by Gerry McInerney with four minutes remaining put us ahead – then I followed up with a point, but we were beaten by a goal right at the death. Seamus Power's 21-yard free was saved by Denis Corry, but Liam Maher crashed home the rebound to win the game.

I THINK THE standard of Clare's preparations dropped during this time.

Whether it was a resignation amongst people that had them thinking... *You know what... we're just not good enough...* I don't know.

This was after the 1981 result effectively confirmed what had happened in the other Munster finals – 1972, '74, '77 and '78 – that we couldn't win a title. With that backdrop, there wasn't much enthusiasm as to who was going to be manager after Fr Harry, along with Jackie O'Gorman and Mick Moroney, stepped away after the drubbing against Cork in '82.

There was no one lining up. 'The Scene' that Duke talked about just wasn't there.

To compare Fr Harry, Justin McCarthy and Colm Flynn with Fr Michael McNamara, 'Trixie' Toomey and Robert Frost who came in – you just couldn't begin to put them up against each other. It was just different. I know they were trying their best, but the levels among everyone dropped.

Trixie was a big influence on a lot of players' careers, but he would arrive to training and put a pair of boots on over his suit trousers – he always wore a waistcoat – and trained the team that way.

We moved back into where we were before the revolution that Fr Harry presided over. Tim Crowe was brought in as fitness coach and he made a difference to things – he'd been with Limerick when they won the Munster titles in 1980 and '81. Then Éamonn Cregan came to us as hurling coach.

I told Cregan straight out that he was mad to come to Clare – he was playing up to 1984 and then came in to train the enemy the following year, while at the same time he was training the Limerick under-21s.

It was never a good move for him to come. I honestly don't know what he was thinking. I could never get around his dual mandate, but it didn't cost him a thought.

'One won't interfere with the other and it doesn't concern me at all,' he said, adding, 'Limerick seniors rejected me out of hand, so why should they label me a turncoat.'

We travelled to training in Ennis together and I told him he was being set up. Loughnane was resisting him, others were resisting him too. This was raw. Cregan represented Limerick at its best and its worst. Fr McNamara brought him in, but he wasn't wanted.

We were in Division 2 that year and won all our games to reach a quarter-final, where we beat Kilkenny after a replay. Then we beat Galway in the semi-final, prompting once scribe to claim, *The renaissance continues, Clare's rebirth as a hurling force was further demonstrated.*

ANY RENAISSANCE AND rebirth was well and truly quashed in the final when Limerick beat us by 11 points. I was in my usual right half-forward position and failed to score, but I wasn't alone as the only starting forward to muster a score from play was Pat Morey.

Jimmy Carroll beat us that day, while it was as if the retired Joe McKenna hadn't gone away, as his replacement at full-forward Pat McCarthy gave us more nightmares when scoring 2-1 from play as they beat us in a canter.

As a result, there were seven changes for the opening round of the championship. Three of them in the forwards, as myself Syl Dolan and Mike Guilfoyle were dropped, with Enda O'Connor, Val Donnellan and Kieran McNamara coming in.

AFTER THE HAMMER fell that Thursday night after training, I went straight to Limerick to meet Siobhán, who was attending a bank event in Kennedy O'Brien's. The plan was to collect her and go home, but inside the door I met Padraig Conlon from Tulla and Brendan Sliney from Cork.

I knew them well, so I just called the barman and ordered a pint.

They knew straight away that I had been dropped. I had that pint and then had a second, but left it at that. I was livid. I never expected it.

I could have had more drink, but didn't, because I was driving.

As my road rage showed on the Sunday, my anger was slow to pass away, but at the same time I was still trying to remain positive after being dropped for the first time in my senior career stretching back to the 1972 Munster final.

After I arrived in the Auburn Lodge, Éamonn Cregan came over to me and said, 'You're playing wing-back'. To my knowledge he had no role in the selection of the team, so I just said, 'Did you not hear the news at all… I was dropped'.

'No Loughnane is out… you're in!'

'And I'm going on Nicky English? You're joking.'

Part of the reason for dropping me in the first place was that I had been carrying an injury. That wasn't true, I was injury free. But now I was being put in the defence for the first time in my career to mark Nicky English, who already had two All Stars to his name at that stage.

Next thing, Fr McNamara was reading out the side and he came to left half-back, called my name and said, 'Éamonn will have a word with you'. That's because I didn't get on with any of the three on the management team of Fr Mac, Trixie Toomey and Robert Frost.

I was part of the 'old guard', a boy of the old brigade and they were the new brigade. Even at that stage, we were defined by whether you were pro or anti-Harry, even though he was gone.

It was still there as the background music. There were a lot of us who were part of the club, which meant they would have met with a lot of resistance. I'm not saying they were the problem, because someone had to manage the team.

In my pomposity my attitude was… *They might have at least told me I was dropped*. But that's bullshit. I was well wide of the mark in my thinking that I'd be entitled to that from the management on the Thursday night.

There was a little snug at the back of the reception area of the Auburn Lodge, and Cregan and myself went in there to talk about it.

'I'm being set up here Éamonn.'

'Ah for f**k sake, what are you talking about?'

'I'm telling you, they won't be blamed for this… but you will, you'll get the blame… and I'll be blamed for it'.

I was paranoid at this stage.

'You can't lose. You're playing left half-back, when you're normally playing right half-forward, so you're in the same position on the field. Just get it and go forward, and if it goes pear-shaped you never played there before and it will be a case of… What the hell were they thinking about?'

I wasn't convinced, far from it. At the back of it I was excited about playing and getting a reprieve – and I wanted to play, but …

There was a but, because the resentment that was there from the Thursday night when I had those few pints in anger, was still there. I didn't go out for pints on any of the remaining nights before the match, but I wasn't a happy hurler.

Far from it.

AFTER THE TEAM meeting we moved onto Cusack Park and as we were going towards the tunnel area Mícheál Ó Muircheartaigh was coming against me.

'Well Johnnie… No. 7 today!'

'Yeah!' and I threw my eyes up to heaven.

'A hurler can play anywhere Johnnie.'

It wasn't that a good hurler can play anywhere, just a hurler. It was nearly the best thing that was said to me all day. It was a jolt. If you're a hurler, you can go and play.

And what Mícheál said was completely well-intentioned and non-partisan.

It was a lovely interlude in a fleeting second when we were passing each other – we were going out as he was coming in from the field. In the dressing-room, loads of lads came over to me and said, 'Give him timber Cal'.

Pat O'Connor was a sub. 'Cal, you don't know how to timber anyone!' he said.

'Just play your own game'.

They were the two best bits of advice I got. It was great.

I had a good game. Sean Stack was centre-back and Donie O'Connell was centre-forward. We were defending the Tulla end goal in the first-half and Nicky English went in and stood about 10 yards away from Donie. I had played a bit of centre-back for Clarecastle, so it was fine.

I was 30, Sean was 31 and our thinking was that our legs were slowing down a bit so the tighter it was the better. It meant a lot of the time we were running towards the sideline for the ball, whereas the danger was that if he stood over five yards from the sideline and ran at me, I'd be in trouble. It meant I handled him.

We should have won the game. Val Donnellan had a great game that day. Cyril Lyons hit 0-4 and Tommy Guilfoyle got a goal but we couldn't kill them off, even though we had plenty of chances to bury them.

Nicky claims that he got one puck that day, the equalising point. He then got two goals in the replay and we were hammered by 11 points.

As I wrote at the time, *To be beaten by great Tipp teams would be bad, but Tipp presently are not a great team.*

It was a bad day, in what was a very bleak period for the county team.

As for the club in those years, it was worse.

◄ ◄ ◆ ► ►

After taking the great Newmarket-on-Fergus Blues to the wire in the 1978 county final, Clarecastle faded quickly into obscurity for a few years. For all comers the Magpies were easy to shoot down.
– Clare County Express

CLARECASTLE'S TROUBLES DATED back to the fall-out from the 1978 county final. It hit the club very hard and had a ferocious impact on everyone's morale as we faced into the 1979 season.

It wasn't just that season though, because it continued into 1980 and '81 as things went from bad to worse, and we made no impact whatsoever on senior hurling. Some days we were the whipping boys, other days pride alone meant we competed, but over those three years the records spoke for themselves.

We played nine championship games, winning just one against the St Flannan's amalgamation that took in Ennistymon, Inagh and Kilnamona. The worst day of all was against Sixmilebridge in 1980 when they hammered us by 2-14 to 0-3. The 1-13 to 0-4 defeat to Kilkishen the previous year was just as bad. The results showed just how far we had fallen.

For a few years it was very hard to get selectors – we couldn't get anyone to train the team; it was hard to get club officers. It was even harder to get players.

We would have had to give walkovers in the Clare Champion Cup that first year, only for the fact that we had the assistance of Ballyea players at senior level. Lads just gave up and were so pissed off with what had happened.

In 1980, the chairman Patrick Kelly proposed at the AGM that we would go down to intermediate level. It may have been a deliberate move on his part to try and provoke a reaction and get people going, but we were so low at that stage that intermediate or below was our level.

I remember saying that if the club was regraded to intermediate, I was going to transfer to Claughaun in Limerick. I don't know if I would ever have left, but maybe I would.

It wasn't any better in 1981, but then that winter Michael Slattery got things going again. I would have been critical of his role after the county final in '78 but he was a great man to circle the wagons. He had the enthusiasm and was like a dog with a bone. The club meant so much to him and people followed him.

Paschal Russell had transferred to Wolfe Tones. It was partly because he was living and working in Shannon, but also because there was nothing happening for him to stay with us. Haulie Russell had transferred to the Banner. For training I was coming from Ardnacrusha and Paschal was coming from Shannon. Then we'd have Anthony Scanlan, Rogie McMahon and Noel Daly – they were the only ones we'd have for senior training. We were all getting sick of it. For those few years we never had more than seven or eight at training. We were in the lowest place.

In the end Michael Slattery came in and got it going again.

The first job was to get the Haulie and Paschal back. That was no big deal and they were easily convinced. Then fellas like Tom Howard, Pat Tuohy and Victor O'Loughlin were coming of age and making the senior team.

We got to the *Clare Champion* Cup final in 1982 when we played Tubber, who had been beaten in the county final the year before. That final went to three games – they were huge for us considering where we were coming from.

Winning that cup was a massive boost for the club, while we also won the Junior A Football championship that year, which was equally significant in lifting everyone's morale.

I'd be seen in Clarecastle as anti-football, which has no basis in fact, but the victory and the progress we made in subsequent years was very important to our recovery. Brian 'Charlie' Donnellan, who was a League of Ireland player with Galway United, was a great footballer. Barney Lynch was better; he was county standard. We were well able to play the game, when we wanted to – it was just about putting the work in. The less kicking the better, and the hand-passing game suited us well.

In St Flannan's, I wanted to play football but I didn't really want to train for it. I always had a bit of a problem with training for football, there was no excitement in it. I was getting on county minor panels, but didn't play senior for the school because of my aversion to football training. When I went 'up the field', it was for hurling only.

Still, I played minor and under-21 football for Clare and I came on against Kilkenny in a National League game one year – and played against Cork in the Munster under-21 semi-final in 1976 when we were narrowly beaten.

It was a big deal to eventually win the Junior A title, beating Naomh Eoin in Miltown. It took us an awful long time to get home that evening.

Then we won the intermediate title in 1984. We played the final in Cusack Park on an October Bank Holiday Monday. The week before we had played against Dublin in the National League and I broke a bone in my hand. I was telling Paschal Russell about it and he said, 'What about it… you'll only be half as bad with one hand'.

There was no pressure with the football. That's what made it so attractive for the players. We didn't train, but we were good enough to win. It was a hugely important element in getting the thing going again and beating Kilfenora by 0-3 to 0-2 was celebrated hard.

After going up to senior in 1985 we beat reigning champions Kilkee in the first round of the senior championship. After that win, Barney Lynch said, 'We should watch the next match to see who we will be playing.'

After about 10 or 15 minutes I told him bluntly, 'I'm not learning anything here…I'm gone'. Not that I was going home; instead it was to Declan McNamara's, the nearest pub to the pitch in Kilmihil, across the road.

Within minutes, most of the crew followed me.

That's what we really thought of football. At the same time there's no doubting the big role the game played in getting us back together as a club, when we thought we might have *no* club.

We took some notable scalps in senior football; in addition to Kilkee, we beat Shannon Gaels and Kilrush, and put it up to Doonbeg in a county senior semi-final in those years.

« CHAPTER 20 »

11am Monday, July 21, 1986 – the morning after another Munster final beating. What can be said? And yet thousands of post-match wounds have said... what can now be done? The game and every ball will be played over in people's minds but the result won't change. We gave it our best shot but it wasn't good enough. Cork's patronising with 'Clare's time will come' must be ignored and firm resolution and hard work undertaken because a team's time does not come.

It must be made.

– John Callinan, 1986

WHEN THE FINAL whistle went in the 1986 Munster final in Killarney, I had a feeling that my time was up. Thirty one years of age – another Munster final lost. It brought the number to six. Too many.

Maybe it was time to stop the clock? *No Mas*, as the great fighter Roberto Duran exclaimed in the ring, as he was being out-smarted by Sugar Ray Leonard.

Again, yet again, we'd been close. Very close as Cork just outpaced us in the second-half to win by three points, 2-18 to 3-12. But it could have been us. The glass ceiling could finally have been broken that day. *If.*

Retirement was on the horizon. Little did I think it would arrive within seconds of the final whistle as I walked off the field with Martin McKeogh.

Along the way I was telling him, 'That's me gone... I've had enough of it now!'

We were inside the 21-yard line and going towards the gate at the bottom corner of Fitzgerald Stadium that leads to the dressing-rooms, but were interrupted by a Clare supporter roaring over from somewhere in the stand.

'CALLINAN... CALLINAN... OVER HERE!'

I turned, saw a fella with a paper hat on waving towards me frantically, so I traipsed over. Maybe he just wanted an autograph for his son or daughter? Or he wanted to say hard luck. Something?

'Give me the oul hurley, you won't be wanting it again.'

I hadn't a clue who he was, but he had his face up to the wire and I wanted to take a swing and hit him. I lifted to swing, but he backed off and I didn't follow through. I was after telling Martin McKeogh that I was finished, but it was alright for me to say that. Not for anyone else.

I WAS MAD. Mad that we had lost again, but mad because I was being told I was finished. Bad and all as 1977 and '78 were, I was still only 22 and 23 in those years, and my hurling life was still ahead of me and not behind me. Now it was coming to an end. Behind me, or very nearly behind me.

But there was perspective. Loads of it.

For a few years after getting married in September 1978, Siobhán and I didn't want children, because we were both so young. However, after a few more years we both had to come to terms with the fact that we couldn't have children. We went through all the medical stuff and it just wasn't possible.

It was a huge disappointment to both of us.

Then it was a case of thinking... *What are we going to do?*

In our early thirties, we began to enquire about adoption and went through the whole vetting process. Adoptions were becoming scarcer then. I'd say we were among the last couple to be lucky enough to adopt two children.

For us it was a very smooth process.

When we were approved for adoption, we were told we might have to wait for up to 18 months for a child. However, after just six months, Aoife came into our lives at only three days' notice. This induced something of a panic.

A couple havng a child naturally have the normal period to prepare for the arrival, and to deal with the fundamentals, like a cot, clothes, so many vital things.

We were both working away, neither of us expecting to get a child so quickly, but Siobhán's sister, Majella and her sister-in-law, Marion, both recent mothers themselves, came to our rescue. Everything was done, but when we climbed the drab stairs of the Mid-Western Health Board's offices on July 4, 1986 – situated over a pub on Catherine's Street in Limerick – Aoife encountered very nervous parents.

Crash courses in making baby feed and changing nappies were taken.

The birth mother of the adoptee child signed a preliminary Consent to the Adoption, but had a period – usually not less than six months – to withdraw this consent and take her child back. A formal Order of An Bord Uchtála, a branch of the High Court, had to be made to confirm the adoption. This can not take place without the birth mother's second and final consent.

We did not expect this to take place until well into 1987, so when we were called by our kind and efficient social worker in the middle of December 1986, to know if we could go to Dublin as An Bord Uchtála was convening pre-Christmas to finalise a number of adoption orders, including Aoife's, there was more panic – though this was good, very happy panic.

Ardnacrusha to Dublin was a longer journey at that time, and with the 'shorter' days, we decided to stay overnight.

The three of us travelled to Dublin and attended with a number of other excited couples at 64-65 Merrion Street on December 18. Our application was heard at 2.20pm. It was quite formal. The board comprised a number of members and was chaired by a retired High Court judge. The registrar was John W. Cronin. The board, having formally reviewed and approved the paperwork, asked us some questions and made the Adoption Order in respect of Aoife Marie.

The Chair, a kindly man, enquired how Aoife, and Siobhán and myself, were getting on? Aoife was probably the youngest of the children present on that particular day. The Chair also enquired about William Leahy, my solicitor boss in Limerick. The hearing was over fairly quickly.

To celebrate, we didn't slum it. We drove the short journey to Jury's Hotel in Ballsbridge and stayed the night. We enjoyed a nice celebratory dinner and travelled home the following morning – Siobhán and myself on cloud nine!

Aoife, 'ours' from July 4, 1986, the most beautiful baby in the world the minute we saw her, was now legally ours.

We often think of the circumstances that gave rise to Aoife's birth mother putting her child up for adoption, and our gratitude to her is tinged with the societal guilt that can cause those circumstances.

Aoife had arrived to us just 16 days before the Munster final against Cork in Killarney. Marian O'Donovan, the mother of one of Clare's 2013 All-Ireland winning heroes, Domhnall O'Donovan, looked after Aoife for the day to allow Siobhán to go to Killarney to watch me in my last Munster final.

There was a lot of perspective around that particular match.

Two years later, we received another call, and we were offered a male child. Eamon made us a family of four.

The process was just as smooth and the order was made again by An Bord Uchtála – the board travelled on this occasion to Limerick. We celebrated Eamon's Order in the Lakeside Hotel in Killaloe, just the four of us, and to our surprise – a total coincidence – the members of the board were also staying in the hotel that same night and having dinner together.

THE NIGHT BEFORE that Munster final we stayed in the Aghadoe Heights Hotel that was owned by former Clare great Dan McInerney. Aidan Tuttle, who by then had become famous as a commentator for match videos shot by Michael O'Sullivan and Paschal Brooks, was staying in the same hotel.

I didn't sleep particularly well the night before the match and was up and about very early – when I was coming back to the hotel at about 8am I met The Tut and we went on another walk.

We talked about politics, the world, a bit about the match and I told him about Aoife. Later that afternoon when I was running out onto the field Michael O'Sullivan zoomed in on 'the near veteran' and on commentary the Tut said he'd... 'like to welcome the arrival of Aoife to Siobhán and John'.

It was the perfect wording.

The Munster final was big, but it wasn't really *that* big.

The Tut captured it. I was showing that video to Aoife until she was about 15 years of age. Nearly every year she'd ask me about her name being mentioned in the commentary on Munster final day and we'd load up the video tape. It's something I treasure to this day.

It was the Tut at his very best, being able to put the right words and right sentiment out there and it meant so much.

The Munster final, any Munster final, was life and death.

Or was it?

I wanted to win one very badly, as much in 1986 as I did in my first one 14 years earlier. My time was running out and this was possibly my last chance at it, so it was everything, but the new life was here and that really *was* everything.

It was more important.

Aoife was the Killarney Munster final baby.

We still could have won the game though.

We had a great chance.

◄◄◆►►

Ger Cunningham and some of the other Cork players who were in attendance in Ennis left with wide grins feeling very confident about the Munster Final. Hopefully, we can burst this balloon of confidence.
– John Callinan, 1986

YOU WOULDN'T HAVE given much for our chances of contesting a Munster final in 1986 when looking at the way the 1985 season had finished in both league and championship. Hammered, and hammered again.

And there was more bad news coming because there was no Tony Nugent for 1986 as he emigrated to America that year. Tony was a huge loss to the team. He was in the John Fenton or Jimmy Carroll mould, going up and down the field. He was a gifted hurler and could do so many things.

There were a lot of good players lost during those years between 1981 and '85. Barry Smythe got injured, but if it had happened when Fr Harry was there you know he would have gone as far as the Mayo Clinic in America to try and get him right and sort it out.

There was no one to do that once Fr Harry was gone – when that type of motivator like Fr Harry wasn't around, it was impossible to get players like Smythe to come back and play. He wasn't the only one.

But there was a change in management in the autumn of 1985 and from there things turned around. Seamus Durack came in as manager, with Martin

McKeogh as coach and Fr Harry and Mick Moroney as selectors. McKeogh was a very good coach and to us was a big step up from what had gone before.

We were back in Division 1 and went fairly well that winter and spring. In the first league game we were well beaten by Cork but then had big wins over Dublin and Limerick before losing to All-Ireland champions Offaly. We should've won that game but were beaten by a point.

Then before Christmas, I got a call from The Duke asking me to meet him for a drink and a chat. We met in O'Driscoll's in Corbally.

'How do you think things are going?'

'The results are better than the performances. We've gotten a few results.'

He started arguing with me.

'Do you only want me to tell what you want to hear?' I asked him.

The team went on to do early morning training that season, going to Lahinch, so it wasn't just in 1995 that this kind of regime was put in place by Ger Loughnane. The Duke was the first to do that and organised it, but that's not to say he was at all the sessions himself.

My line to him that day we met was, 'Do you think Tommy Guilfoyle gives a f**k how many kitchens you sell in Tulla or Bogner Regis. He doesn't!'

We had it hot and heavy. He called me because he wanted to be reassured. He called me because we were kindred spirits on so many levels and I had, and have, great time for him. We were in all the trenches together over the years. I don't think he held it against me, because if friends can't have a disagreement then they're not friends.

Still, all during that season we disagreed over where I should be playing on the team. I played six out of our seven National League games and was right corner-forward on every occasion – I hated playing there, even though I got 2-1 against Limerick in the third round.

I wanted out of the corner, but come championship I was still there.

Against Limerick in the quarter-final at Cusack Park I was in on Pat Herbert. My uncle was in the army and he rang me the night before to warn me about him, as if I didn't know about him. Pat was a tough operator.

Limerick started really well that day. The late Danny Fitzgerald was on fire and they went 0-8 to 0-1 up in the first quarter, but goals before half-time by my full-forward line colleagues Syl Dolan and Gerry McInerney got us back in the game and we dominated in the second-half to win by six. Then back in Cusack Park two weeks later we beat Tipperary. After they had beaten us in 1983, '84 and '85, it was some revenge and redemption, but from my own point of view I was still in the same corner and got well cleaned out of it by Seamus Gibson.

Still, we were back in a Munster final, in with another shot at that elusive title. And, we had every reason to be hopeful.

That's because there was no fantastic team around that year. There was no Cork side of the quality of that three in-a-row side; there was no side as good as the Limerick side that won Munster back-to-back in 1980 and '81.

On top of that, the great touch for us was that the Munster final was out of Thurles. Getting the game on in Killarney was a big thing for us. Maybe our luck would finally turn there.

BEFORE THE GAME, I pleaded with Duke not to play me in the full-forward line. I felt all I was doing there was bringing up the average age of that line of the attack. I was in the right corner, Tommy Guilfoyle was full-forward and Syl Dolan was in the other corner.

To me the forward line was all over the place. You had Gerry McInerney at wing-forward – that was crazy. Alan Cunningham was at centre-forward – even crazier, as he was a wing-back and then Seamie Fitzpatrick was on the other wing.

I asked him to give me 20 minutes out on MacCurtain. I had no grá for MacCurtain. He was a bête noire of mine. I didn't like him and I don't think he liked me. He was one of the only ones I didn't like.

I played on other lads like Sean Foley and Liam O'Donoghue and had no issues. Iggy Clarke was the best I played on. (I like to have amnesia regarding Ger Henderson). He was quick, a serious hurler and he could step forward and get a point off you which was a big thing then – a wing-back scoring off you was a real black mark in those days. He was a classy fella in lots of ways.

With MacCurtain, it's just that I didn't like him, even though I didn't know him at all. He had a strut about him and moaned all the time to the referee. I'd regard him as a small man, but he was no smaller than myself. If we were on a Munster team together, I'd be sitting with Tom Cashman and not Dermot MacCurtain, for no obvious reason. That's why I begged the Duke to put me on him, just to see what I could do.

I felt I could do well there. I was convinced of it.

'Gimme 20 minutes on him and if I don't do it, take me off.'

He wouldn't do it. I thought I should be wing-forward and Val Donnellan should have been in the corner. Instead, I was on Johnny Crowley and not that much play came my way. Meanwhile, playing McGow at wing-forward had worked as he had scored 1-1 off Denis Walsh and he was on fire. Tommy Guilfoyle was also playing very well at full-forward and Syl Dolan was holding his own in the other corner. Eventually they switched me out wing-forward and Seamie went into corner-forward.

After I moved out I could hear the Cork selectors, Jimmy Brohan, Pat McDonnell, Johnny Clifford and Dónal O'Grady in a knot talking. They all had All-Irelands and were planning switches. They were about to switch Tom Cashman out on McGow, but our selector Mick Moroney came down along and got Alan Cunningham to switch with McGow.

The Cork selectors didn't have to make the switch – we made it for them.

I did alright when I went on MacCurtain, even though I didn't set the world on fire. It was mainly to get it into Tommy Guilfoyle.

The game itself was a bit like a horse race. It was a case of which team had its head up or head down at the finish. It was a great chance, but there were some soft goals conceded by the defence.

Ger Loughnane was on Tomás Mulcahy, who was in the left corner. Tommy Keane always only played at No. 4, but Mulcahy and John Fitzgibbon switched corners and Loughnane followed Mulcahy. Tommy was lost at right corner-back; he just didn't have his bearings and Fitzgibbon got a goal.

Jimmy Barry got a goal without having had a puck before that because John Moroney had a very good game on him. Kevin Hennessy was coming in and as John Moroney went to meet him, he hand-passed to Jimmy Barry, who first timed it to the net past Eoin McMahon.

That was it and another chance had gone.

What if? Yet again!

For long periods it appeared as if the unthinkable was about to happen, noted Dónal Carroll in the *Irish Independent*, because, *No-hopers Clare gave not a hoot for reputations.*

But it wasn't enough, with Peadar O'Brien lamenting in *The Irish Press* that,

The great Clare dream of hurling glory lies shattered once again.

Clare proved the cynics wrong, mused Vincent Hogan, also in the *Independent. No, they did not collapse. No, they were not overawed. But ultimately, they failed to break the tradition of decades.*

Only an incurable romantic could reasonably argue that agony will help them in future battles. It will not. To be near and yet so far brings bitter trauma. Nothing more.

After the match I drowned my sorrows over a few pints in Jimmy O'Brien's, the famous football pub in Killarney. Billy Loughnane from Feakle got me in there, because the place was packed.

Then on our way home we stopped in Rathmore (where my Cork father-in-law, Tim O'Donovan stopped on his way home to Kilmallock after Munster football finals) and went into another pub.

There was a Cork fella inside.

He didn't know who I was but he turned to me. 'The match wasn't worth a damn. There wasn't skin lifted... or a hurley broke'.

I said nothing. I was finding defeats harder to take.

Definitely, it seemed like a good time to retire.

But still, it wasn't the right time.

« CHAPTER 21 »

The isolation and solitude of the Burren was disturbed by a flock of Magpies never previously seen in that part of the country at this time of year. Like the feathered variety these Magpies were looking for silverware.

— John Callinan, 1986

IN 1984, WEARING my GPA hat, I'd used my platform as a columnist with the *Clare County Express* newspaper to cast a players' gaze at the administration of the GAA as the association went about its business in its centenary year.

I didn't put the boot in at the start of the year as the GAA prepared to celebrate those 100 years. It was more a case of trying to point them through an open door and in the direction of some action.

Something new, something different. Surely they had it in them? I wrote...

From what we know the founding fathers of the GAA were radical far-seeing men from wide-ranging backgrounds, unafraid to break old moulds and new ground. Now the GAA is the establishment and is a bit unsure of its role straddling on the one side the games organisation and on the other the cultural, political and social movement.

Let's get on with it. Let's analyse and see what faults there may have been in the first 100 years. It was a good first century but there should be no sitting on boards or clapping on the back. Let's have some clear thinking, with clear objectives and less journeys on meaningless and at times dangerous tangents.

To put it mildly, I was very disappointed at what they came up with – finally putting the boot in at the end of the year. *There was little critical analysis within the GAA of the past year with a view to improving matters in the coming decades, rather there was a defensive and sometimes arrogant head in the sand reaction to analysis and questioning of certain positions taken by the GAA.*

In the end, what little change there was came at a local level when the Clare County Board departed from the norm by fixing its county finals in hurling and football in Gleann Cíosóg, Carron, in homage to Michael Cusack and the place of his birth.

The football final went ahead there, but the hurling was cancelled at the 11th hour. It wasn't a hurling pitch because it was too narrow, but after reaching the county final we would gladly have played there. Just being back in a county final after what the club had been through since 1978 was huge – we'd have played that match in a carpark or a farmer's field.

OUR OPPONENTS SIXMILEBRIDGE, however, wouldn't go to Carron, so Cusack Park it was. The 'Bridge were in their third successive final – their fifth in three years if you take in the two replays in 1982 and '83 against Éire Óg. They were very strong, as they proved after beating us and then going on to win the Munster club title for the first time.

But we could have beaten them.

What sticks out is when I was kicking the ball to safety towards the end-line for a '65' as we held on to a narrow lead. Out of nowhere, Gerry McInerney appeared and with the slightest of deflections guided the ball inside the left hand post. That was a hugely important goal late on in the match and they went on to beat us by a point.

Two years later we got back to the final and this time we were going to Carron, as it came up to the requirements laid out by the county board. It certainly was time for us to win the big one, as we squared off against O'Callaghan's Mills, who hadn't won a title since 1937.

We went up by bus to Ballyvaughan and had tea and sandwiches in Hyland's Hotel, and then went for a walk down to the pier. Looking out on Galway Bay an hour before a county final was really strange and weird.

Barney Lynch was always the best craic around any Clarecastle team. At the flick of a switch, he'd make the most serious thing sound hilarious. As we walked around Ballyvaughan village that day some of his jokes were questionable, while others were just plain bad. They were so bad we had to laugh at them, but it meant that we were totally relaxed when it came to the game.

The dressing-rooms in Carron were tiny, so we couldn't even stomp on the spot to warm up before going out. The crowd were on the touchline and nearly on top of us. All this with the backdrop of Mullaghmore mountain.

It was a strange experience even before we got to puck a ball.

I was doing the team warm up and Dermot Fitzgerald was huddled over in the corner having a fag for himself. He wasn't going to be running over and back the field and warming up in public. He didn't need to and played well, just like we all played well. It was a game we controlled from the start, leading all the way before goals in the last few minutes from George Power and Victor O'Loughlin gave us a comfortable 10-point victory.

At the end of the game, I made my way to my old friend and sparring partner, Paschal Russell. We hugged.

'Is this it?' I began. I was a bit under-whelmed at winning my first senior championship.

'No,' he replied, 'the Munster club'. He was right, though that did not prevent us celebrating for several days.

We played a good Mount Sion team in Cusack Park in the Munster quarter-final and beat them well. Then we beat St Brendan's from Kerry in the semi-final back at Cusack Park, with the final against Borris-Illeigh in Limerick.

We didn't play well and the game was over at half-time when they were leading by 1-8 to 0-2. We got back into it in the second-half to get within four but we were never going to win. Noel O'Dwyer beat us that day with nine points from frees. I was being marked by Bobby Ryan and I didn't have a good game at all.

By then I'd decided to give one more year with the county team. I didn't need much persuading as the lads asked me to be captain. I was flattered.

APART FROM BEING captain, I was moved out from corner-forward to midfield, and then to wing-back. I was in a part of the field where I got be influential and still had a bit left in my legs. Corner-forward, to me, was kind of a rest home before you got dropped for good, so being moved was a new lease of life for me.

And I had a decent season hurling wise.

By this time, myself Stack and Loughnane had started to become the three-hand reel on the team. The fellas who were beaten in all the Munster finals going back the years. A recurring theme amongst journalists was, 'Let's get the three fellas who were beaten in all the Munster finals together'.

It was a case of… *If a Clare story is needed, we'll talk to the three boys.*

We were all happy to soldier away for the cause – and for ourselves – and that season we had a great run in the league, with way less intensity in our preparation when compared to other years. Maybe a bit of the Brendan Vaughan thing came in there – throttling down in the league and not pushing it, and then building it up gradually for the championship.

We could have won the league along the way, though. Galway prevailed in the end by 3-12 to 3-10 for a victory that kickstarted a golden era for them, but in that stand-alone game it could have been us.

We got a great start and led by 0-4 to 0-1 in the early stages, but it was the goal chances that decided things. Joe Cooney struck first with two in the first-half – they led 2-4 to 0-7 at the break.

Early in the second-half we hit back with two within the space of a minute – I centred a ball to Tommy Guilfoyle, who slammed to the net, before Gerry McInerney fired home a free to put us back in front.

However, when Galway responded quickly with their third through Anthony Cunningham, it proved the critical score of the game. They were never headed after that, even though our third from Syl Dolan still gave us a fighting chance going into the closing minutes. Gerry McInerney had his chance right at the end that could have snatched it for us.

'If I'd hit it cleanly, it was a certain goal,' he said afterwards, 'but the ball was in a hole so I tried to flick it out before shooting. I mishit it, it was a real sickener.'

Afterwards, we were in the Ragg for a meal and the Duke was complaining about us not winning and the opportunity that was lost. Lifting the National League trophy would have been huge for me – after all, I would only have been the fourth Clareman to do it after my clubmate Haulie Daly, and Jimmy McNamara and Sean Stack.

But I wasn't hugely disappointed either, because we had put very little into the league. I felt we should have done more, but I was annoyed with the Duke because I thought the whole object of the league was about performance, not about where and how it ended. We had put in a decent performance and were going places, and it should have been looked at in those terms.

But in response to losing the final the management started to change the team in subsequent challenge matches. I used to travel to matches with James Shanahan from Broadford. They switched me from midfield to wing-back, and James was gone to centre-forward.

There was a lot of chopping and changing. It was as if not winning the league final seemed to unnerve the lads. They got cross, felt the need to make wholesale changes and appeared to lose confidence in us.

We had beaten Tipperary in the league semi-final. After that, Babs changed his team around completely. He had to because otherwise they were going nowhere. When we played them in the first Munster semi-final in Killarney, we were lucky to draw with them – then they hammered us in the replay.

People ask me, what happened between the drawn game and the replay against Tipp that year? I say, what happened in the six weeks between the end of the league and the championship. A lot happened.

We were terrible.

BEING BEATEN BY 4-17 to 0-8 on my final day as a Clare player and as captain was not a good way to go. I didn't even make it to the end of the game as I got injured before half-time trying to tackle Joe Hayes.

I always loved the physicality of county hurling and was strong for my size. There were shoulders in the chest that time, which I got and gave, and I always felt that if a fella caught you with a shoulder in the chest it was your own fault, not his. In the 1981 Munster semi-final Cork's full-back Dónal O'Grady buried me and only that I was in good shape, I would not have recovered from it.

I got caught in this game though and there was no way back.

I was trying to 'do' Hayes, to bury him with a hit.

It was right in the middle of the field. Joe was down over the ball to rise it and he missed it – I had him, expecting him to come up. I was going to put him into the next parish with a shoulder. Instead, he stayed down and I went right over his shoulder, but my leg got trapped and I injured my knee really badly.

That was it. Not the way I had planned to go, but it was over.

◄◄◆►►

Seanie O'Leary is supposed to have said that it is better to have people asking you why did you retire rather than why don't you retire. Given that nobody asked me why I retired I must presume they have been asking the other question for a while and I have been stone deaf. Either way I think the old phrase of a good run being better than a bad stand covers the situation. I have had a long innings. I am disappointed at not achieving my ambition of Munster and All-Ireland championships, but there are no regrets. I have got a lot more out of it than I have put into it. It is time for a new broom.

– John Callinan, 1987

IT WASN'T HARD to walk away.

The difficulty was going quietly. I wasn't able to, so much so that less than two months after our championship exit, I marched into the August meeting of the Clare County Board to have my say.

There was a big crowd in the West County Hotel as the election of a new manager to succeed Seamus Durack was on the agenda. My old team-mate Sean Hehir got the job, but that's not what I was there for.

I was there because of what was said at the July meeting of the Clare Hurling Board. I thought the criticism was naive, uninformed and destructive – that the team were 'over-trained and tired' and that Clare teams didn't prepare like they do in other counties.

As outgoing captain, I wanted my say and my club delegate asked the permission of the top table to allow me to speak. The request was ruled out of order by the chairman Robert Frost.

Being a Clare player and the team's captain for that year didn't mean speaking rights could be conferred on me, because I wasn't an official delegate. I was silenced, so I left the meeting there and then.

That night, I penned my thoughts in the *Express*.

The remarks from the July meeting shows us to be innocent almost to the point of simple-mindedness. I don't have the answer for the collective failure of the team, but over-training or too much physical wasn't the problem. The people that propound this theory, that first achieved notoriety in the late 1970s in a column of The Clare Champion written by a prominent board officer under a pen name, are dangerous to the ambition of any Clare team. They speak from no practical background of team preparation.

They have no idea of the physical and mental preparation necessary at inter-county level. Further, they induce an unwillingness to work hard while naively believing every word that drops from the mouth of the successful. They are not even-handed or fair in their comments. I did not hear any praise for the trainer when the team was being lauded after last year's Munster final when we kept coming back at Cork. The trainer was the same both years and the preparation was very similar. We will win nothing unless we are physically and mentally prepared. Neither will the successful tell us how to be successful.

I clearly needed to put that down. It was a cleansing exercise and maybe it was a way of retiring on my own terms and making a clean break before turning my attention back towards the club as we set about trying to retain our senior title.

CLARECASTLE HAD NEVER done that before, but from my own point of view that title defence had begun nearly a year previously after we lost the Munster final to Borris-Illeigh in the Gaelic Grounds.

On the way back the team bus stopped somewhere between Newmarket and Clarecastle, and I jumped up and said a few words. 'We are all going to get pissed and pissed for a week, but this is not the way this group should finish. We'll have another cut at this.'

My words were motivated by the fact that I was really cross with the way I played myself. I had no status when I stood up in the bus to try and rally everyone for the following year. I wasn't captain; I wasn't the elder statesman. Patrick Kelly was the trainer of the team, but I became trainer in 1987 and wanted the job badly.

We got back to the final where we faced Feakle, but it was the semi-final when Kilmaley took us to two replays that really made us. Feakle were waiting for us in the final for six weeks. They were the coming team after winning four under-21 titles in-a-row, but we had it over them and they couldn't beat us. I started that county final at wing-forward.

The two Guilfoyles and Val Donnellan were key men for Feakle – it was Mikey who would start the runs and open it up for Tommy or Val. I was adamant, 'He has to be stopped, he can't make these 30 or 40 yard runs… it will kill us'.

Very early on, Mike went on one of those runs but Tommy Howard met him after he had it laid off. I was about 20 yards away and could almost hear the air going out of Mikey's lungs. He was nailed.

I'd been there myself when on the receiving end. When it happens, you're wondering if you're ever going to get a breath again. But when it's on the other side, there's no sympathy.

'Get up Mikey for f**k sake!'

Val and Tommy were then jawing at me.

'You're over the hill Callinan.'

'I got up the hill more than you did Val.'

Then Val was taking the free and there was more.

'Put it over the bar if you're a man.'

He lifted the ball and it was only gone five yards and I knew it was going over the black spot. By the time it was gone over, I was long gone from Val. I'm not necessarily proud of that, but you did what you had to do to try and get that edge.

In my entire career, I hit one player deliberately with my hurley and that was in this county final. I don't think I was dirty and never saw any great value to be gained out of dirty play. I had seen dirty play in Clarecastle and saw that it got the club nowhere, apart from winning us a bad reputation.

In this instance I hit Tommy Guilfoyle, because I just couldn't stop him.

It wasn't a moral decision, but it was a pragmatic decision.

I always loved the physical contest in hurling. I liked hitting fellas with my body. I won't say I liked getting hit, but if I got hit that was part of it as well.

That's a bit macho, but I liked that part of it.

I HAD MOVED to centre-back from wing-forward to mark Val Donnellan.

Tommy was full-forward. Val was calling for the ball and I was sledging him…

'Call for the ball when he's hitting it out, there's no point calling for it when it's in the crowd'.

Val put his hand up and I hit him a good slap.

'Put the f**king hand up when the ball is coming'. He had to do it then and I cleaned the ball out of his hand.

Then Tommy came out.

It was like the eclipse of the moon when he stood in front of me. Victor O'Loughlin was midfield and he was backing and backing into me after Liam Moloney pucked out the ball and I thought he was going to challenge in front of Tommy.

I was two yards behind Tommy and he caught it cleanly between the two of us and turned, and I went off square and went for him with my shoulder – he was running at me and something just tempted me, fear maybe, and as I got in close, I brought up the pole of the hurley and gave him a belt into the jaw. I was making it look like I shouldered him.

It stopped him.

The belt into the chin stopped him. The referee, Michael Quinn was running in and I was running back. Mikey Guilfoyle was running out to have a go at me, with Anthony Scanlan saying, 'Go on… go on!' But there was no fear of Mikey hitting me.

By the time I made it to the '21' Quinn came over to me.

'What's your name?'

'For what?'

'Give me your name now!'

'Is this a man's game or what… are you not allowed shoulder someone anymore?'

'And how would you account for his head coming back?'

'Get your hand off my shoulder… give me your name before I send you off.'

GER LOUGHNANE NEARLY won that county title on his own for Feakle. He was brilliant, but in the second-half Kenny Morrissey took the wind out of his sails a bit. Kenny was 21 then, but didn't start the final. I was livid with that but had no say, because even though I was the trainer, I wasn't a selector.

We were out in the Auburn Lodge before the game and Kenny turned to me and said, 'I'll help us win it yet'. I thought it was a great attitude and he came on without 15 minutes to go and he soon buried Loughnane with a shoulder. George Power was on Loughnane at that time and got booked for it by his first cousin Michael Quinn.

Afterwards, Seamus Gardiner told me that when I went to centre-back I didn't hit many balls down the middle. I told him I'd hit it into the river rather than down the middle, just to keep it away from Loughnane. He was that good that day.

It was the most enjoyable match I ever played for Clarecastle. I had the satisfaction of training the team, I was playing, and I played well and we won.

People always talk about the first one you win, but the second one was a lot better for me. It was in Cusack Park, it was more like a county final.

« CHAPTER 22 »

I think it was about the Thursday after the great day before it finally sunk in when I saw a sticker on the back of a car proclaiming that we were the champions in colours that were definitely ours and not anybody else's. We had now taken our place among the hurling nations. No more will columnists, television, radio people and amateur psychologists and psychoanalysts wonder what is deficient in the Clare psyche. No more will we be asked why can we not win. For that alone we should be most grateful to this great team of players and mentors.

— John Callinan, 1995

IT WAS OVER, but it's never over.

It wasn't over because you're always hurling, even if you mightn't be holding a hurley in your hand and never again will.

Seventeen years pulling on a Clare jersey since my first day as a minor against Tipperary through to my last day as a senior against the same opposition. In that time there were 29 senior championship appearances and 93 in the National League for a grand total of 124 senior outings.

A nice figure, with some great days along the way, but plenty of dark days too. I'd change some of it, but I loved to play and I loved the contest. Every ball was a contest, so every match, every half hour and every ball I was going for was a contest.

I loved that duel element to it.

Sometimes, I was ahead in the contest, sometimes I wasn't. The contest was the big thing, what attracted me to hurling.

And the craic was great.

People might say to me, 'You were very unlucky!'

Yes, we had big disappointments and never reached the mountaintop, but my answer is, 'You've no idea how lucky we were!'

People have also asked, 'Wouldn't you have loved to win a medal?'

I'm not actually sure a medal would have given me any more joy. It probably would have, but I don't think I would have been happier in my heart if it had been me winning that All-Ireland medal in 1995, rather than being a supporter.

It would have been a different satisfaction but in terms of what the win in 1995 meant for hurling people, going back to the time of my father, Dónal Carey, John Hanly and all the people who had promoted it and kept it alive, there was a huge satisfaction in what was achieved.

WE WERE PLAYING in the best of times, when we could nearly decide how much we trained. We weren't on GPS. We were proper and serious amateurs, which is really what we should be.

They shouldn't be preparing the way they are now, unless they're professionals, which they're not.

Many times since Clare's glory years in the 90s Anthony Daly has told me that my generation had the best of it when we were hurling – that we took it very seriously, but that we still managed to have the craic and along the way we also had an unbelievable time.

My answer to him is always, 'Give me your medals and you can have the craic!'

But he's right in what he says every time.

It was a great time to be hurling, and hurling gave the Clare teams I was part of for 17 years far more than any medals we won or lost on the field.

Lots of things happened in our time. I'm talking about socio-economically. Free-Education, people having work, having cars that allowed them travel to Thurles, to Wexford, to Kilkenny... anywhere they wanted to go.

It was a generation that was starting to get on the move. There was more and more work in Shannon; there was less emigration and we represented that kind of movement and change in Clare, but not just in Clare.

Without Shannon, Clare would have been backward. We recognised that at the time. We were cocky enough. We fancied ourselves in lots of ways and we loved the limelight of representing the county. We had a decent rapport with the supporters, and had great fun.

We were comfortable together. We regarded ourselves as close friends. Loughnane and Honan weren't big drinkers, so they wouldn't have been out and about as much as some of us. Loughnane was a small bit of a loner, but we were all tolerant of that.

Sean Hehir was a complicated and complex fella – so serious and so intense and hard on himself, but everybody loved him. We used to have great craic with Hacker, but I don't know if he realised it was craic.

A lot of us have been at each other's weddings. I was Colm Honan's Best Man. He and I trained in the gym in the NCPE, now the University of Limerick, and later in my 'home made' gym in Ardnacrusha. Enda supplied the car for my wedding. He was my closest friend. I usually travelled with him to games and we were never far apart. Duke wasn't far away either.

Maybe 'The Scene' was unchallenging, maybe it was a bit too tight and maybe it was harder to get off the team than on it for a few years. But we all wanted the same thing.

WHAT WOULD IT have been like to win a Munster and an All-Ireland?

We'll never know.

Thing is, I never played to win the championship. I played to win the match, and then the next match.

I saw that with Kilkenny and Tipperary fellas. They played to win the medal. I was the other way around. Maybe it was a quirk of my own personality and this sounds like I was easily satisfied.

I wasn't.

I was a horrendous loser.

After a big defeat I'd be nobody's company for two or three days, at work or at home. I hated those days and as the years dragged on, I got worse.

I was always that intense, be it club or county. At the very end of my career, I thought we could have achieved much more at club level – an example is that

I absolutely resented giving the 1988 championship to Feakle. That's the way I saw it.

We lost to Ruan in the semi-final that year and I was out of order after it. We were going for three in-a-row and I was angry that we didn't achieve it.

I attacked Anthony Scanlan, one of the most decent and nicest fellas you could meet in life. He had retired in 1988 and I challenged him down in Power's about it.

'Why did you retire?'

I said the same to Dermot Fitzgerald. Mrs Power had to come out from behind the bar and tell me to quieten down. Another time, I had words with a good young fella who won a Harty in 1976 and played one or two matches with us, but then didn't play at all.

We came from Navin's over to Power's and he turned at the counter and said, 'Jesus, ye went down badly today'. Mrs Power was just arriving with two pints and I had my fist up. She nearly let the two pints fall.

'I'm very, very sorry Mrs Power.'

WE HAD THREE widows running pubs in Clarecastle at that time – Mrs Power, Mrs Navin and my mother. I was looking at Mrs Power and was thinking of my mother. I walked down the lane and got home as my mother was closing up and she said, 'Were you fighting up the street?'

The word had travelled down.

I probably experienced more depths.

I'd go deeper than I'd go high. We didn't have that many wins, but when we didn't have that many, you'd think that we'd get very high when they did come.

The depths of defeat and the over-analysis of what should have been done – what I could have done myself and what other fellas could have done – got me down. Never to a clinical state, but I would have got myself drunk for a couple of days when we'd talk even more rubbish and become even more depressed.

In the late 80s I genuinely felt Clarecastle had a chance of winning four in-a-row. We played in the county final in 1989 and got beaten by the 'Bridge.

I could have been off the team in '89, but how bad would that have been with the young guns like Anthony Daly, Fergie Tuohy, Alan Neville and all these guys coming through. I wanted to be part of it.

After that I played with Parteen in 1990 and '91. I thought I wasn't going to be a huge loss to Clarecastle and because I was living in South East Clare for so long, I thought I'd give them something for a few years.

I didn't even know the colour of the Parteen jerseys when I joined, but I think I gave the club a bit of a lift. They were Junior A and I had a few good games with them. It was a perspective I'd never seen before.

In my first year with Parteen I also go involved with the Clare under-21s. Seamus Durack was manager, with Fr Willie Walsh, Ger Loughnane, Enda O'Connor and myself with him.

In 1991 we got sponsored by Noel Keating of Kepak in Meath; Noel was originally a Kilrush man. In doing that we were almost operating independently of the county board. We had our own little independent republic going. There wasn't an awful lot of money involved, but getting the sponsorship was a statement nonetheless.

We had fellas like PJ O'Connell, Ger Moroney, Stephen Sheedy, Pat Healy and Pat Minogue on that team. We had a decent team and played loads of challenge games. I remember one night PJ O'Connell roasting Pat O'Neill, who became a bit of cult figure with the Kilkenny seniors afterwards.

But when we came to pick the team for the Limerick match in Kilmallock, it was completely different to the one that played a lot of the challenges. I had a falling out with Durack over it because I felt it was a compromised team.

Limerick had Ciaran Carey as their main man. If he was wing-forward, Ger Moroney was supposed to be on him, if he was midfield Stephen Sheedy would pick him up.

We had ended up with nobody's team.

Walking around the field beforehand, Loughnane said to me, 'If we don't beat this crowd by 10 points we're going nowhere!' My answer to that was, 'If we don't beat them we're definitely going nowhere'.

Pat Heffernan beat us on his own that night.

The following year Durack stepped down and he wanted me to be the manager for 1992. I told him to go away and organise that with Brendan Vaughan, and see how he'd get on. I never heard anything after that. I got no phone call and wasn't surprised. Enda O'Connor didn't either.

Instead Ger Loughnane got the team, with Louis Mulqueen and Mike

McNamara with him. That was Loughnane's third year with the 21s.

This was the team that had reached the All-Ireland minor final in 1989. I brought my son Eamon to the Munster final against Waterford in Thurles; it was the first big match he was at. I was going to start him off with a winning Munster final.

It didn't work out.

THERE WAS ALWAYS the club.

That year, in 1992, Ger Ward who was team manager asked me to train the seniors. When I agreed, he said that I might as well transfer back and play a bit of intermediate. I ended up playing a few league games for the seniors.

About four weeks before the championship Ger asked me did I want to play or train the team, because I couldn't do the two.

I was waiting for him to make that proposition, or else I was going to say it myself. It was agreed between us – Ger took over the training of the team, but then turned around and left me off. I couldn't believe it.

I was livid. As mad as I was on the day of my father's funeral 30 years earlier when they played without me. We were playing the old enemy Newmarket in the first round and us older lads in the squad were convinced that the younger lads didn't appreciate them or respect them enough.

They had three goals in the first 10 minutes. Paddy Quinn and myself were brought on at half-time. We were playing into the Tulla goal and Newmarket had a young fella, Tom McNamara corner-back – they used to call him 'The Hound'.

He ran out towards me. I accelerated and drove my shoulder into his chest and rocked him. Then I ran straight for Seanie McMahon who was full-back; he just turned his back and walked towards the goal. I couldn't shoulder him in the back.

There used to be a handful of Clarecastle supporters – call them the ultras – who used to gather at the back of the goal under the scoreboard, and I roared up at them. They got going. I was just livid with everybody, with whole world really.

The first ball came in and I got it, turned and beat my man, and Seanie McMahon met me and drove me back and I put the ball over the bar. Then I ran at Seanie again and he turned his back again.

'You f**ker Seanie.'

'I wasn't going to go fighting with you to get Clarecastle going… that's all you were doing,' he said to me later.

That was the whole plan in my own mind – go in and cause a bit of havoc. *If I need to get put off here… get put off!* I got another point.

We made a bit of a fight of it but it wasn't enough. As defending champions, we were unceremoniously dumped out of the championship.

That was it then.

My last senior game.

I was still mad going off the field.

WE'LL CALL IT our Doonbeg moment. That game against Newmarket came seven days after the Clare footballers had won the Munster championship. A couple of our more eminent players went back to celebrate Clare's win in the Munster football final. They had a long night in the Long Village.

I felt that they should have been training with the club.

They should not have gone drinking.

I'd been at the Munster final myself. Living in Ardnacrusha at the time and just a few miles from the Gaelic Grounds, at about 2.45pm, just under an hour before Paddy Russell threw in the ball, it was a case of… *Jesus, I better show some face and go in and watch them on their big day.*

Then after John Maughan's side famously beat Kerry to win Clare's first Munster senior football title in 75 years I was with a crowd afterwards in Begley's Bar in Clonlara having a few pints.

We were celebrating, but we were hurling people, not football people, so when someone piped up… 'It's not really us', there was wasn't much else left to be said.

It was great, but we were *hurling* and this was *football*.

It didn't mean as much. It couldn't.

Still, we went to the All-Ireland semi-final against Dublin, just to see a Clare team play in Croke Park. It was a day never to forget – parking the car outside Conway's Bar on Parnell Street where Pearse had surrendered to the British after the 1916 Rising, then turning the corner to make my way to the Royal Dublin Hotel to meet my Clarecastle teammate and great footballer, Barney Lynch, and seeing another uprising as Clare supporters were taking over both sides of O'Connell Street all the way to Croke Park.

Writing my column in the *Clare County Express* afterwards I parked my hurling allegiances and bias. *This group of Clare footballers and their mentors have raised the self-worth of the whole of County Clare, east and west… it was indeed great to take one's place amongst the counties of the world to paraphrase a great patriot.*

The football gave us that and I could appreciate what those few months had done for county Clare. When it happened for the hurlers three years later, it was just the same, only magnified.

AS A SUPPORTER and an old hurler, I could see what the game and the success meant.

The night of the Munster final win.

The team stopping in Clarecastle; we had organised a lorry. It was fantastic.

The Ryans, a family of musicians, were playing and I lost the run of myself, calling them the Hogans, their mother's maiden name. I was the MC!

Loughnane and Daly were brilliant that night.

The Galway match in 1995 was just a day out, like the footballers' semi-final was. I didn't care. Then after the All-Ireland I met my old teammate Tony Nugent out on the field.

It was personal to everybody.

I was on Limerick 95 radio and made a mess of saying, 'Tiocfaidh ár Lá'. The amount of people that heard it amused me. Hego would have loved… 'Tiocfaidh ár Lá' though.

The day had arrived. By then, in August 1995, we had moved from Ardnacrusha back to Clarecastle. Good timing.

Afterwards, as we came home through Limerick and they were clapping the Clare cars at Hassett's Cross down from Thomond Park. There was hardly anyone in Clarecastle that Sunday night. I was wired, had very little to drink and got up the following day to go to the office, but there was nobody around.

Then we spent all day waiting for the team to come back.

Those days and nights, I understood why Dalo and the boys needed to head into the west for Doonbeg that night in 1992 and to drink through the night with everyone else instead of taking the pledge for the Newmarket game.

They had to see it.

They had to see it, in the hope that it could be them, and could be us, as hurlers. And when it was them and us in 1995, it's why I turned to Ger Loughnane on the podium in Clarecastle.

'We've won that Munster championship at last… we can die happy now'.

I really meant it.

I never meant anything more in my life.

That's what hurling has meant to me.

EPILOGUE

Epilogue

SOPHIA WAS IN her push-buggy, and I was walking her to Clareabbey, where my mother and father are buried. It was late afternoon. A Friday, late summer in 2019, and the end of another ordinary week, when I took a call from Liam Hayes and we chatted, for the first time, about the idea of this book.

This book of memories.

My *memoir*! Something I had not given any thought to, ever before, not until Liam informed me that his company Hero Books would like to publish my story as part of their 'Legend's Series'.

An autobiography?

An official legend?

I didn't believe I qualified for an autobiography.

And legend? In Clare, and also in Clarecastle, I would not be near the front of the line of hurlers deserving such a title. Liam suggested I put that 'difficulty', that 'doubt' of mine, to one side to begin with – and we never did get back to talking that bit through.

He wanted to talk about the good reasons I should have for writing a book. I had none, not really. We talked.

He wanted me to think of bringing people – readers of this book – back to another time and another place. Different times, different places, and in each introduce readers to a cast of characters who populated my life. This book is about them, too, Liam told me.

And he told me to picture myself on stage – he actually mentioned me sitting in the front row of the Gaiety Theatre, and looking at all of the people on the stage.

'You're going to be in the middle of the stage!' he told me, and then he told me not to worry about that.

So, here I am walking off that stage, and I am doing so happily. But first I want to remember that walk with Sophia and that first chat.

And if there was one good reason to have this book published, then it was because it gave me the opportunity of dedicating it to the special little girl in our lives, Sophia, who is now three years-old. I also get to dedicate this book to my beautiful sister, Mary who has now passed after she battled cancer, but never let the cancer break her.

Two great reasons, in fact, that leave me not in any way stressed about producing any other reasons.

So, Sophia and I were heading to Clareabbey. It's a nice walk, and I like to head there, not just for sentimental reasons. About 20 minutes. I never brought Sophia for longer walks than that, in case she 'lost the head' with me. Not that she ever has.

Sophia is a huge presence in our lives. She is a special child in every way, not least because she arrived into this world an awful lot earlier than she was expected to, and weighed less than two and a half pounds.

Her birth, and her survival, is a story of the toughness of nature… the fight and strength in all of us, even those amongst us who first appear so delicate and tiny. When we look at the photographs of her now, we can only shake our heads in wonder.

She remained in the hospital for a long time. I sneaked in once to catch a glimpse of her, though only after Sophia's two grandmothers sneaked in the week before me! In one photograph, all you can see is Sophia's head. The rest of the photograph looks like an empty blanket.

But everything went smoothly enough, once the brilliant midwife insisted that Louise go into hospital, that scary day for Eamon and Louise, and all of us.

Nature, indeed!

We had Sophia's arrival into this world, and Mary's imminent passing. One person leaving this life, one person arriving.

Sophia and Mary were, and remain, two people who gave me good reason to have the story of my own life – and portions of the lives of the people I have known – published. Like everyone else, when you are first asked to consider having a memoir published, your initial thought and fear is of having your 'privacy' disturbed, and perhaps rudely so!

So, be it.

This book has been an opportunity to tell Sophia and Mary that I love them, tell my wife Siobhán how much I love her, and also our children, Aoife and Eamon. And it was also an opportunity to thank so many other people who have been there for me in my life.

AS I'VE SAID, it was an 'ordinary' week in the summer of 2019.

None of us knew anything about, or suspected, the extraordinary events that were just around the corner and how all of our lives were going to be, not just 'disturbed' but thrown upside down, and upside down again, because of Covid-19.

In early February 2020, I went to see Mary for the last time.

Mary lived in England, in south London. There were five of us siblings all sitting down to dinner together in a nice restaurant; Anne hadn't been able it make it over. Mary always had such a great smile. In the earliest photographs, there was always that smile, and if you looked at us sitting at the table in the restaurant you would never know which member of the Callinan family was dying.

Mary was smiling, still full of life.

We were in the early stages of the first rumblings of the worldwide pandemic. We all found it scary, didn't we?

In London, however, there appeared a foolhardy disregard for what was descending on our lives. So, when we needed to talk to Mary after that memorable dinner, we resorted to Skype and Zoom meetings, all of which were difficult, because of the lack of intimacy, the lack of warmth.

We all understood, at that point, that we would not see our sister alive again. With that thought, I became really low in myself, and miserable. I had never felt so low. April 12, Easter Sunday, was my 65th birthday… and *was* I especially *miserable*!

Leo Varadkar wasn't helping. When I listened to him, I thought the end of the world was upon us, and on the day of my birthday, it was one wet, awful day.

I could not even get out for a walk, to clear my head. I looked to read something.

I had been reading about Hemingway and Roald Dahl... don't ask me why! They were in the same house during the terrifying Spanish Flu. They were cocooning, in this house, somewhere in the south of France.

One of them said they had better check provisions, in case they needed to hunker down and stay out of harm's way for a long, long time. They did their check-list... wine, brandy, absinthe, whiskey... enough bottles of other things to make cocktails for many months!

Ok... I told myself.

And I spent the next couple of hours distracting myself, seeing in our case if we had enough of everything in our house to get through a pandemic.

We had enough alcohol, anyway.

That was my lowest day in 2020, until the day that Mary died. Her failing health was distressing for all of us. She has a husband, Brian and two daughters, and Brian caught the virus. Mary also caught the virus, and survived it. The virus did not end it for her.

Brian, the girls, and our brother Eamon, were all in London at the time, all of them in quarantine. I had a dread for days, that Mary would die and that none of them would be able to leave the house. That Mary's body would be brought out alone, and that she would remain alone.

Mary died in May.

Everything about our everyday lives was abnormal. We were coming to terms with living our lives in lockdown. In the last week or so, I found Skype harder still. It was not how I wished to remember Mary.

As always in England, there was a long delay before the funeral could be held. The pandemic did not help. I had no idea what to do. Finally, I decided I needed to go...

I drove to Dublin. Stayed overnight in an airport hotel, and the next day flew out... double masked and gloved, goggles too. There were only about 15 people on the Ryanair flight. I had a taxi booked from Gatwick airport to Mary's home.

I got to say goodbye to my sister.

I CAME HOME to Ireland the following day.

And into two weeks of self-isolation. I stayed in my room, though I went out and walked the land on my own, without seeing a soul. I also sat out in the backgarden, all alone, thinking, about life, about everything.

Aoife, my daughter, brought me my one 'hot' meal of the day, leaving it on the window-sill.

I got my own breakfast in my own 'quarters'. But my days of solitude were taken up with work, and were never an eternity. IT introduced itself to me and Aoife brought home files from my office in Ennis.

The second Wednesday, with another three days to go, I was invited to play a game of golf. I could not say yes. I remained half-terrified that I had brought something back from England. I hadn't, thank God.

On the Saturday morning, I packed the car.

Fourteen days had ended, and Siobhán and I headed off to West Cork for a fortnight's break. Where we have holidayed all of our adult lives, and Siobhán before. In Ballydehob, where Siobhán's father's family had first taken root.

West Cork.

Where the pandemic was forgotten, or at least pushed back for a little while, and we got to live for a little while as though life was almost back to 'normal'.

CLOSE TO THE end of her life, a couple of weeks before she passed after a long illness, my mother say to me, 'I should never have given up the fags!'

My mother, who died from leukaemia, had stopped smoking seven or eight years previously. But she had been a smoker all of her life.

She was in hospital in Galway for treatment and, remarkably, had enjoyed 18 months of excellent health before she relapsed. This was 1990, and I got to spend a great deal of precious time with her, as I frequently brought her to the hospital for her visits and her chemotherapy.

She was a classic Irish mother, but because my father had died so young, she literally became *everything* to us. She was not overly religious. However, religion still played a huge part in her life. It was there for her, and for us, she believed.

Particularly for her, during the harder times in her life, I expect.

Near the end, she was on morphine in the hospital, where she would eventually pass on a Monday night. On the Sunday morning, Mary had been with her, having spent the night by her bed. I arrived at about 8.0am.

She was not saying very much at this stage.

A youngish priest suddenly arrived into her room, someone I had not seen before. I was looking at him and wondering… *So, where have you been while she was suffering here all these weeks… and really needed you?*

Maybe I was being unfair to him, I don't know.

For those last few days she had been lying on her right shoulder in the bed, as she always did, hanging out over the edge of the bed. Looking at her, I had to fight the urge not to push her back into the bed fully. I wanted to see her more comfortable, more at ease in her final days and hours.

The priest, who might have been in his twenties, I'd guess, was by the side of the bed. I felt he was looking at me, sitting there in the only chair in the room. I felt he wanted to sit down in the chair.

I got up.

He sat down. About two feet away from my mother, and he said… 'Mary…'

There was no sign of life in my mother.

I was standing over the priest's right shoulder, when he said, 'Mary… we'll say a few prayers'.

I don't know why I was agitated by his presence, but I was… *She could have done with you here a week ago!*

When she could actually see you… hear you!

'We'll say some prayers for a comfortable passage!'

My mother suddenly opened an eye.

Her left eye, and she looked up at him.

'Does that mean… I'm dying Father?'

The poor man nearly died on the spot himself. But that was my mother. She was always so strong, but she was also a ball-hopper with people. As a publican most of her life, she had to be ready to meet and duel with everybody and anybody in all kinds of conversations. I thought, at times, she over-did the slagging.

But those were the last words I heard her speak… 'Does that mean… I'm dying Father?'

I liked to think that there was a twinkle in her left eye as she put the poor man back in his box.

She was only 67 when she passed. A young woman, very young still I realise, now that I am only one year younger than she was that same year she passed.

I was 35 years of age in 1990.

My mother's only brother, Peter Hayes is still alive. He's 99 years young, living in Dublin! There were just the two of them in the family.

Anne, who was 14 when our father died, minded us in those years, Anne and Mary were like second mothers, but my mother was never all that busy in the pub, or The Shop as we called it, for long periods of the week. It was a country pub. I now wonder and try to re-imagine her life during those years.

But it is always hard to get a full picture in my mind of my mother… because, I suppose, your mother is your *mother*! You don't stop as a child or even a young man, to look at your mother and think about what she's *thinking*, or what exactly is happening in her life. She's your *mother*.

What do I know? I know that she was wonderful. Strong and caring, and brilliantly ordinary in handling the whole lot of us. Though she was a big educationalist. She saw that we all needed to achieve everything and anything that we could possibly achieve.

She wanted us all to do right by ourselves.

I suppose that might also have been her view of my hurling career, in addition to my life in law. Mary Callinan, however, was not a pushy mother when it came to my sporting life. She watched.

And, I always saw her as being gloriously underwhelmed.

UNLIKE DAN CAREY.

Dónal Carey, who helped me and supported me at every crossroads, and twist and turn in my hurling career.

It was no real surprise that he himself enjoyed a successful political career, because I always saw him as a bit of Joe Biden. Like President Biden, Dónal forged alliances with like-minded people.

He is a man to whom I owe so much. But, with all of our lives too foolishly busy, I have not spent enough quality time with him these last few years. We will always feel close to one another – and I am honoured in be godfather to his first born, Leonara – though he has not come to the village all that often these last few years.

Life moved on for both of us. For me as a solicitor, and for Dónal as a TD spending increasingly large amounts of his time in Dublin and Dáil Eireann.

However, when my uncle Peter came down to Clarecastle, to see the village for the last time, the first man I wanted him to meet was Dónal Carey.

Dónal had always been, and will always remain, a central pillar in my life.

TOM HAYES'S PUB?

The Shop? When we all left home, Eamon stayed by my mother's side and ran the place, and he was a good man behind the bar. Quieter than my mother, less talk out of him for sure, but good at the job.

But it was, like all rural pubs, a hard enough business in the years after my mother passed. The pub was left to Eamon, but in the late-90s the decision was taken to sell it. It was the right decision.

I seldom call to the pub anymore.

For me, it is a place I will always hold fondly in my heart, of course, but it is also a place that inhabits a different time, with different people.

A previous lifetime. It has nothing to do with the owners now or their patrons – Eileen who runs the place now is a lovely woman – but I felt slightly uncomfortable in there the last few times I ventured through the doors.

When my Uncle Peter was in the village for the last time, a couple of years ago, we walked the street and passed the pub. We headed for the bridge. It was a Saturday afternoon, and as we were passed the pub again on the way back, I said to him that we should go in… for one!

'We should,' he agreed.

'What'll we drink?' I asked.

Peter told me that when 'big farmers' would come to a Fair in older times they would drink half pints of porter.

'Two glasses of Guinness, please!'

We supped like two 'big farmers', and Peter pointed over my shoulder and he said he had been born in the room just above us.

We finished our two glasses, and to doubly distinguish ourselves as 'big farmers' we ordered two more… glasses.

IN THE MIDDLE of this pandemic, in the summer of 2020, I decided to call certain people and see how they were doing?

Fr Harry Bohan was the first person I called.

But phoning Fr Harry was the ruination of my best of intentions of calling several others that same afternoon. Because Fr Harry and I were quickly back in the summer of 1977, the Munster final... and how we were 'done'!

He's now in his early-eighties, working away in Sixmilebridge parish. That was, I think, his first parish too, his first pastoral role, because Fr Harry was, if you like, a 'Minister without portfolio' and living in Shannon and tending to so many things – and not just our hurling dreams – for the largest portion of his adult life.

He remains the busiest man in Clare, the busiest in the west of Ireland still. He told me he found the lockdown forced on us all during the pandemic, to be helpful in a sense. He found in his life more space for himself, for once, and more time to write.

Talking to him, even about games that disappointed us in the end and ruined our ambitions, I was reminded of how lucky I have been in my life.

Dónal Carey, and Fr Harry.

Two amazing men, who were central pillars for me. The game brought us together. The puck of the ball. Was I seeing both of these great men as substitute father figures, at different times in my younger life? I honestly don't know. Maybe.

All I know is that the game brought us together, and allowed us build such friendships through losses and victories.

When we think about it, and leave medals to one side, we all have so much to thank the game for.

I HAVE LIVED two very separate lives.

The life of a hurler

And life in the legal professional. I qualified as a solicitor in 1977, which leaves me 44 years at work as a solicitor – a lot longer than the years I spent on the field of play.

My 'real' career has been a huge part of my life, of course, and it would be easy to say that being a solicitor defined me, but I don't believe it does. The same could be said of my life as a hurler.

A senior counsel whom I worked closely with for a long number of years would often start talking to me about hurling. I felt, that he felt obliged to talk to me about nothing else, but hurling! He wasn't a huge hurling man himself.

I stopped him one day to remind him that I held views on many other things...

on politics, on literature, on so many other things that are kicking off every day on this planet.

I suppose, those of us who have spent a lifetime in the GAA can all easily get defined by others. We give our lives to the pursuit of the ball because, as I have sought to explain in this book, we love the act of being on the ball, challenging for the ball… it is a physical, joyous act.

And, after our playing days end, we go back to the club or the county to help others be the best they can be in the same act. I have remained involved with Clarecastle down through the years, as an administrator, and as chairman for a period, because we need to develop the club and make it better for the next generation.

That, I also found a joyous act, even if there was no ball ever at my feet.

Law and hurling are an unusual combination. I was talking to a man in the UCD Law Society recently and I did not know him, but he said to me, 'You used to play hurling!' I know I never once walked into a lecture during my college years with a hurley in my hand. Neither did I have any legal background, when I decided to study law.

Those two careers have run parallel, and never had to cross paths, and seldom did except for the 1978 county final. I did not make a bad career decision, because the law has given me a very good, satisfying life. Did my life as a solicitor, once I retired as a hurler, replace the cut and thrust, the chase and massive joy, of being out on the field? No.

There are always some nerves when you stand up in a courtroom. You are performing a significant role on behalf of a client… and there is a performance, you have to *perform*.

The courtroom is also a public place, like a GAA field. There is an audience. There are winners and losers, when cases end. And you have to walk away, either way, and start again the next day.

I do less court work now, than I did in my earlier days as a solicitor. But I have been lucky enough to take great satisfaction away from almost my entire career to date. I have worked with some very fine people. And that satisfaction increased when I started working for myself, and then partnered with the future Judge Marie Keane. Partnering in Limerick, and in Galway, I worked with the best of people.

Same as I hurled with the best of people.

THE ONE FIELD, I think of most of all these years later?

The one, special field, that holds the greatest memories. It's Tulla, naturally enough. It was always special, smaller than Cusack Park or Croke Park, Fitzgerald Stadium or Semple Stadium, or Limerick's Gaelic Ground and the other historic grounds I found myself in.

Tulla was different for us, and special in a way that all of those other magnificent grounds could never be; it was like a GAA ground found in a body of work from the hand of JKR Tolkien or JK Rowling.

Magical. A field, now when I close my eyes, that appears like a field from a fantasy.

That was Tulla.

Windswept, more often than not.

Never the prettiest, and never the most splendid to look at.

In the middle of nowhere.

It's a place that does not need an extra lick of paint or a hint of grandeur, in order to rise above every other GAA field I have ever knows or visited.

TULLA SAW SOME foul deeds on the field.

Of course, it did. When we all look back at games we played in, in a different age, we cannot honestly say that we are happy with everything we did, everything we saw. Hurling and Gaelic football could be filthy in the 70s and 80s, and it often was just like that.

I am not beating myself on the chest. And I am not being smug when I say that I was not involved in many underhand or nasty incidents myself – I looked into my heart in building this book, and I do not have much more to confess.

But when I came of age for senior hurling in Clarecastle there was a culture, an unhealthy relationship between neighbouring parishes in particular. But, thankfully, the game changed the longer I played.

The game became more respectful – and parishes became more respectful of one another. Teams fed less and less on old memories, injustices of the past, and scurrilous incidents that might have been left unresolved. School, college and work-places brought people together.

Sure, I was on the field at club and county matches, when there were actions that were simply awful. It's right to look back now and condemn those actions, and say good riddance to them. And the code of silence, which I was party to, I admit, is also gone.

Those GAA days are over, and that is a good thing.

I'm going to revisit one game now, and I am not going to mention the names of others. That's not adopting that code of silence, rather, I am re-telling this little story to openly admit that morally we all walked very thin lines a generation ago in the GAA.

I was at an age when I was coaching a team, and the first-half had ended on a sour and bloodied note. All hell was breaking loose in our dressing-room. Everyone was in our dressing-room.

I brought the team into the toilets... the fifteen players on the field for the second-half, not even the substitutes. We were not missed for the next five minutes.

The biggest man on the team was told to put his shoulder to the door, and told not to budge. Nobody was getting in.

I told our full-forward to deal with the opposing No.2 who was guilty in our eyes of hitting one of ours.

'Consider it done!' he replied.

I continued. 'The next thing we have to do is the beat these f***ers!' I told them. 'But... everyone has to keep the head!'

I reminded the team that one amongst them, and only one, was going to do what had to be done. But nobody else had to deliver retribution.

Back out on the field, our full-forward told their No.2... 'It might be the first minute... or the 31st minute... but you're... DEAD!'

Nothing much happened in the second-half, other than a good game of hurling was played. But I ask myself now, where was the morality in what I had asked for during half-time. Our full-forward never acted in the end, as things turned out. He didn't need to.

But I had been prepared for him to act, and to act on our behalf. We were all guilty, every last one of us, in one way or another, during that lawless age in the GAA's history.

IN 1995 AND '96 I took charge of the Clarecastle senior hurling team for the first time. Was I the manager? I was in charge, and I was doing the training and the coaching, so I guess you could call me the manager.

Obviously, the summer of '95 was consumed by the county's Munster and All-Ireland triumphs, so our county championship was 'run off' fairly quickly in the autumn. We survived the first game, but we were then beaten by Cratloe, which was a bit of a disaster. We had six county stars on the team, but we weren't sufficiently organised.

We regrouped in 1996 and made it to the final, where we met Wolfe Tones.

These were such exciting times for Clare hurling. We were All-Ireland champions, but in addition four Clare teams ruled club hurling in Munster through the second half of the decade – Sixmilebridge, Wolfe Tones, ourselves and St Joseph's.

It was a phenomenal period of dominance for the county.

Wolfe Tones beat us in the final in 1996, and progressed to rule Munster. Brian Lohan actually *beat us*. He came out of defence with six or seven balls that made the difference between the teams. It was 1-11 to 1-8 in the end. It was a huge disappointment.

But, things happened before the final itself which upset some people in the parish. Our team selection did not go down well with everybody.

My abiding memory of 1996 is not of losing the final to Wolfe Tones, but instead it remains centred on the personal hurt felt by too many good people in the parish

As a management team, we resigned at the end of the year.

In 1997, Ger Ward, Roger McMahon and Oliver Plunkett took charge of our seniors, and they and the team did everyone proud. We were Clare champions again, and we beat Patrickswell to lift the Munster title. We only lost to Birr in the All-Ireland semi-final after a replay.

And 1997 was the perfect summer.

Clare were All-Ireland champions once more and, into the bargain, we beat Tipperary twice in the same championship to doubly prove our worth.

And all of that was followed by Clarecastle proving ourselves the very best in the county and also in Munster.

We could have won the All-Ireland aswell but, still, it remains *my* perfect summer of hurling.

IN THE LATE-90s, I was approached by the Offaly County Board.

Babs Keating, then the Offaly senior hurling manager, had made his unfortunate 'sheep in a heap' remark and lost his job. It was 1998. The Offaly board wanted to know if I was interested?

I was flattered at the approach and I considered it for a number of days, and I made enquiries with Eamonn Cregan. Certain remarks had been made by Offaly men, like... 'You will be well looked after!'

I was curious then, and still remain curious, as to what that means in relation to inter-county managers.

Offaly were an outstanding team at the time and would have been attractive to anybody to manage. However, I had a problem with loyalty. Even though I played in a few different coloured jerseys, I believe I could only really be truly loyal to two jerseys – the Clarecastle jersey and the Clare jersey.

I had an arrangement to meet with the Offaly board in Killaloe on a certain evening but in the course of that same day I decided to call the secretary and indicate that I would not be in a position to take up the offer. I am not suggesting that I was the only person they were speaking with, but I know that they were serious.

The secretary encouraged me to go to the meeting, but I felt that I would be going under false pretences.

Imagine? 1998?

What a bullet I possibly missed. Events may have turned out differently, who knows, but I certainly would not have wanted to be the manager of the Offaly team in the three-match saga against Clare, and all that went with it at that time, arising mainly from referee Jimmy Cooney's unfortunate mistake in the second match.

As I say, a bullet missed.

I HAVE ADMITTED that in my time setting up the Gaelic Players Association we were not aggressive enough in presenting our demands, or even our wishes to anyone in Croke Park running the GAA.

But we served a function. We did present ourselves.

Today's GPA have achieved a great deal and much more than we ever did, but I would not be the greatest fan of the modern version. This GPA is elitist and because of its presence, the formation of a Club Players Association was required.

When we were wishing for more in the 70s and 80s we were mad to become more organised, more professional in very possible way. We wanted everything to be done correctly at a time when so much was not being done right. Today this *want* amongst those talented players in the country has gone too far.

And the young men playing our games are experiencing careers which – despite the riches that are being distributed by the GAA through the GPA – border on the abusive in my mind. No doubt the female hurlers and footballers will require the same.

Instead of complaining about the symptoms of mental and physical health issues which affect its membership, the GPA might try working at easing the pressures and stress being applied on too many young men and women in the modern games of hurling and football and camogie.

It is notable that the GPA absented itself on the fixtures and closed season issue but took a position against the new rules against cynical play. Strange.

The GPA must do more itself to helps its own members, but of course it's now inside the GAA tent with all of its goodies on offer.

They could seek to have the demands on their members lightened.

Over-coaching and over-professionalising has harmed our games. A number of industries have grown up and become 'well off' from the games that our players play and not just at county level. For me, the more a game is coached the more it needs to be cared for and monitored by non-coaches.

Coaches and managers have a specific job and that is to be the best they can be and win at almost any cost. They have, in my view, allowed the game of hurling to be severely influenced and I would say damaged by paying too much attention to what can be seized from other games such as football, rugby and basketball.

Hurling, over a number of decades, but much more so in recent years, has become a 'possessional' game when I believe it was created to be a 'propelling' game. Of course a game evolves, and I don't want to go back to shinty but we should not be fooled by coaches who have their own agendas, some of which might not be in the best interest of the game - or in the best interests of players and spectators.

At least one person who has heard me on this issue would be disappointed if I did not mention the 'roll-lift' – I would ban it. It is a stationary skill in a dynamic game and perpetuates the ruck.

The industries around our games include coaches for individual positions, strength and conditioning coaches, statistical personnel... it is taking 20-to-30 people to make a team fit to win an All-Ireland title; it is unseemly and destructive in the long term. The other industry that disappoints me is 'punditry'. This industry, to a person, appears to be a cheerleader for the modern game and can apparently see no wrong in it.

Players continue to say they do not wish to become fully professional, but is this actually true? What athlete would not want to spend the best four or five years of his or her life playing the game they love and being paid to do so? Why do they not admit to this?

This leaves us with a situation where players in the GAA are living the life of a 'professional' athlete, without the very attractive list of rewards which come with 'professional' careers in other sports. There are, I presume, some non-obvious rewards.

I think this conundrum is one for the GPA, which of course has its own fully-professional management.